THE
RUSSIAN NOVEL
IN FRANCE

THE
RUSSIAN NOVEL
IN FRANCE
1884–1914

BY

F. W. J. HEMMINGS

OXFORD UNIVERSITY PRESS
1950

Oxford University Press, Amen House, London E.C.4

GLASGOW NEW YORK TORONTO MELBOURNE WELLINGTON
BOMBAY CALCUTTA MADRAS CAPE TOWN

Geoffrey Cumberlege, Publisher to the University

PRINTED IN GREAT BRITAIN

PREFACE

THIS book is a slightly abridged version of a doctorate thesis prepared at Oxford between 1946 and 1948. I was fortunate in having my studies directed by M. Gustave Rudler, at that time Marshal Foch Professor of French Literature. In paying my own tribute to the unfailing generosity with which he put the rich store of his unique experience and erudition at my disposal, I shall be only one of the last of a long series of British students who over many years have had reason to express a similar indebtedness.

I would wish, too, to express my thanks to Professor S. Konovalov, of Oxford University, and to Professor L. C. Sykes, of University College, Leicester, who read the typescript before it went to press, for their suggestions and corrections; and finally to Mr. H. R. Leech, of Balliol College, Oxford, for his patience in verifying an important point of detail in the Paris libraries at a time when I was unable to visit them myself.

F. W. J. H.

LEICESTER

December 1949

CONTENTS

I

THE LAUNCHING OF AN INVASION

RUSSIAN troops marched into France in 1814, with the armies of their allies, to restore a dynasty and impose a peace. But the invasion to be chronicled here took place seventy years later, caused no blood to be shed and no maps to be re-drawn. It was an invasion by the printed page, which restored certain aesthetic ideals that had been languishing in exile, and imposed, for a brief space, a compromise peace on the turbulent Parisian world of letters.

This is what happened. In the three decades that preceded the First World War, the general public in France learnt for the first time that there had been flourishing in Russia for rather less than a century an important vernacular literature. They were told, and were able to see for themselves, that this literature (above all that part of it classed as 'prose fiction') had many enduring qualities, would repay intelligent study, and might even successfully pilot a *fin-de-siècle* generation of writers who had lost their spiritual bearings. The 'invasion' was one of translations and commentaries, of serious explanatory manuals and breezy newspaper articles. Current evidence of it might have been gathered by scanning railway bookstalls, but also by eavesdropping on conversations in literary cafés and drawing-rooms, and (most interesting of all for posterity) by reading carefully the latest French works of fiction, where might be detected conscious or unconscious reproductions of the themes and preoccupations of Russian literature.

The subject of this book is simply the course and immediate effects of this invasion.

The term is not a far-fetched formula adjusted over the event by an historian enjoying the advantage of the mid-twentieth-century perspective. The phrase: 'the invasion of French literature by the Russians' was used to describe current happenings by more than one clear-sighted eyewitness. In 1886, when the process was beginning to make itself felt, a contemporary jokingly declared that Paris was suffering the Russian *revanche* for the burning of Moscow in 1812: but instead of setting the city on fire, the 'Cossacks' were content to drown it under floods of printer's ink.

Most successful invasions (by force of arms) have two characteristic qualities. They are sudden and sweep all before them;
and they occur when least expected, their origins are concealed.
The (pacific) Russian invasion of France had both these
qualities.

It was sudden. For suddenness there can be few analogies in
French literature or any other to the blaze of glory that played
around the names of Tolstoy and Dostoevsky almost as soon as
they became familiar to the intellectual and artistic strata of French
society. For the spear-head of the invasion was represented by
these two novelists. The point is fundamental and we shall revert
to it. Nineteenth-century Russia produced a rich store of poetry,
a few stage masterpieces, a succession of brilliant and profound
pieces of literary criticism, and a series of works that rank among
the most interesting achievements of the modern European novel.
And among the exponents of the last-named class of writing, none
can have conquered more readers outside Russia, none stirred the
collective imagination of Europe more and prompted more self-
examination among other novelists, than Fyodor Mikhailovitch
Dostoevsky and Lev Nikolaevitch Tolstoy. Yet at as late a date as
1880 their very names were unknown to anyone in France but the
merest handful of specialists. By the end of the decade, however,
so suddenly did events move—by the end of 1886, almost—their
names had become household words, everyone had read, or pretended to have read, their chief works, young novelists were imitat-
ing them, older ones reading them for inspiration.

The invasion was unexpected, unforeseen, because it was by
nature unplanned, an irruption of barbarians. There is no single or
obvious reason why it should have occurred when it did instead of
ten years earlier or twenty years later. Russian literature as a whole,
before it could gain recognition in France, had to await the discovery
of Tolstoy and Dostoevsky: it was only when they were confronted
by these two giants that the French began to interest themselves in
other neglected figures that might be lurking in this uncharted
wilderness. But how is one to account for the complete absence of
synchrony between the coming of celebrity to these novelists in
their native land and in France? Tolstoy had written his greatest
works many years before the French began to devour them with
such voracity; when Dostoevsky died and was all but awarded the
honours of a national funeral, he was totally unknown in France.

It is no answer to say that translations were not available: if a demand had been sensed, the commodity would have been supplied. There was simply no market; proof of this lies in the fact that a perfectly satisfactory translation of *War and Peace* was produced at St. Petersburg and offered for sale in Paris as early as 1879: scarcely anyone bought it then, but six years later the book was a best-seller.

It is hard to avoid the conclusion that, to have created so electrical a sensation, the Russians must have made some special appeal to Frenchmen in the late eighties, an appeal which would have been ineffective earlier. The high qualities and deep interest of their books would eventually, no doubt, have attracted wide attention; but the process would have been a slow one, resulting in part from painstaking efforts of interpretation by a small band of enthusiasts. In the event, universal admiration burst over them like a shower of gold before they were at all well known in the bulk of their work.

This 'special appeal' that it is necessary to postulate, can be traced back to numerous sources. Once these are isolated and examined it will be legitimate to venture certain conclusions about the scope and nature of the influence of the Russian novel in France. The analysis will hold an incidental interest because the reasons for the spectacular success of the Russians are intimately bound up with the spiritual mood of France during the last fifteen years of the nineteenth century.

For the greater part of the century, Russian institutions, culture, civilization, and artistic achievements, were scarcely considered in France a subject for serious study. An occasional traveller, having visited the country, would find on his return a market for a not always very trustworthy narrative of his experiences.[1] But by and large in France there was no sustained interest in Russia. At most, one or two enthusiasts had chosen this field for their researches; their enterprise was considered by the public at large to be about as fruitful as mapping the mountains of the moon.

Even in purely academic circles, Russian studies received little encouragement in France, in spite of the establishment, in 1840,

---

[1] Typical of such accounts were the Marquis de Custine's *La Russie en 1839* (1843), Alexandre Dumas's light-hearted *Impressions de voyage* (1860), and Théophile Gautier's *Voyage en Russie* (1866).

of a chair of Slavonic studies at the Collège de France.[1] The truth is that the motives behind this foundation seem not to have been of the purest order. Its sponsors acted less on a disinterested desire to see East European studies placed on a firm footing than in a hope that by this move they might crystallize liberal opposition to the extinction of Polish nationhood. The chair was therefore given in the first place to Adam Mickiewicz, Polish national poet, fanatic Bonapartist, one of the most lionized of the exiles in Paris. In so far as he mentioned the Russians in his lectures (which according to custom were public), his patriotism could never have permitted him to suggest that they were anything but a race of barbarians quite unversed in the gentler arts of civilization.

His appointment was a political gesture, and it was in this light that the foundation of the chair was regarded by all parties. Liberals welcomed it as a standing protest against the settlement of 1815, legitimists viewed it no otherwise and for that reason regarded it with the gravest suspicion. Balzac, in his novel *Le Cousin Pons* (1847), digresses from his narrative to refer scornfully to the creation at Paris 'of chairs of Slav, Manchu, and literatures as little fit to be professed as the literatures of the North which, instead of giving lessons, ought to be receiving them'. Balzac, it might be thought, would have been more kindly disposed towards the cause of Poland; but his devotion to throne and altar was stronger than personal sentiment.

Mickiewicz's first two successors were as little likely as he to foster interest in Russian studies. Cyprien Robert, who replaced the Polish poet in 1845, was an expert on the Balkan Slavs, then under the rule of the Ottoman Empire. He disappeared in mysterious circumstances and in 1856 Alexander Chodzko, a Lithuanian whose interests were mainly philological, took his place and held the post until 1884.

Throughout the mid-nineteenth century, then, Russian (as distinct from Slavonic) studies were at a very low ebb. The events of 1870 had a salutary effect, but even after this date, misconceptions and rank ignorance were widespread. The diplomatic service tended to assume, for instance, that since French was

[1] Details may be sought in Louis Leger, 'Le Monde slave, leçon d'ouverture au Collège de France', *Revue Bleue*, 18 Apr. 1885, and in *Russes et Slaves, 2ᵉ série* (1896), by the same author (chapter on 'La Chaire de littératures slaves au Collège de France').

universally understood in Russia—by the politer elements of
society—the Frenchman going there would be wasting his time if
he tried to learn the language of the natives. In 1873 Louis Leger,
who was to succeed Chodzko at the Collège de France, quoted it
as a fact that there was greater public provision at Paris for the
study of Tibetan and Japanese than for learning the official tongue
of the most far-flung empire of Europe: with the result that doubt
was cast on the very existence of a vernacular literature in those
parts.[1] The situation was admirably summed up in 1886 by Eugène-
Melchior de Vogüé, at the beginning of his book, *Le Roman russe*:
'Until a few years ago we left it to a handful of orientalists to busy
themselves with checking the writings of these Sarmatians. We had
a notion that a literature might exist in their midst, as in Persia or
Arabia; we did not place much trust in it. . . .'

Among those early 'orientalists', pride of place must be given to
Prosper Mérimée. He has many claims to celebrity, as novelist and
story-teller, archaeologist and historian; it is not the least of these
titles that he was the first French man of letters to take a serious
interest in Russian literature.

Having learnt enough Russian from a native teacher to be able
to puzzle out a text without too much difficulty, Mérimée applied
himself to reading and occasionally translating the better-known
authors. His translations unfortunately are few; and they are all of
short pieces—Gogol's satirical play, *The Inspector-General*, four
short stories of Pushkin's including *The Queen of Spades*, and some
(by no means the best) of Turgenev's *contes*. His versions are not
always free from errors,[2] but at least they are intelligent and un-
exceptionably elegant.

Mérimée also wrote a small number of critical monographs on
certain Russian writers, Pushkin, Gogol, and Turgenev. They do
not appear to have stirred up any deep curiosity for his subject
among Mérimée's readers, and for this reason it is interesting to
compare them with Vogüé's which, at a later date, had such a
remarkable popular success.

The first of Mérimée's articles dealt with Gogol,[3] and the conclusions he reached were, on balance, unfavourable. While paying

---

[1] Leger, *Le Monde slave*, p. 266.
[2] See Leger, *Nicolas Gogol*, pp. 209-15.
[3] 'La Littérature en Russie: Nicolas Gogol', *Revue des Deux Mondes*, 15 Nov.
1851.

tribute to the keenness and veracity of the Russian's powers of observation, Mérimée censured him for deliberately preferring sordid subjects and base characters—or, in other words, for being what Vogüé later congratulated him for being, the man who inaugurated realism in Russian literature. Gogol's tireless satire irks Mérimée, who would not deny that (in Russia particularly no doubt) things have a distressful side to them, but wonders whether it is proper to be continually on the watch for this.

In this respect he found Turgenev a more attractive writer. Discussing *The Sportsman's Sketches,*[1] Mérimée emphasized that Turgenev's satire of social abuses is less bitter than that of the older writer; he is not blind to the fact that evil practices flourish in his native land, but he does not denounce them with indecorous violence. He shares with Gogol a love for the insignificant detail ('this delight in, this talent for description is a quality, or if you will a defect shared by most Russian writers'), but there is a difference in the moral quality of his realism which is more elevated than Gogol's. 'He turns aside from ugliness, which the author of *Dead Souls* tracks down so eagerly. You feel in everything he writes a love for what is good and comely. . . . He sees good alongside evil, and even in the uncouth and absurd figures he shows us, he is able to reveal some noble and touching quality.' This last remark foreshadows much of what Vogüé will have to say on the subject of Turgenev's forbearance and sympathy when that novelist is describing the trials and tribulations of his characters.

Fourteen years later Mérimée returned to Turgenev;[2] by this time the critic's pioneer work on the novelist had borne fruit, and the Russian's reputation was firmly established in France. Rather ruefully, Mérimée notes that he is now quoted as one of the leaders of the new realist school. Turgenev steers clear, however, of the disillusioned irony that embitters the outlook of other exponents of the new doctrine (Mérimée was writing on the eve of the publication of Flaubert's *Éducation sentimentale*). Whereas the French school takes a malicious delight in detecting human frailty and folly, Turgenev exerts himself in bringing to light the good wherever it lies concealed. He is the 'champion of the weak and the disinherited'.

---

[1] 'La Littérature et le servage en Russie. *Mémoires d'un chasseur russe*, par M. Ivan Tourghénief', *Revue des Deux Mondes*, 1 July 1854.

[2] With an article in the *Moniteur universel*, 25 May 1868, which was reprinted in Mérimée, *Portraits historiques et littéraires* (1874).

In all this, Mérimée can be seen once more as a forerunner of Vogüé.

Matters literary were only one side of Mérimée's interest in Russia. He spent probably more of his time in researches on Russian history, especially the history of the 'Time of the Troubles' and the reign of Peter the Great. There is little evidence that he took any interest in contemporary Russian literature, apart from Turgenev's works. A single reference to Dostoevsky does, however, occur in one of his letters:[1] Mérimée explains to his correspondent that to satisfy the entreaties of certain friends he has been reading *Crime and Punishment*. It is evident from the few words he says how widely out of sympathy Mérimée was with the experiments Dostoevsky was conducting in the treatment of reality. 'I will tell you frankly', says the author of *Colomba*, 'that, in spite of the author's great talent, this novel does not appeal to me; he is too keyed up, his emotion is pitched too high and this has spoilt the lucidity of his artistic observation.' Mérimée thinks that Dostoevsky owes more to Victor Hugo than to Pushkin, and asks: 'Is it worthy of a Russian writer, having so lofty a model, to follow in the tracks of Hugo and find his inspiration there?' The judgement is peculiarly unfortunate, especially as regards Pushkin's influence. Dostoevsky had an unbounded admiration for the greatest of Russian poets. As a boy he wept on hearing of his death, and as an old man delivered an impassioned oration at his centenary celebrations. References to and quotations from Pushkin are frequent in his works—more frequent than in the novels of Tolstoy or Turgenev.

As a critic of Russian literature, Mérimée had his limitations. Chief among these is his inability to see it save as an off-shoot of the older literatures of France, England, Italy, Greece.... Mérimée was not disposed to admit that the Russians might now be untied from the leading-strings of Western culture; and he was very far from suggesting, as Vogüé was to do, that they might act as an anti-toxic and tonic medicine for French writers. As a later historian[2] said, Mérimée, for all the interest his remarks have, judged Rus-

---

[1] Quoted by É. Halpérine-Kaminsky, *Ivan Tourguénief d'après sa correspondance avec ses amis français* (1901), p. 15. The recipient of the letter, according to H. Mongault ('Mérimée, Beyle et quelques Russes', *Mercure de France*, 1 Mar. 1928, p. 362) was Mme Alexandrina Dmitrievna Longinova (1836–77).

[2] A. Lirondelle, 'Le Roman russe en France à la fin du XIXᵉ siècle', *Revue des Cours et Conférences*, 30 July 1925, pp. 723–4.

sian literature by its external face: Vogüé was the first to judge it by its inner content.

The events of 1870 threw France into Russia's arms: a diplomatic volte-face which culminated in the Treaty of Alliance of 1891. Throughout the century Russia, as a political entity, had been coldly regarded by the French. Bonapartists had never been able to forget that Napoleon's first serious defeat had been inflicted by Russian military power. By republicans, the Empire of the Tsars had been looked on as the major bulwark of autocracy in Europe and the natural opponent of France so long as France remained the champion of constitutional democracy. Finally, Paris had made itself the haven of refugee Polish nationalists after the Congress of Vienna had confirmed the dismemberment of their country, temporarily resurrected by Napoleon; Polish hatred of Russia, rooted after centuries of war, waxed stronger as the result of the new oppression of their country and infected their French hosts. The 'rape of Poland' was a commonplace source of indignation for French liberals of the thirties, and Victor Hugo, enumerating the crimes that tyranny had perpetrated in his day, capped all by a reference to the Russian suppression of the Polish rising in 1831:

> Quand un Cosaque affreux, que la rage transporte,
> Viole Varsovie échevelée et morte,
> Et, souillant son linceul, chaste et sacré lambeau,
> Se vautre sur la vierge étendue au tombeau;
> Alors, oh! je maudis, dans leur cour, dans leur antre,
> Ces rois dont les chevaux ont du sang jusqu'au ventre![1]

As soon, however, as Prussia stood revealed as a new and hostile power across the borders, French diplomacy looked over to Prussia's eastern neighbour as a natural ally against any future act of aggression. This new diplomatic orientation determined a switch of popular feeling in France. The period of 'Russophobia' came to an end, and Hugo's 'Cosaque affreux' became the hero of the hour. The popular theatres staged plays with Russian heroes moving in Russian settings;[2] and readers of the sentimental novel gorged themselves on the productions of Mme Henri Gréville, whose

---

[1] *Feuilles d'automne*, xl.

[2] Examples: *Danicheff*, by A. Dumas fils and Pierre de Corvin, 1876; *Michel Strogoff*, from the novel by Jules Verne, 1880; *Serge Panine*, also from a novel by Georges Ohnet, 1882.

stock characters were officers of the Imperial Guard and wilful St. Petersburg beauties. Mme Gréville, by her real name Mme Alice Durand, was the daughter of Jean Fleury; her father had settled in Russia in 1856, having been appointed Professor of French at the School of Law in St. Petersburg.[1] Her novels first saw the light of day as serial stories in Russian periodicals. In 1876 she found a publisher in Paris, and her books came tumbling out of the press in great numbers. Their titles (*Les Épreuves de Raïssa, Sonia, La Princesse Oghérof, Dosia*) are sufficient indication of their nature: they were novels of Russian local colour, and did open a new vein in France. But this prolific authoress was not capable of plumbing very deeply the peculiarities of the national psychology, and her characters (drawn mainly from the aristocracy), are recognizably Russian only by a certain charming impulsiveness and by the place taken in their lives by the samovar.

Apart from these popular manifestations of a new interest in Russia, there is evidence that a genuine attempt was made in the seventies to place French knowledge of the country on a sounder and more scientific basis. In 1875 the teaching of Russian was started at the École des Langues orientales vivantes, while chairs were founded about this time at other centres of learning besides Paris—at Lille, Lyons, Dijon.[2] Specialists who saw their subject coming into its own at last, were well aware of the political aspect of this movement. 'Russia has been all the rage in France for a few years', wrote Leger in 1880. 'If the truth were known, it is not certain that this enthusiasm is based on altogether disinterested principles. . . .'[3] Vogüé's apologia for his book hinted at this even more discreetly. 'For literary reasons—which I shall go into later—and for reasons of another order that I shall pass over in silence, because everyone will know what I mean—I am convinced that we must labour to bring the two countries together by helping them to imbibe each other's culture—par la pénétration mutuelle des choses de l'esprit.'[4] These are the words of a soldier who had been wounded during the Franco-Prussian War and of a trained diplomat who had represented France at St. Petersburg.

It would be unwise to underestimate the part politics played,

---

[1] See V. Boutchik, *La Littérature russe en France* (1948), p. 23.
[2] See P. Kovalewsky, *Les Études littéraires russes en France* (1933), pp. 4, 5.
[3] Leger, *Nouvelles études slaves* (1880), p. 105.
[4] Vogüé, *Le Roman russe*, p. vii.

even at long range, in directing the attention of the French towards Russian thought and art, a process which culminated in the discovery of Tolstoy and Dostoevsky. Anyone who could or who pretended to be able to pronounce with authority on any subject connected with Russia, was assured of a respectful audience; for it was of first-rate importance to know what was to be thought of this nation on whom France was, to some extent, staking her future: were they merely a barbaric Asiatic horde, or were they one of the youngest members of the European family? The analogy is conceivable with the renewal of interest in Russia which we witnessed in this country, when the Soviet Union became overnight our ally in the struggle against the very same foe as France had faced in 1870.

The chief works that came out as a result of this resurgence of curiosity about Russia after the Franco-Prussian War were, in the realm of literary criticism, Courrière's *Histoire de la littérature contemporaine en Russie* (1875), and Alfred Rambaud's *La Russie épique* (1876).[1] In the field of social study, the pioneer authority was Anatole Leroy-Beaulieu, who published articles on various aspects of Russian life in the *Revue des Deux Mondes* from 1873 onwards. These were later worked up into an extensive work issued in three volumes between 1881 and 1889 under the general heading of *L'Empire des Tsars et des Russes.*

Rambaud's work dealt with the earliest monuments of Russian literature, and does not therefore come within the scope of this study. Courrière's book, however, holds considerable interest if only because it was the first attempt to provide the French with a manual of Russian literature. Courrière introduces his work with the remark that 'it will surprise some readers and afford instruction to many. In our unwillingness to rid ourselves of commonplaces that we found ready-made when we came into the world, we have accepted unquestioningly the proposition that there was no Russian literature, or that if there was, it would have no interest for us.' He regards his book as a small contribution to the post-war drive to acquaint the French more thoroughly with the great nation which will ultimately, perhaps, be their partner in the task of containing expansionist Prussia.

---

[1] Rambaud also brought out an *Histoire de la Russie* in 1878, which Vogüé (in his *Regards historiques et littéraires*, p. 72) called 'excellent'.

Courrière's field is vast; he tends rather to overwhelm the reader by the multiplicity of the names that he quotes, and he inevitably incurs the danger which besets any critic of 'unsifted' literature—he fails to make the major figures stand out among the welter of minor ones.

In his preface Courrière makes two points which will not be overlooked by his successors in the field of Russian criticism. The first is that 'realism', which had been in France only the creed of one school, and then only during a comparatively recent period, is fundamental to Russian literature in every *genre*. The second point is that the Russians share with the English a liking for the didactic, the socially instructive: 'The Russian novel instructs, preaches, moralizes, develops some thesis or other.' The observation, though it needed little perspicacity to make it, is worth emphasizing; for, in the eighties and nineties, it was the implicitly moral tone of the works of Tolstoy, and to a lesser extent of Dostoevsky, that charmed the conservatives among their French readers: Brunetière sang the praises of the Russian novel for no other reason. And, when French novelists began to fall under the influence of the Russians, it was this tone that many of them endeavoured to reproduce.

Courrière devotes, as might be expected, appropriate portions of his book to the works of Gogol and Turgenev, already known to the French thanks to their translators and to Prosper Mérimée, Sainte-Beuve, and others. But he has also some comments to offer about the works of Tolstoy and Dostoevsky, which at that date were quite unknown in France except to the insignificant minority who could read Russian. These remarks are of particular interest if only because they are the earliest extant published pronouncements by a French writer on these two figures, destined to affect French literature so powerfully in future years.

Among Dostoevsky's works, he gives accounts of *Poor Folk*, *Insulted and Injured*, *Crime and Punishment*, and *The Possessed*. *Crime and Punishment* rouses Courrière to an almost rhapsodic flight: the novel, which was later to create a furore in France when translated, seems to have impressed this early French critic chiefly by the nightmarish atmosphere the author succeeds in creating.

From the very first page, you feel yourself snatched up by an invisible power and set down in a strange and unreal world. All your ideas are turned upside down. You barely have time to ask yourself where you are being hurried off to. The further you go, the more this nightmare weighs on you. You read on and on, panting, aghast, unable to analyse or ponder your impressions, to such a degree this monstrous, extravagant world grips you and holds you fast (p. 322).

It is, however, by the 'perfection with which Dostoevsky develops the psychological analysis of the emotions and moral sufferings of Raskolnikov' (p. 328) that the novel has won an outstanding position in contemporary Russian literature. The hero is a 'moral monster; although his mechanism is complete, its mainsprings have become unhinged. You are confronted with the birth struggles of thoughts which thrill you with horror. You ask yourself whether all that can possibly happen! And when the hallucination is past, when reality reasserts itself, you are still quivering with the nervous shock and vague terror produced by this dream' (p. 322).

These words, 'dream', 'nightmare', 'hallucination', will recur constantly in French criticism of Dostoevsky; Hennequin[1] later on made great play with them, perceiving that Dostoevsky's distortion of reality was compounded of the same elements of truth and fantasy that are present, for each one of us, in the world of dreams. The assimilation of Dostoevsky's novels to dream-fantasy was no doubt in part due to the mere strangeness of an unfamiliar type of art. One is reminded of the words of Madame de Staël in an analogous situation, when she introduced Goethe's *Faust* to the French:

The criticisms that may be levelled against such a work of art can be easily foreseen, or rather, it is the type of work that will incur censure, even more than the manner in which the subject is treated; but if good taste was for ever standing guard over the ivory gateway of dreams, to oblige them to take on the conventional shape, they would rarely strike the imagination.[2]

Courrière mentions Tolstoy only for *War and Peace*—*Anna Karenina* and the later works had not of course been written at that date. In Courrière's opinion it is 'undeniably one of the finest masterpieces of Russian literature' (p. 350). Curiously, the character of Natasha, which later French writers were to find so appealing, fails to attract this early critic, chiefly because he is shocked by the vicissitudes of her emotional life (p. 353). Courrière is however on common ground with his successors in deploring the intrusion of

[1] See his *Écrivains francisés* (1889), especially pp. 164–5, 254.
[2] *De l'Allemagne*, book II, chap. 23.

Tolstoy's philosophical theories in the novel—though less because this infringes on the impartiality expected of a realist writer than because of the absurdity of the theory itself (pp. 355–7).

In particular it is Tolstoy's fatalism that jars on Courrière. When the cause-and-effect sequence is very strongly marked in any fictional or historical narrative, there is a natural tendency to conclude that events could not have taken any other turn. This seems to be why Tolstoy, the most exclusively realist of writers, should have conveyed so marked an impression of fatalism in his novels. (It did not form an integral part of his later philosophy.)

Tolstoy's fatalism is most apparent in his treatment of the Napoleonic campaigns, and Courrière expresses grave disappointment that the author of *War and Peace* should have seen nothing in this 'gigantic struggle between two worlds' beyond a linking up of accidents outside the control of the human will. The two Emperors, their generals, and their troops, are 'mere pawns moved hither and thither by the hand of destiny on the vast chess-board of the world' (p. 345). Tolstoy's fatalism, Courrière continues, betrays 'a reasoned, systematic intention to belittle the greatness of events and the importance of the part played by the individual will' (p. 355).

There is little more in the *Histoire de la littérature contemporaine en Russie* to claim our attention here, save an important general point that Courrière makes to start off with in his preface and to which he returns at the end of his book. He asserts on these two occasions that Russian literature owes virtually nothing to French models; and that in spite of the fact that French has always been the language of the civilized stratum of Russian society. The influence of English writers has been greater in Russia: 'Dickens and Thackeray have headed literary movements: Victor Hugo, E. Sue, A. Dumas have been imitated only by second-rate novelists.' Contemporary French literature, although it finds many eager readers in Russia, is frowned on by the critics, who accuse French novelists 'of straining after effects and fine phrasing, of inventing characters and subjects which have no connexion with reality and which are purely imaginary' (p. 360). Courrière thereby counters a couple of decades in advance the parochialist theories of Jules Lemaître and others, who maintained that all Tolstoy and Dostoevsky had done was to digest ideas furnished them by the French and to reproduce them in an exotic guise.

Vogüé has left an impressive tribute to the work of Leroy-
Beaulieu. He is 'the man who was our forerunner and who remains
our guide';[1] his name dominates those of other French students of
Russia who have done no more than walk in his footsteps and
glean where he had reaped. 'If truth and justice are not idle words,
when the man comes who will write the history of the discovery of
the Slav world by the French, he will credit this stalwart, persever-
ing spirit with the main effort, and assign him the largest share of
honour as being the first cause of the great effects.'[2]

François Buloz, the enterprising editor of the *Revue des Deux
Mondes*, was responsible for dispatching Leroy-Beaulieu on his
mission of investigation. Leroy-Beaulieu found his subject was
almost completely virgin: no Russian, no German even, had
attempted an encyclopedia of Russian life and manners such as he
contemplated. Consequently he had to resort throughout to first-
hand evidence; he made several tours of Russia, and by questioning
individuals of every occupation and officials of every degree, he
gradually, over a period of many years, built up his compendium
of knowledge.

Leroy-Beaulieu was first and foremost an economist and a student
of political history, and literature plays a subordinate role in his
magnum opus. The first volume (published 1881) deals with the
land and its inhabitants; the second (1882), with the civil institutions. The third volume, which deals with religion in Russia (the
established Church and the innumerable dissident sects), did not
appear until 1888, and is therefore posterior to the period immediately under review: but it was this volume which was probably of
greatest interest in literary circles, and in any case it had come out
in instalments in the *Revue des Deux Mondes* over the previous few
years.

In his pages Leroy-Beaulieu revealed the existence on the other
side of Europe of a peasant culture deeply imbued with faith in the
doctrines of Christianity and in the idea of holiness common to
Catholicism and Orthodoxy. The ordinary folk in Russia had learnt
the lesson of the Cross; the moujik 'has not forgotten the value of
suffering; he appreciates its virtue; he feels the efficacy of atonement and relishes its bitter-sweetness' (p. 45). The writer draws
attention to Tolstoy's affinities with the peasant sectarians of Rus-

[1] Vogüé, *Regards historiques et littéraires*, p. 70.
[2] Id., in a letter published in the *Revue Hebdomadaire*, 9 Apr. 1910, p. 152.

sia and to Dostoevsky's development of their favourite doctrine of
expiation through suffering, and goes on to show how Russian
literature, although practised for the most part by free-thinkers, is
at bottom essentially religious, being steeped in the same preoccupations—the enigmas of Life and Fate—as have from time
immemorial troubled saints and sages.

The real service to literature rendered by Leroy-Beaulieu was
that he drew a sober and reliable picture of the Russia of his day.
Future readers of Tolstoy and Dostoevsky would be able to verify
the accuracy of the reflection these writers gave of the Russian
'panorama' and to supply for themselves the factual basis of many
imaginative passages: the mixture of brutality and saintliness in the
composition of the Russian peasant as displayed in *The Power of
Darkness*; the monastery scenes in *The Brothers Karamazov*; the
characters of the nihilists and the populists who play so large a part
in *Fathers and Sons*, in *Virgin Soil*, and in *The Possessed*; the
arraignment of bureaucractic injustice and corruption which
inspired so many Russian novels from *Dead Souls* to *Resurrection*.

Dostoevsky's death in 1881 passed almost unnoticed in France.
Not quite, however. Eugène Yung, director of the *Revue Politique
et littéraire* (later to be known familiarly as the *Revue Bleue*), had a
correspondent on the spot at St. Petersburg, who was able to
furnish him with certain details about the life and works of this
little-known novelist. This was Jean Fleury, the father of the
novelist, Henri Gréville, whose works we have mentioned in
passing. The article he wrote for the *Revue Bleue*[1] deals also with
the novelist Pisemsky, whose death had occurred at the beginning
of the year.

It is noteworthy that Fleury does no more than touch on that
quality of Dostoevsky's work which Vogüé was to stress most
emphatically: his religion of pity. 'His works are marked', writes
Fleury, 'by irony, wrath, a contempt for humanity, accompanied
by a deep sympathy for those that suffer, for the "Insulted and
Injured".' That is all.

Fleury is bold enough to measure Dostoevsky against Émile Zola
(the parallel will be drawn later by Vogüé), and the Russian does
not suffer in the comparison. Noting that *Crime and Punishment*

---

[1] 'Deux romanciers russes contemporains', *Revue Bleue*, 26 Feb. 1881.

and *Thérèse Raquin* came out about the same time and are both
founded on much the same subject, Fleury declares that 'the Russian novelist is closer to reality and to truth, is more human, and
the impression given by his book is more frightening. The French
author is superior by the art of his novel-construction and by his
analysis of sensations. There is more of the man in Dostoevsky,
more of the brute in Zola.' Vogüé will do little more than extend
and illustrate this observation and add the rider that the French
novel would find a brighter future if it turned its back on Zola and
turned to Dostoevsky for inspiration.

Fleury registers astonishment at the behaviour of Dostoevsky's
characters: an astonishment which will be prolonged and re-echoed
in every key until it is pointed out (by Gide),[1] that Dostoevsky's
creations only appear abnormal because they are free: they act as
any one of us would act if our behaviour were not perpetually
governed by a factitious desire to be 'true to ourselves', which leads
us most of the time to be quite false to our real selves. Fleury
acknowledges the realism (i.e., the power to convince) of the
characters in Dostoevsky's books; but their behaviour, he thinks, is
entirely inexplicable by ordinary rational canons. 'They are copied
from nature, they are certainly living creatures, they are gifted even
with a superabundance of life [ils sont plus que vivants même]: but
we Westerners cannot help being profoundly astonished by them,
because logic is powerless to explain their actions, and their intellectual faculties are unbalanced.' Unbalanced; the unvarying cry,
reiterated unwearyingly in the next thirty years, of those who
recoiled before the frightening potentialities Dostoevsky revealed
in the 'Underground Man'.

Dostoevsky's illogicality, maintains our essayist, does not stop
short at his psychology. The way he writes, his vaguenesses and
digressions, derive from the same irrationalism. Here again Fleury
anticipated innumerable complaints made at a later stage in France
about Dostoevsky's prolixity, his alleged inability to stick to his
subject.

Fleury's unpretentious article probably caused only the smallest
ripple of interest among subscribers to the *Revue Bleue*. It is hard
for a critic to arouse enthusiasm when he is dealing with writings
inaccessible to the ordinary reader. Perhaps Fleury may have caused
certain progressive publishers to wonder whether these novels

---

[1] But not until 1923. See his *Dostoïevsky*, p. 170.

might prove a happy speculation, if a translator could be hired to do them into French. To any such, the professor at St. Petersburg issues a warning which will be, regrettably, taken to heart when the time comes: 'To be appreciated by the French public, Dostoevsky's novels would need to be recast and overhauled like certain German works of erudition.' Timorous injunctions of this kind, recapitulated by Vogüé and others, encouraged a Halpérine-Kaminsky in his disastrous tinkerings with *The Brothers Karamazov*. Those who made such suggestions failed to foresee that the 'recasting and overhauling' was almost bound to be entrusted to men who, without the slightest inkling of Dostoevsky's artistic intentions, would cut and trim the original works with a view to pandering to the thirst for sensationalism of the widest possible circle of readers.

If Courrière's references to Tolstoy had been a trifle summary, such deficiencies were met to a large extent by an article, 'Lew Tolstoï: un pessimiste russe', inserted in the recently founded *Nouvelle Revue* on 1 June 1883. Of the author, E. de Cyon, I have been able to discover no particulars of interest; but his monograph is precociously illuminating, and as a critic he deserves special mention as a noteworthy, though little regarded, forerunner of the author of the *Roman russe*.

Tolstoy is defined by de Cyon as a 'realist writer in the best sense of the word, gifted with an extraordinary creative power', who is in addition 'an exquisitely delicate psychologist and an audaciously original thinker'.

As far as his realism is concerned, de Cyon observes that, as with all realists, 'the narrative is highly circumstantial, the descriptions extremely minute'. Tolstoy takes little heed whether 'such and such a detail is pleasing or displeasing, is essential or unessential to the subject, ennobles or debases the character to whom it is attributed' —even if this character appears to be one of those for whom the author nourishes a secret preference. De Cyon strikes a note here which will have infinite reverberations in French criticism of Tolstoy. The author of *War and Peace* struck the imagination of the age as the most honest and most vivid chronicler of the world as it was; he sailed into port under the flag of Realism. In all the welter of criticism that ensued on the revelation of Tolstoy's works to the French, the starting-point was always to judge him as a realist; to praise him in so far as he was thought to conform to realist procedure, to damn him as he was deemed to depart from it.

Adverse criticism of Tolstoy's realism centred chiefly on the very meticulousness and luxuriance of his descriptive passages; they were sometimes felt to be laboured and overdone. Such cavilling did not enter into de Cyon's estimate of Tolstoy. The Russian novelist could never be fairly accused of indulging in long descriptive passages just to display his powers of observation, or even with the mistaken idea that the whole truth involved counting every fly on the wall. He saw the external world and described it always through the eyes of the principal character of the moment.

The horrors of the battlefield are shown through the eyes of Andrew Bolkonsky, the tragic spectacle of Moscow in flames through those of Pierre Bezukhov, the heady swirl of a ball-room waltz is conveyed by an account of Natasha's impressions, and so forth.

If the point seems to have been a little neglected by de Cyon's successors, it cannot lightly be dismissed if we are to reach a fair assessment of the influence Tolstoy may have had on the French novel after the eighties. Such long descriptive passages as are encountered at the beginning of many of Balzac's works and were an outstanding feature of Loti's books—passages in which the author is obviously recording an impression he himself has received at some point—are much less frequently to be met with in the twentieth-century novel. To some extent this may be attributed to the example of Tolstoy, consciously or unconsciously followed by French authors.

It will be recalled that the second quality de Cyon attributed to Tolstoy was that of being 'an exquisitely delicate psychologist'. Among all the critics who came after de Cyon, there was never one that dared dissent from this proposition. One would indeed be hard put to it to cite a novelist in any literature who had mastered more thoroughly the art of laying bare the mental and spiritual mechanism of his characters. Tolstoy is like the devil in Lesage's story: but he takes the roofs off people's minds, instead of just taking them off their houses like Asmodée. One of the few past masters of psychological realism in France who can stand comparison is Stendhal; and de Cyon draws the parallel with insight and discretion. The two writers, he observes, have much in common; both had an early experience of military life, which is reflected in their works; both 'contracted from their earliest childhood the habit of watching themselves think, which trained them to read the hearts of others with consummate perspicacity'. Finally, their prose styles have identical qualities of mathematical precision and unpretentious sobriety. Tolstoy, however, is superior to Stendhal by the fertility of his imagination. The unending series of characters he presents is something quite unknown in literature outside the *Comédie Humaine*: and yet all these characters are perfectly distinct one from another, however lightly they may be drawn.

De Cyon had denoted Tolstoy in the title of his article as 'a Russian pessimist'. Discussing this pessimism, de Cyon maintains that it is one of the qualities that link him up with other writers in his country: melancholy laps the Russians round like an impenetrable fog. De Cyon suggests various reasons for this—the cold winters, the vast distances which separate men from one another, the tyrannical administration, 'the apathy born of the conviction that every well-intentioned effort is fated to remain sterile'.

Belittlement of the efficacy of personal endeavour is one of the salient characteristics of *War and Peace*. Courrière, as we have seen, made much of this.[1] 'Never', says de Cyon, 'does Tolstoy forget to show the futility of our projects, the vanity of what we call the effect of our wills.' In his view, Tolstoy is here reflecting a national failing of the Russians—the lack of tenacity that cuts short enterprises enthusiastically embarked upon, the quick discouragement as soon as difficulties present themselves: a facile generalization which the more recent history of the Russian nation may be held to belie.

All these essays—the work of earnest but on the whole unconsidered writers—add up to an unconcerted and largely ineffectual crusade to arouse interest in these two foreign novelists; and all the while their works remained almost completely unknown in France. Two things were now needed: that the French should be given the opportunity to read the novels in their own language; and that a fresh critic, writing with sufficient power and persuasion to capture the ear of a wide public, should undertake a full examination of the new works.

The crying need for translations was seen clearly by no less a

[1] And after him, Adolphe Badin: see his review of *War and Peace* ('Un Roman du comte Tolstoï', *Nouvelle Revue*, 15 Aug. 1881).

man than Turgenev. With customary urbanity Vogüé later summed
up the two sides of his activity in France with the words: 'Turgenev had come to us as a missionary of the Russian genius; by his
own example, he proved the high artistic merits of this genius.'[1]
It has been seen that Mérimée first mentioned him in connexion
with *The Sportsman's Sketches*. Turgenev made his name in France
with this work, of which two translations appeared in quick succession in the fifties. His subsequent novels, all translated at short
intervals after their appearance in Russia, increased his reputation;
their qualities of compression and clarity, of realism not darkened
by dreariness, impressed many a discerning French reader. The
friendships he made in Paris eventually persuaded him to remain
there, a voluntary exile from his native land. Mérimée knew him,
but was not the only nor even the closest of these friends. Turgenev was greatly attached to George Sand and to Flaubert, both
of whom he outlived; he was a guest at the table of the Goncourts,
and cultivated the acquaintance of writers of a younger generation,
Zola, Huysmans, Maupassant, and many others.

Although with the passing years Turgenev lost touch more and
more with his own country, he loyally used the very considerable
influence he had with French writers and publicists in order to
advertise other Russian novelists. In particular he was most anxious
to see Tolstoy appreciated at his true value; and this in spite of a
fierce personal antagonism which had at all times estranged the two
writers. He made it his business to find a publisher for Princess
Paskevitch's translation into French of *War and Peace*, and when
in 1879 this work appeared at St. Petersburg, he dispatched copies
to his friends Flaubert, Zola, and Daudet, and to leading critics:
Taine, Edmond About, Philippe Burty, André Theuriet, and
others. Auguste Dorchain, who met Turgenev in Paris in 1878,
related many years later how one day Turgenev had pulled out of
his book-shelves three volumes with a pale green cover, saying:
'Here is one of the finest books of the century, a novel by one of my
countrymen, Leo Tolstoy. Although it has already been translated
for some time, hardly anyone has spoken about it, and no one has
said what an extraordinary masterpiece it is. It is called *War and
Peace*. Read it, and tell all your friends they ought to read it.'[2]

Another literary novice, Paul Bourget, first learnt the names of

---

[1] Vogüé, *Le Roman russe*, p. xliii.
[2] Dorchain, in a letter to *La Plume*, 15 Dec. 1913, p. 271.

Tolstoy and of Dostoevsky from the lips of Turgenev whom he met at Taine's house. 'One of the finest impressions of my younger days', Bourget later wrote, 'was the generous impartiality of the aged Russian novelist rendering an honest and noble tribute to his more youthful rivals.'[1]

And it was not only lip-service. On one occasion, when asked for a contribution by the editorial staff of *Le Temps* (a paper in which some of his stories had already appeared), Turgenev handed in a French translation of Tolstoy's *Sevastopol*, and asked for that to be published instead.[2] In a letter to Tolstoy dated 9 January 1879, he offered to undertake a translation into French of *The Cossacks*: nothing appears, however, to have come of this project.[3]

If Tolstoy did not become widely known in France at an earlier date, this was clearly through no fault of Turgenev's. It has been enough that his efforts failed for suspicions to have been cast on their genuineness; was it a chance slip or deliberate malice that prompted one memorialist to describe Turgenev, many years after his death, as 'sly and envious—he never opened his mouth about Tolstoy or about Dostoevsky'?[4]

Between October 1883 and June 1886 Eugène-Melchior de Vogüé, the vulgarizer that the hour required, published the six articles that were gathered together to form the *Roman russe*; and over the same period a quite considerable mass of translations of Tolstoy and Dostoevsky were thrown on to the market. The 'Russian invasion' had been launched.

Meanwhile, articles and essays about the two novelists were becoming increasingly commonplace, but our record may safely confine itself to alluding simply to three representative critics: Arvède Barine, Ernest Dupuy, and Francisque Sarcey.

The appearance of the first translations of Dostoevsky in the summer and autumn of 1884 was the occasion for a fresh article in the *Revue Bleue* dealing with the Russian novelist.[5] This time the contributor was Arvède Barine (Mme Vincens) who was later to

---

[1] Bourget, 'Eugène-Melchior de Vogüé', *Revue des Deux Mondes*, 15 Jan. 1912, p. 252.
[2] See Halpérine-Kaminsky, op. cit., p. 204. The translation duly appeared in Apr. 1876.
[3] See I. Pavlovsky, *Souvenirs sur Tourgueneff* (1887), pp. 29, 31.
[4] Léon Daudet, *Quand vivait mon père* (1934), p. 16.
[5] 'Un Grand Romancier: Dostoïevsky', *Revue Bleue*, 27 Dec. 1884.

acquire a reputation for her vivid biographies of historical and literary figures. In her article Arvède Barine furnished a few details about Dostoevsky's life up to the time of his sentence of penal servitude, and also summed up his qualities and defects as a writer in two or three sentences which contain the essence of most of what Vogüé will have to say about him: 'Dostoevsky is often prolix and diffuse, like a true realist he spares us nothing, not even the chattering of fools and the raving of madmen. He has too little thought for the art of novel-construction. He is occasionally tedious. These blots are lost in the lustre lent to his work by a phenomenal knowledge of the human heart, a very lively dramatic sense, a powerful imagination and a strength of sympathy which recalls George Eliot.'

The following year Arvède Barine wrote a further article for the same periodical, this time on Tolstoy.[1] Her study of Dostoevsky had anticipated Vogüé's by little more than a fortnight: that of Tolstoy came seventeen months later than Vogüé's article on the same author in the *Revue des Deux Mondes*, but Arvède Barine contrives to avoid repeating anything he had said by confining her comments to *Anna Karenina*; Vogüé had refrained from discussing this work since, at the time he was writing, the translation was only just being brought out. Arvède Barine testifies to the rapid growth of Tolstoy's popularity in France over the past few months, and she herself clearly thrills to the magnificence of Tolstoy's genius.

When you have praised the luxuriance and strength of his imagination, the intuitive power that allows him to follow the most fleeting and secret impulses in his characters' souls, his dramatic sense that caused Flaubert to compare him to Shakespeare,[2] the sublimity of his thought, the fruitfulness of his views on all subjects, the poetry of his landscapes, the atmosphere of kindliness in which the work is steeped, you may feel, if you have not chanced to be born and bred in Russia, like a traveller who contemplates from afar an enormous peak looming above a chain of mountains.

All this reads more like publisher's 'blurb' than a real attempt at critical analysis; and it is remarkable how the same phrases spring

[1] 'Le Comte Léon Tolstoï: à propos d'*Anna Karénine*', *Revue Bleue*, 5 Dec. 1885.
[2] Flaubert, in a letter of thanks to Turgenev for sending him a copy of *War and Peace*, wrote of the book: 'C'est de premier ordre! Quel peintre et quel psychologue! . . . Il me semble qu'il y a parfois des choses à la Shakespeare. Je poussais des cris d'admiration pendant cette lecture.' See Halpérine-Kaminsky, op. cit., p. 130.

to Arvède Barine's mind when she speaks of Tolstoy as when she wrote about Dostoevsky. Both her articles wear very much the air of being written to order, after a hasty perusal of the books she was reviewing and the small stock of information readily available about the personalities of the two authors.

Ernest Dupuy's work (*Les Grands Maîtres de la littérature russe*, 1885) is, in spite of its title, unpretentious. It was Dupuy's misfortune that his work preceded so closely Vogüé's much more masterly and better-documented work. Dupuy is not always trustworthy over matters of fact; Leger took a sardonic pleasure in demolishing a theory he had advanced that Mérimée's *Matteo Falcone* was plagiarized from Gogol . . . by pointing out that *Taras Bulba*, which Dupuy had alleged was the original, appeared six years later than Mérimée's story![1]

The 'great masters', according to Dupuy, are Gogol, Turgenev, and Tolstoy—not Dostoevsky, nor even Pushkin. He normally contents himself with giving a straightforward analysis of the outstanding works of the authors.[2] He is careful not to be tempted into comparisons, invidious or otherwise, with contemporary French writers—thereby distinguishing himself sharply from Vogüé both in his procedure and aims. In his discussion of Turgenev, however, Dupuy draws a distinction between the Russian novelist and contemporary French realists which is of some interest in view of Vogüé's judgements on the relative merits of the two schools. 'The observations of our realist writers', says Dupuy, 'are cold and systematic; those of the Russians and particularly of Turgenev are always natural and in most instances impassioned' (p. 207). In his very first work, *The Sportsman's Sketches*, Turgenev 'had the courage to show not only his pity, but his affection for the Russian peasant' (p. 169) and every succeeding novel from the pen of Turgenev is marked by its pathos, a pathos which by the simplest means sometimes attains the sublime. The error of French realists— Dupuy makes an honourable exception of Alphonse Daudet—is 'to

---

[1] Leger, *Nicolas Gogol*, pp. 99–103. See also Duchesne in the *Revue de Littérature comparée*, 1929, p. 140.

[2] Olga Smirnoff, 'Études et souvenirs', *Nouvelle Revue*, 1 Dec. 1885, mentions it as a fact that Dupuy was assisted by two Russian collaborators. This would explain how he manages to include in his chapter on Tolstoy accounts of (among other works) *The Cossacks*, and *The Journal of a Billiard-Marker*, of which the first was not translated until 1886, while the second appeared as late as 1888.

mistake unresponsiveness for strength, and they set up to be very strong fellows. Turgenev's great superiority is that he does not set up to be anything, not even a specialist in vulgarity and earthiness' (pp. 213–14).

Generally speaking, Dupuy's book, useful as it may have been as a work of propaganda and vulgarization, is practically negligible as a serious contribution to the study in France of the Russian novelists.

Francisque Sarcey's contribution was modest but not without originality. It consisted of a series of seven articles which appeared in the *Nouvelle Revue* between August 1885 and September 1886, each one giving an account of one or other of the new translations which were being published about this time. Sarcey, unlike Vogüé or Arvède Barine, had no knowledge of Russian and no special qualifications for speaking of Russian literature; but the value of his remarks is thereby, if anything, enhanced: one feels the impressions he records are those of the average educated Frenchman happening on these rather strange works of art after a lifetime of wide and intelligent reading. Sarcey was older than most of the other writers who played a leading part in introducing the French to the Russian novel, and he was armed for his task by a long experience of literary (and especially dramatic) criticism.

Of the various novels of which he gives an account, it is *Anna Karenina* which seems to have chiefly impressed Sarcey. 'I don't think I know any story more moving, more absorbing, more instructive and more moral at one and the same time. . . . I beg of you, read *Anna Karenina!*'[1] *War and Peace* is recommended a little less warmly, largely because of its alarming dimensions: but, since it is summer and the afternoon heat will keep his readers indoors for four hours a day, this three-volume novel will fill in their time as amusingly and as profitably as any other reading.[2]

Tolstoy's emotionalism, more than any other quality of his writing, appealed to Sarcey. In *War and Peace* he finds particularly affecting the passage in which Generalissimo Kutuzov bursts into tears when he hears the French have started the retreat from Moscow; the hard old father of Andrew Bolkonsky has his 'moments of soft-heartedness' while his daughter is 'kind-heartedness itself'.[3] As for *Anna Karenina*, Sarcey defies anyone to read the chapter

---

[1] Sarcey, 'Les Livres', *Nouvelle Revue*, 15 Jan. 1886, p. 406.
[2] Ibid., 1 Aug. 1885, p. 634.   [3] Ibid., p. 632.

where Anna pays secretly a visit to her little son, without bursting into tears. 'The whole story is impregnated with a tenderness and a pity quite beyond words.... As I write these lines, I feel my heart leap in my breast and tears filling my eyes, so vivid the impression it has made on me.'[1]

Dostoevsky he puts frankly on a lower plane than Tolstoy. Comparing the two works which gained for each his reputation in France, Sarcey writes:

> *Crime and Punishment* is the book of a Gaboriau[2] turned philosopher: it is the work of a Balzac tarred by mysticism. *War and Peace* is an admirable epic. *Crime and Punishment* is a highly curious and amusing novel. The ladies would rather read *Crime and Punishment*. *War and Peace* will satisfy the gentlemen better.[3]

Crime and Punishment was the work on which, more than on any other, Dostoevsky's reputation in France was founded. This harrowing story of the duel between a murderer and the internal forces which crumble his moral fibre and drive him to acknowledge publicly his crime, seems to have curdled the blood of very many Frenchmen in the eighties, and perhaps the novel owed its sweeping success largely to these less reputable allurements. As years passed, however, and *Crime and Punishment* continued to be read with scarcely abated interest, it became clear that the fascination of the book sprang from something deeper than the mere capacity to thrill; and in 1888 Lemaître (who could never be accused of partiality where the Russian novelists were concerned), corrected Sarcey's somewhat deprecatory judgement, remarking that 'if Dostoevsky's novel had no more in it than a tale after the style of Gaboriau, it would not have stirred us so deeply.... *Crime and Punishment* is not just a detective novel; it is, above all, the history of a soul.'[4]

The fact remains, however, that Dostoevsky's book first made its name in France as a novel of terror; and thus far, Sarcey faithfully reflects public opinion. He records that from the moment of its first appearance the work caused a great commotion 'among the educated younger generation at Paris', and confesses for his own part that for twenty years no book had had such an effect on him.

---

[1] Sarcey, op. cit., 15 Jan. 1886, pp. 405–6.
[2] Gaboriau: a popular French writer of detective novels who wrote in the 1860's.   [3] Sarcey, op. cit., 15 Aug. 1885, p. 869.
[4] Lemaître, *Impressions de théâtre, 4e série*, p. 249.

'If the primary merit of a work of literature is to capture the imagination of the reader, to people his sleep with horrible nightmares, to abash his reason and to wring his heart, it is certain that *Crime and Punishment* is one of the most marvellous novels that have appeared for half a century.'[1] But it was not only Sarcey's hair that bristled: other contemporary writers give similar accounts of the trepidation caused by a first reading of the novel. Léon Sichler, in a hack manual of Russian literature which came out in 1887, tells how he lent the book to one of his friends, a hard-boiled fellow, who was worn to a shadow after a night spent 'between sleeplessness and nightmares, so shaken had he been by the first pages of *Crime and Punishment*.'[2]

Sarcey can hardly be blamed for finding in Dostoevsky a great deal to disconcert him; for the Russian needed to wait until the French had grown more familiar with his method of writing, and had had the opportunity of reading the other works at that time untranslated, before justice could be done him; and his canonization was, on the whole, a task reserved for the generation still at the lycée at that time. Of the famous scene in *Crime and Punishment* when Raskolnikov confesses himself to Sonia, Sarcey remarks 'nothing more astonishing for us Frenchmen than this evening's conversation. . . . It is not ridiculous; it is *different*.'[3] The situation in *Insulted and Injured*, where Natasha's lover discusses with her former suitor whether the latter should marry the girl or not, is equally strange. 'This *ménage à trois* is the oddest thing for us Frenchmen.'[4] Dostoevsky's reputation for 'un-Frenchness' is in the making.

In stressing first and foremost the emotional qualities of Tolstoy's novel, and in failing to penetrate beneath the disconcerting surface-level of Dostoevsky, Sarcey betrays a limitation in critical acuity which, as we shall discover, mars Vogüé's work as well: a circumstance which may suggest that the reactions of these two men to the new form of art were not dictated solely by personal taste and prejudice, but were in some degree a reflection of the 'spirit of the age', and in particular of the spirit of the upper middle classes to which they belonged, traditionalist but not necessarily reactionary, highly cultivated, a little unimaginative but not unintelligent.

[1] Sarcey, op. cit., p. 855.
[2] Sichler, *Histoire de la littérature russe*, p. 319.
[3] Sarcey, op. cit., pp. 867–8.   [4] Ibid., 1 Sept. 1885, p. 184.

II

THE ONSLAUGHT ON THE NATURALIST CITADEL

IN 1876, Eugène-Melchior de Vogüé, then aged 28, was appointed secretary to the Embassy at St. Petersburg. This was his second diplomatic post, his apprenticeship having been made at Constantinople. At St. Petersburg the young attaché found time, in the midst of his official and literary activities, to learn Russian; in this he showed uncommon zeal, for in this city where French was the accepted medium of polite conversation, few foreigners troubled themselves to master the vernacular tongue. Armed or partly armed with this knowledge, he set about discovering for himself the literature of the country and cultivating the acquaintance of its leading writers. He met N. Leskov, the noted novelist and short-story writer; V. Soloviev, the philosopher of religious idealism; B. Markevitch, a popular novel-writer; and no doubt many others.[1] He attended the funeral of Dostoevsky, whom he had known during the last few years of the novelist's life. He was at any rate in correspondence with Tolstoy. In 1878 his marriage to Alexandra Annenkov, maid of honour to the Tsarina, set a seal on the bonds that linked him to the people he was shortly to interpret to his fellow-countrymen.

The idea of this interpretation was, it seems, suggested to him by the wife of the poet-novelist, Alexis Tolstoy. Perhaps too the success of Leroy-Beaulieu's articles on Russian institutions gave Vogüé the idea of writing a rival series to deal with an aspect of the Russian spirit on which Leroy-Beaulieu had on the whole kept silent. As early as 1879, in a brief review of *War and Peace* written for Buloz's *Revue*, Vogüé hinted at the general study he was preparing. The first of the five[2] articles which were later remodelled and published in book-form, was on Turgenev (*Revue des Deux Mondes*, 15 October 1883—on the morrow of the novelist's death). Tolstoy followed, in the issue for 15 July 1884, while the studies

---

[1] See Halpérine-Kaminsky, preface to Tolstoï, *La Mort* (1886), p. iv.

[2] An article on Pushkin, which later became chapter II of *Le Roman russe*, was the only one not to appear in the *Revue des Deux Mondes*: it was published in the *Revue Bleue*, 29 May 1886.

of Dostoevsky and Gogol appeared 15 January and 15 November 1885. On 15 May 1886 the *Revue* published, under the title 'De la littérature réaliste à propos du roman russe', Vogüé's summing-up of his findings. This article was an extract from the preface of the *Roman russe*, which was registered as a publication in June 1886.

Vogüé added and retracted little more than was necessary to bind up the individual studies and make of them a coherent book. Some of his remarks (e.g. concerning Tolstoy in the opening pages of the article) were omitted since they had an application in 1884 which was out-moded in 1886. Generally speaking, the article on Tolstoy was the most subject to revision; this is what might only be expected, since the author was, unlike the others Vogüé treated, still alive and writing very actively.

The *Roman russe* was more than just one of the instruments by which the French were introduced to a virtually unsuspected and little-known galaxy of writers. Its importance as a landmark in the history of nineteenth-century literature has been widely recognized. The judgements Vogüé passed on the Russians coloured French appreciation of the newcomers for a generation; his main thesis, that Russian realism held a lesson for contemporary France, made the book almost a literary manifesto. Admittedly the *Correspondant*, the organ of the Catholic-conservative wing, gave it a cool reception on its first appearance;[1] but as time wore on, the spokesmen of the Right were disposed to count the publication as a date in the history of literature.[2] Even a man like Ernest-Charles, who was no admirer of the Russians, agrees that the *Roman russe* appeared just when it was most needed and revealed Russian literature to the French when it would have been unpardonable for the mass of the reading public to continue in ignorance of it: Vogüé's book, although its 'eloquence is greater than its erudition', was superficial only to the degree necessary, at that time, in order to

---

[1] Ph. Douhaire, 'Les Romans russes', *Le Correspondant*, 25 Aug. 1886, p. 762: 'Cet ouvrage est plein de thèses éblouissantes, mais plus spécieuses souvent que solides, ou qui du moins demanderaient à être plus fortement établies qu'elles ne le sont.'

[2] For instance, F. Brunetière: 'La Littérature européenne au XIXe siècle', *Revue des Deux Mondes*, 15 Dec. 1899, p. 679; J. Lionnet, *L'Évolution des idées chez quelques-uns de nos contemporains* (1903), p. 51 (footnote); V. Giraud, 'Eugène-Melchior de Vogüé', *Revue des Deux Mondes*, 15 May 1910, p. 296.

'start a literary, intellectual and ethical fashion in Parisian drawing-rooms'.[1]

To what extent was Vogüé's book responsible for the 'Russomania' of 1886? He remarks himself that his final article, which became the preamble to the *Roman russe*, 'has struck home very deeply, especially among younger people. I have evidence of that in the form of letters from people of varying positions, of visits from younger men and pieces of gossip which come back to me from every quarter.'[2] It also appears that the articles on Tolstoy, preceding by a few months the publication by Hachette of *La Guerre et la Paix*, helped to secure for the latter what Halpérine-Kaminsky calls *un succès foudroyant*. The translation, published first at St. Petersburg in 1879, had been on sale in France since that date; but whereas, according to the same authority, less than 500 copies had been disposed of before the publication of Vogüé's article, during 1885 over 20,000 copies were sold.[3]

On the other hand, Romain Rolland, recalling (admittedly after twenty-five years had blunted the edge of his impressions) the exuberance with which his generation devoured the works of Tolstoy, says 'the majority of us, myself among them, had not been acquainted with Eugène-Melchior de Vogüé's book until after reading Tolstoy; and his admiration seemed very restrained compared with ours'.[4] Vogüé himself notes that 'the Russian novel found its real public among the educated youth of every walk of life'[5]—and is it likely that these young enthusiasts subscribed in any overwhelming numbers to the *Revue des Deux Mondes*?

When one speaks of Vogüé's 'revelation' of the Russians, the phrase should not then be taken to mean more than that he secured them the ear of a far wider audience than would otherwise have been their lot at the start. Rolland's 'normaliens', and generally speaking all those with fresh minds and a curiosity for what was new and off the beaten track, would no doubt have read the Rus-

---

[1] J. Ernest-Charles, *Les Samedis littéraires* (1903), p. 331.

[2] Vogüé, letter to H. de Pontmartin, 26 May 1886.

[3] Halpérine-Kaminsky: 'Lettre inédite sur les études russes', *Revue Hebdomadaire*, 9 Mar. 1910, p. 144. The figure seems incredibly large, and d'Haussonville (preface to Vogüé, *Les Routes* (1910), pp. xxii–xxiii) sounds nearer the truth when he says that in the *five* years after 1885 'more than 10,000 copies' were disposed of.

[4] Rolland, *Vie de Tolstoï*, p. 3.

[5] Vogüé, *Le Roman russe*, p. lii. Unless otherwise noted, all quotations from Vogüé in this chapter are from the *Roman russe*.

sians and thrilled to them to exactly the same degree if Vogüé had never written the *Roman russe*. But Vogüé must be credited with having ensured that the cult of Tolstoy and Dostoevsky did not become at the outset an esoteric mystery. The prestige of the periodical in which he was writing, his own eloquence, and evident sincerity—all these must be allowed to have given great impetus to the rapid popularization of Tolstoy and Dostoevsky in France after 1886.

But the most important cause of the book's effectiveness was the appeal it made to the very large body of opinion which had, by 1886, grown tired of the methods and ideals of the Naturalists. It is not in the unexpectedness of Vogüé's presentation of the Russian novel but in the application he made of his findings that the true revelation is to be looked for. It has been wittily observed (and here translation would fall down) that the main purpose of the *Roman russe* was to 'tailler des croupières à la littérature française alors en vogue', and that 'M. de Vogüé a doublement aimé le roman russe: d'abord pour lui-même, et ensuite contre le roman français'.[1] The significance of Vogüé's masterpiece cannot be grasped unless it is seen as an attempt at utter demolishment of the naturalist aesthetic theory: it can be viewed, for instance, as a counter-blast to Zola's *Roman expérimental*, which had come out only a few years previously (in 1880).

All through the lengthy introduction to the *Roman russe*, in which, Vogüé told a friend, he had put the core of his thought,[2] the critic is describing the sorry state of the realist or naturalist movement in France and contrasting it with the far healthier condition of realism in Russia. Without attempting to deal with all the novelists that Zola had claimed as 'Naturalists', Vogüé goes straight to the father of them all, Gustave Flaubert (and discards Balzac and Stendhal whom he rightly regards as mere predecessors).

He attacks Flaubert on two scores: he denounces, firstly, his 'impassiveness', and, secondly, his 'pitilessness'. The Russian novelists, he maintains, are exempt from these vices.

By 'impassive' art, Vogüé is referring to the allegation that Flaubert designedly banished all emotion from the treatment of his human material, refusing to take sides in all questions of sentiment,

---

[1] A. Hermant, *La Vie littéraire*, 1ère série (1918), p. 143.
[2] Vogüé, letter to H. de Pontmartin, 26 May 1886.

even by implication. This view of Flaubert's attitude would be deprecated to-day as an over-simplification; but in any case it is certain that the novelists who followed Flaubert, and hailed him as their leader, moved farther and farther away from this ideally dispassionate, non-committal standpoint. Maupassant himself, Flaubert's personal disciple, in his very first work of fiction, where he might be expected to have been most under Flaubert's influence, enlists the reader's sympathy in no uncertain way on the side of Boule de Suif, and satirizes caustically her 'social superiors': a certain class-consciousness, a concern for the under-dog, is characteristic of nearly all the naturalist school in France. Nothing is more misleading than Vogüé's description of them, in this introduction to the *Roman russe*, as a school of 'acrobats, strolling entertainers' who 'profess a fine disdain for the bourgeois author who meddles with instructing or consoling mankind' (p. xxxiv).

The Russians, of course, do 'meddle with instructing and consoling mankind': Courrière had said it long ago: 'The Russian novel instructs, preaches, moralizes, develops some thesis or other.' This is what Vogüé has at the back of his mind all the time, and this is what he is leading up to.

The second fault which Vogüé found with Flaubert's novels was his 'pitilessness', the inhuman irony with which he pursued his hapless characters. 'Since he is unaware of the existence of a higher source of charity, he divests himself of all pity; in all the universe he sees only stupid or obnoxious animals, subjected to his experiments, the world of Bovarys and Homais' (p. xxxiii). *Bouvard et Pécuchet* is callousness pushed to the point of sadism: 'The unhappy Flaubert pursues that idiot [Bouvard] savagely; he forgets that moral infirmity is as worthy of compassion as physical infirmity . . . he has forgotten or scorns the voice which commanded respect for the poor in spirit, calling them blessed' (pp. xxxiii–xxxiv).

The criticism here seems strangely harsh, and seems to have been dictated more by Vogüé's Catholicism than by his concern for letters. And here we strike through to the core of Vogüé's hostility to Flaubert, Zola, and their brood, and his advocacy of Turgenev, Tolstoy, and Dostoevsky. If there was one metaphysical principle on which all French realists worked, it was scientific determinism. The supernatural, or simply the inexplicable, never intervened in their stories; once given the postulates of initial temperament and subsequent upbringing, the characters behaved in strict accordance. This realism left out of account any independent moral Agent: metaphysically, it was atheism.

Now this repelled Vogüé as it had repelled every Catholic before him, beginning with Barbey d'Aurevilly. But they had pleaded and blustered without avail: naturalism had gone its way and piled up one masterpiece after another. Vogüé's attack struck home because he was able for the first time to set up against the achievements of the French realist school those of a contemporary school of writers, also realists, whose works did have overtones of the other-worldly. They were not 'impassive' because, convinced of the existence of a divine Guide and Judge, they showed themselves anxious about the moral state of their characters. They were not 'pitiless', because this anxiety forbade them to take malicious delight in watching the struggles and downfalls of the men and women they wrote about.

True, the Russians were not Catholics. But (more from a spontaneous urge than in accordance with set convictions), they steeped their works in the Christian virtues of charity and forbearance. Turgenev, Tolstoy, Dostoevsky, 'swing in the breeze of every doctrine imported from abroad, sceptical, fatalist, positivist; but without realising it, in the very core of their being, they always remain ... Christians' (p. xlv). At the end of his book Vogüé speaks further of the Russians' 'forlorn efforts to expand the charity of the Gospels beyond its proper bounds', which have led them into cherishing 'a wild tenderness for Nature, for its humble offspring, for the disinherited and the sufferers' (p. 344). Russian realism is 'ennobled by moral emotion, by a concern for the divine and by sympathy for mankind' (p. 342).

Vogüé's contention was that this leaven of fraternity and charity would, if taken over from the Russians, transform French literature: he maintained that he already detected certain traces of its workings. Those who read the Russian novels with such avidity have been attracted, not by the local colour and spice of novelty, but by 'the spirit of life which informs these books, the note of sincerity and sympathy. The younger generation has found here the spiritual nourishment which our imaginative literature no longer affords, and being starved for it, they have fallen to with great appetite' (p. li). And Vogüé concludes categorically—formulating briefly his challenge and fundamental argument: 'My conviction is that the influence of the great Russian writers will be wholesome for our exhausted art . . .' (p. liii).

This, then, is Vogüé's approach to his subject: it is in this light that he will make his 'revelation'. We are less likely to be disappointed in the *Roman russe* if we regard it as being primarily a polemical work and only to a subordinate degree a work of pure criticism.

The title, *Le Roman russe*, is a loose one, embracing a series of monographs not all of which deal with novelists. The two chapters in which Vogüé argued most cogently his central thesis, are those on Dostoevsky and Tolstoy; and since these two writers, in years to come, were to mean more to the French than all other Russian literary figures, the other parts of his work may be passed over here, in the main, in silence. It is, however, worth observing that whether Vogüé is writing about Gogol or Turgenev, Tolstoy or Dostoevsky, his main argument never falls far into the background; and whenever he happens on a story or novel in which the moral overtones transfigure the realism to a notable degree, then he tends to dwell on the work irrespective of its intrinsic worth or significance. Thus he singled out, in his chapter on Gogol, the short story, *The Greatcoat*, for special attention. In this odd composition he found the germs of the 'compassion for humanity' which marked so strongly the works of Gogol's successors; and he does not forgo the opportunity of contrasting once more the 'pitilessness' of the Flaubert of 1880 with the sympathy which the Gogol of 1840 betrays for his wretched hero. Akaky Akakievitch has much in common with Flaubert's two celebrated comics, Bouvard and Pécuchet: like them, he is a copy-clerk, and, like them, a weak-minded and ingenuous creature. But between the realism of the French master and that of the Russian, yawns a gulf. The material, the treatment, are entirely different. Flaubert draws a caricature, makes a butt of Bouvard, jeers at him, spits on him; Gogol jokes about his hero gently and with a secret compassion. 'For the first, the man of weak intellect is nothing but a detestable monstrosity; for the second, he is an unhappy brother' (pp. 97–8).

In Turgenev, Vogüé was dealing with a writer whose works were readily accessible in translation, and who did not as an artist stand noticeably aloof from accepted European traditions. But for all the French influence on his art and thought, for all the personal links that bound him to Flaubert and the naturalists, Turgenev, in Vogüé's view, swims in the mainstream of the Russian novel, for he never relapses into the cult of 'impassiveness', he never relinquishes his interest and sympathy for the little world of his creation.

Vogüé illustrates the differences that separate Turgenev from the naturalists of contemporary France by suggesting how the latter might have treated one of the stories in *The Sportsman's Sketches* (*Living Relics*—the sportsman comes across a peasant woman, abandoned and wasted with sickness, who tells him the story of her life in a tone of quiet resignation). 'In this broken body there is a soul, purified by suffering, angelically meek, uplifted, without losing any of its peasant's artlessness, on the heights of absolute renunciation' (p. 160). This theme, which Turgenev treats with so much discretion, the followers of Zola, 'the illustrious friends of Turgenev's old age, would not have failed to turn into a lecture on pathology; they would have delighted in the dissection of these stiffened limbs, these hidden sores. They would have pointed out all the flaws in the nervous system and diagnosed idiocy' (p. 162).

Vogüé praises *The Sportsman's Sketches* chiefly as a work of political and social usefulness: it was a fearful blow dealt against the institution of serfdom. The book parades before us a gallery of peasants degraded by forced labour and the deprivation of personal liberty, and of nobles perverted by the enjoyment of absolute power. It is not, however, open war. Turgenev did not conduct a frontal assault on this survival of feudalism: the censorship would have made short work of any such an attempt. Russian writers dare only be pathetic, trusting their readers will grow indignant. It would be curious if the 'social pity' of the Russians, the mainstay of Vogüé's thesis, reduced itself to a subterfuge rendered necessary by a muzzled press. In Republican France 'social art' could not be a substitute for direct social criticism: if 'social art' was to be given preference over 'art for art', this would have to be on its own merits.

'Voici venir le Scythe, le vrai Scythe, qui va révolutionner toutes nos habitudes intellectuelles. . . .' This apostrophe, which Vogüé had originally applied to Tolstoy,[1] is placed at the beginning of the

[1] Vogüé, 'Le Comte Léon Tolstoï', *Revue des Deux Mondes*, 15 July 1884, p. 267.

chapter on Dostoevsky as if to mark the contrast with the 'westernized' Turgenev he has been discussing. In many respects, Dostoevsky is the very antithesis of Turgenev; but the two writers 'have one common characteristic . . . human sympathy'—a sympathy which in Dostoevsky swells to a 'desperate pity' for all who are sunk in distress and misfortune of every kind.

Poor Folk, Dostoevsky's first book, is a 'work of tenderness, springing from the soul in a single burst' in which the writer 'reveals his whole nature, his morbid sensitivity, his need for pity and devotion, his bitter conception of life, his fierce pride, always smarting' (p. 216)—but it is not until after his imprisonment in Siberia that the 'religion of human suffering' can really be seen in evolution, and to begin with, in Dostoevsky's memorial of this terrible passage in his life, the *Letters from the House of the Dead*.

Vogüé recalls that Dostoevsky's one intellectual recreation during his years of penal servitude was the reading of the New Testament; and so suffering becomes a true 'religion', fortified and illustrated by the authority of the Gospels. The characters of *The House of the Dead*, 'these extremists, are steeped in the spirit of a New Testament which has passed through Byzantium; they are fashioned by it to asceticism and martyrdom. . . . These people come directly from the Acts of the Apostles' (p. 238). Vogüé makes much of the episode of the Old-Believer, sent to Siberia for having burnt down an Orthodox church, who spends his leisure time reading prayers, and who throws a stone at the commandant 'solely in order to be flogged, "to submit to suffering" '; the scene illustrates 'the mystical value which the common man in Russia attributes to suffering, sought after for its own sake, for its propitiatory virtue' (p. 228).

Vogüé is careful to indicate the difference between Dostoevsky and the French naturalists, with whom certain lurid descriptions in *The House of the Dead* might appear to link him. There is no indifference in the Russian writer. 'The observer throws a cloak of broad sympathy over all the "unhappy folk" who surround him . . . he avoids thinking of their crimes, in order to bewail the sadness of their atonement, to look—for that is his constant care—for the divine spark which prevails always in the most degraded wretch' (p. 226). Nothing is glossed over in his account of the convict-prison. Dostoevsky surpasses the French naturalists in the atrocity of the scenes he evokes; and yet he is not of their school. Why?— because he has a moral and social purpose which transfigures the sordidness of the paths he treads. 'A man who visits an alms-house out of sheer curiosity, to gaze on picturesque sores, would be judged hardly; he who goes there to dress those sores, deserves interest and respect. Everything depends on the writer's intentions' (p. 236). Dostoevsky 'wrote to bring healing . . . *The House of the Dead* achieved for the deportees what *The Sportsman's Sketches* did for the serfs: it was the alarm-bell which hurried on reformatory measures' (p. 237).

This observation is not one of Vogüé's happiest, and later French critics rectified his mistaken view of Dostoevsky as an advanced liberal after the fashion of Turgenev.[1] Vogüé, in exalting Dostoevsky at the expense of the naturalists of his own country, overlooks the Russian's political record and at the same time ignores the strong reforming zeal of the leader of the school he decries, who had declared that

people will soon set about relieving extreme poverty, the day they decide to know it with the suffering and shame it involves. I am accused of retailing filthy inventions and spreading deliberate lies about poor people who have brought tears to my eyes. . . . My one desire is to show them as society has forced them to be, and to arouse such a pity, such a cry for justice, that France will at last cease to allow herself to be devoured by a handful of ambitious politicians, and will busy herself with bringing up healthy children and providing for them.[2]

In his study of *Crime and Punishment*, Vogüé develops the idea of the 'religion of suffering' of which he detected the germ in *The House of the Dead*. In the confession the criminal-hero Raskolnikov makes of his crime, and in Sonya's acceptance of exile with him, Vogüé sees the essence of this 'religion': 'Here we are back once more on the ground to which Dostoevsky always returns, the fundamental conception of Christianity among the Russians: that suffering is good in itself, especially suffering undergone in fellowship, that it is a sovereign remedy for all difficulties.' One cannot speak of the bond that unites this pair (Raskolnikov and Sonya) as Love: 'we have to restore the etymological meaning of our word *compassion*, as Bossuet understood it: suffering with or by another' (p. 250). And since every religion has a ritual, Raskolnikov falls at

---

[1] Thus Ossip-Lourier speaks of Dostoevsky's 'vie réactionnaire, rétrograde' (*Psychologie des romanciers russes* (1905), p. 160) and twits him with his abject professions of loyalty to the Tsar.

[2] Zola, letter to F. Maynard, 4 Apr. 1885, *Les Lettres et les arts* (1908), p. 254.

the feet of Sonya and proclaims he is kneeling before all suffering humanity.

The cruelty of certain scenes in *The House of the Dead* had been excused by Vogüé in consideration of the social reforms the book had implicitly urged. In the same way the dreadfulness of *Crime and Punishment* is justified, in the view of the French critic, by the moral intention of the author. And regarding this intention, there can be no doubts: Dostoevsky 'hopes to deter men from committing such actions by the picture of the torments of mind that follow them': but he reckoned without the perversity of men who are sometimes tempted to imitate the evil they are warned to eschew. Vogüé illustrates the point by the story of the Moscow student who, after reading the novel, reproduced in deed the crime Dostoevsky had imagined as fiction. Consequently he admits he is highly perplexed how he should assess the moral value of the work (p. 254).

The question is scarcely one which, it might be thought, would concern a literary critic; but Vogüé, having already in his introduction thrown down the glove to the pundits of 'art for art', cannot allow himself to neglect such considerations.

In the Russian novel—whether the author be Gogol or Turgenev, Tolstoy or Dostoevsky—Vogüé is searching all the time for the same two features: firstly, a faithful picturing of Russian, and human society, a microcosm reflecting the macrocosm of the world; and, secondly, an implicit moral commentary on this image which should fit in, as far as possible, with his own ideas as a mildly progressive Catholic democrat.

Hence it was that he found little to please him in Dostoevsky's later writings, at that time still untranslated. He saw only a falling-off after *Crime and Punishment*. The realist technique was, it seemed, abjured: 'the action is no more than a loose embroidering which can be fitted to all the author's theories'; the characters are no longer taken from real life but are 'conjured out of the inferno of his fancy . . . a shadow-theatre of figures flitting in and out the story' (p. 255). In his discussion of *The Idiot* and *The Possessed*, Vogüé attempts heroically to view the first from the standpoint of the Christian moralist and the second from that of the bourgeois politician. Myshkin is an incarnation of the Gospel commandment: 'Be as little children . . .': 'always the writer returns to his fixed idea, the supremacy of the simple-minded and the sufferer' (p. 259).

The Possessed is a precious document for students of the nihilist movement in Russia—no more, no less: Vogüé prefers it to Turgenev's *Virgin Soil*, but only because it is a more powerful treatment of the same theme. The shortcomings of Vogüé's critical armoury are startling when one considers that he regarded this latter-day masterpiece of Dostoevsky's purely as a treatise on the sources and strength of the social revolutionary movement in Russia, while André Gide, who devoted more space, in his essay on Dostoevsky, to *The Possessed* than to any other of the novels, hardly once mentions the nihilists.

The rifts and flaws in Vogüé's interpretation of Dostoevsky had an incalculable effect on the fortunes of this novelist in France. Vogüé's summary dismissal of *The Brothers Karamazov* made editors and translators shy of presenting it for a long time save in mutilated form. *The Idiot* and *The Possessed* received very inadequate treatment, and there is no mention, for instance, of so fundamental a work as *Letters from Underground*, or of the important novel, *A Raw Youth*. Those whose business it was to produce French versions were only too ready to accept Vogüé's word for it: *Letters from Underground* was miserably mangled in Halpérine-Kaminsky's translation, while French admirers of Dostoevsky had to wait till 1902 before they could read *A Raw Youth*.

Vogüé has been so severely taken to task by André Gide for the inadequacy of his presentation of Dostoevsky, that it seems almost unkind to labour the point. It has, besides, been pertinently observed that Vogüé's best excuse is that Gide himself for a long time recoiled before the difficulty of the subject.[1] Gide remarks sardonically that it was precisely the cavalier treatment of the later novels by 'ce grand dadais de Melchior' which prompted him originally to read them![2] 'M. de Vogüé,' he says elsewhere more graciously,

M. de Vogüé, who made the noble gesture of presenting to France on the silver salver of his eloquence the iron keys of Russian literature, excused himself, when he came to Dostoevsky, for the uncouthness of his author. . . . With the result that we are not too sure which feeling is uppermost: gratitude, for he was, after all, the first to open our eyes—or

[1] M. Arnauld, '*Dostoïevsky*, par André Gide', *Nouvelle Revue Française*, Aug. 1923, p. 151.
[2] Gide, *Journal*, 5 Mar. 1927 (Ed. de la Pléiade, p. 832).

irritation, for he offers us, seemingly against his own will for there can be no question about his good intentions, a deplorably reduced, incomplete, hence untrue picture of that extraordinary genius.[1]

It should be borne in mind, however, that Vogüé may have been tempering his own more favourable opinion of Dostoevsky in order to suit the conservative tastes of readers of the *Revue des Deux Mondes*. Those of his pronouncements which were not intended for the *Revue* give, in fact, quite a different picture of Vogüé's attitude to Dostoevsky. In a letter to Pontmartin (31 December 1884) he says, about Dostoevsky, 'he is an enormous figure. . . . Taine was telling me the other day that MM. Zola, Daudet, de Goncourt and company are not worthy to unloose the shoe-latchet of that man.' Elsewhere[2] Vogüé seems to hint that Dostoevsky's works will please an élite, the 'spirits who range the world in quest of new horizons', but he fears that the novels 'will utterly scandalize the ordinary habits of reasoning such as can be bought ready-made from the stores'. There is a note of derision here in his reference to those who could not stomach the genius of Dostoevsky and whose minds are dressed in 'decent standard suits, within anyone's reach, perhaps a little tightly cut, but which save the wearer a lot of trouble'. Admittedly Vogüé is here writing a foreword to one of the translations, and in the circumstances he was practically bound to express himself favourably with regard to his author. None the less, there is no reason to suppose that he was insincere in this instance; and in another foreword, placed at the beginning of Derély's translation of *The Idiot*, Vogüé's treatment of Dostoevsky is altogether more generous than it had been in the *Roman russe*. Here he seems genuinely anxious to smooth the path for his author, to combat the prejudices that might turn his French readers against him.

He seems to have felt that the main impediment to full appreciation of the Russian author was the strangeness of the behaviour of his characters. The impression these characters give of being dominated by their impulses, instead of dominating them as would a good sound Latin, 'renders them unacceptable for the good people in our parts'. There is a slight ring of irony in this 'good people'— Vogüé is palpably taking Dostoevsky's part, though one suspects it

---

[1] Gide, *Dostoïevsky*, pp. 2, 4.
[2] In the preface to Neyroud's translation of *The House of the Dead*.

is with an effort. The power of the intellect, in the characters of the Russian novelist, is undisciplined, uncontrolled. The book (*The Idiot*) is mad, it will be said: so are the figures it describes and the incidents it relates. Has literature the right to concentrate thus on morbid aberrations?

It is remarkable that Vogüé had, in the *Roman russe*, himself thrown up his hands in dismay at Dostoevsky's 'morbid preoccupation with exceptional types' (p. 279). He had complained that in the later novels particularly, all the characters were perpetually in a state of simmering emotion. They are never shown eating: they seem to subsist on strong tea if they are not addicted to vodka. They scarcely ever sleep, and if they do, it is to dream. They are nearly always in a fever. 'Among the numberless characters invented by Dostoevsky, I do not know one individual that M. Charcot could not claim on some ground or another' (p. 257).

Vogüé, in his preface to *The Idiot*, tries to defend Dostoevsky against these objections (although he had been one of the first to formulate them), by arguing that all imaginative literature that deals with the passions is more or less a study of minds unhinged; for what is passion if not a temporary suspension of the reasoning faculties? Do not Oreste, Phèdre, Hermione, by the disorder of their emotions and ideas, show themselves to be at the mercy of that very insanity which the psychotherapist examines in his clinic? 'Thus literature, willy-nilly, studies a disease, gives us a course in mental pathology, every time it describes a highly developed condition of passion.'

The great distinction between the classical authors and Dostoevsky is simply that the former did not realize what they were doing, whereas Dostoevsky is fully aware of the close kinship between passion and madness: from his point of view, madness is the norm, not the exception.

Vogüé concludes here by making a quite remarkable prophecy. He says that Dostoevsky's work will need to wait a couple of generations before it earns the full appreciation to which it is entitled.

In fifty years' time, when the science of mankind has enforced on the general public the slow, inevitable revolution we are witnessing, when it will be necessary to expunge from dictionaries many old terms, the over-narrow meaning of which no longer corresponds to our present state of knowledge—and chief among them the words *mad, madness*—then it will be seen that this daring Russian probed many a problem which will be then, if not solved, at least frankly accepted by all.

The fifty years have elapsed, and in the interval the writings of Freud have revolutionized our ideas on the motives of behaviour. Nowadays scarcely anyone would attempt an interpretation of Dostoevsky without reference to the new science of the sub-conscious, which, if it has not abolished the word 'madness', has at any rate made it, as Vogüé foresaw, a term altogether too gross for precise application. Such intuitive flashes as these go far to redeem Vogüé's alleged obtuseness with regard to Dostoevsky, stigmatized so caustically by André Gide.

The viscount's blend of irritation and enthusiasm, of short-sightedness and penetration, makes it hard to pronounce one way or the other about his Dostoevsky criticism; but assuredly Gide was a trifle unjust to his predecessor. Dostoevsky found in his first French interpreter one who grasped at the handle if he did not push open the door; who saw his limitations without realizing his profundities; and whose findings were perhaps more tendentious than well-founded. The chief value of Vogüé's essay on Dostoevsky is that it is eminently representative of the middle attitude of the French reader of his generation: full of curiosity for such extra-ordinary productions, but full of misgiving none the less.

Vogüé's chapter on Tolstoy is the most objective of all the mono-graphs in the Roman russe: and for that reason no doubt the most successful. Only towards the end (pp. 321–7), when he tries to establish comparisons between Tolstoy and the French realists, does the tendentious note creep in. But in the main, his account of Tolstoy's literary achievements is impartial and inspired with an unfeigned admiration which he succeeds in communicating to his reader.

Not everything, however, that Vogüé advances about Tolstoy can be passed unchallenged. His fundamental starting-point is that Tolstoy is the supreme exponent of 'realism'. Vogüé had, whenever possible, viewed the Russian novelists as realists, but he had been compelled to admit that every one of them, at one stage or another, violated the commandments of the realist doctrine. Gogol provided an early example of a work of realism in Dead Souls, although the realism of his earlier compositions is compromised by a leaning towards romantic fantasy and caricature; Turgenev, towards the end of his life, fell into the error of allowing personal prejudices to bias his vision; Dostoevsky, in his later works in particular, was apt to float out of the world of reality on the flood-tide of mystical effusions. But Tolstoy is the realist *par excellence*. He had anticipated naturalism. A modern reader, picking up Tolstoy's *Family Happiness* (written 1859) 'would think he was reading the work of one of our young novelists who teach him a disillusioned approach to the world; he would be surprised to discover that the plain unvarnished reproduction of the realities of middle-class life was invented in Russia thirty years ago'.[1]

To say that Tolstoy was realist because he reproduced the realities of life, because he was 'concerned to imitate real life', (p. 305) means in practice absolutely nothing: Vogüé is turning in circles. It needs little reflection to put him the question: 'How can you tell Tolstoy is reproducing the realities of life? How do you know that his inventions are nearer to what actually is, than the inventions of Dostoevsky—or indeed of any other writer?' Vogüé said that Tolstoy was 'gifted with unequalled lucidity and powers of penetration for the scientific study of the phenomena of life. He has a clear quick analytic view of everything that is on earth, both inside man and outside him' (p. 282). But the most that can surely be said is that Tolstoy's view of life and reality coincided with Vogüé's, and probably with that of most men of Vogüé's generation and upbringing. In another generation however, or among men with a different social and intellectual background, Tolstoy's view of reality might seem quite inadequate or even false—unreal; they might find a greater measure of 'reality' in the account of life given by an altogether different kind of writer: Dostoevsky, for instance.

With this reservation, that Tolstoy's 'realism' was by no means equivalent to 'the Truth', as Vogüé suggested it was, we may pass on to consider his analysis of the means by which Tolstoy gave the impression of 'reproducing reality'; and here we shall find Vogüé on firmer ground.

---

[1] Vogüé, *Le Roman russe*, p. 292. Vogüé first made this observation in 1882, applying it to Tolstoy's short story, *Three Deaths*, in a foreword he wrote to his own translation of the tale: 'Bien avant qu'on eût inventé chez nous et réduit en formule la littérature dite *naturaliste, impressionniste*, M. Tolstoï avait été conduit, non point par une théorie, mais par la nature de son esprit, à photographier la vie dans ses plus cruelles réalités, dans ses plus fugitives nuances.' (*Revue des Deux Mondes*, 15 Aug. 1882, p. 913.)

Tolstoy, remarks Vogüé, in the first place never romanticizes, that is, he will never exploit the emotional and irrational content of any situation he describes. Tolstoy writes of his childhood, shunning completely the sentimentality that such a subject usually compels (pp. 288–9). He visits the Caucasus, a land radiant, for a young man with literary aspirations, with the romantic aura cast over it by the poetry of Pushkin and Lermontov; but in the novel he writes (*The Cossacks*), the turbulent fairyland becomes a province of the Russian Empire, divided into so many administrative areas (pp. 285–6). He takes part in the Crimean campaign, but in his descriptions of war, in *Sevastopol* and in *War and Peace*, his writing, Vogüé maintains, has the authentic ring of truth about it; feats of courage are accomplished by men whose minds are filled with the most trivial concerns. At the most 'through sheer simplicity, the narrator sometimes draws tears to our eyes for these heroes unconscious of their heroism' (p. 299).

In the second place, Tolstoy disregards all the acquired and non-essential dignities, the physical and intellectual adornments of men and women. Vogüé believes that the secret of Tolstoy's genius is his refusal to be blinded by the ordinary conventions of nobility, greatness, sublimity, his inexorable reduction of all humanity to the lowest common denominator; herein he is to be distinguished from Balzac, the 'father of French realism'.

The lowest common denominator, for humanity, is the physical, the animal being; and in Tolstoy the highest of the high are brought down to the level of the lowest by the attention the author gives to the corporal detail. And so Vogüé reminds us (p. 302) how Napoleon in *War and Peace* is described on the eve of Borodino at his toilet, his fat naked body being sponged down by a valet. Nowhere more than in his treatment of Natasha is Tolstoy's rejection of the romantic convention more evident—the 'seductive maiden quivering with life' (p. 314) becomes in the Epilogue a mother of children, limiting her interests to her household duties. And the final answer to the metaphysical questionings of Bezukhov is provided by the 'poor in spirit' Platon Karataev, the unintelligent half-animal, 'good-hearted, however, vaguely fraternal' (p. 312).

It is through this reduction of humanity to a common level, the view of a god-like Being contemplating the world of his creation, that Tolstoy attains 'impassiveness'. Now Vogüé had castigated Flaubert scathingly for his impassiveness: he smoothes over this contradiction in a far from satisfactory way by claiming that Tolstoy's moral greatness justifies this attitude which in a lesser man would be overweening! Tolstoy's impassiveness does not revolt Vogüé as does the affectation of indifference in the French realists —Stendhal, Flaubert: the irony with which they handle their puppets arouses a certain irritation in the mind of a sceptical reader; their claim to pass judgement on their creation seems impertinent. Such is not Vogüé's feeling when reading *War and Peace* or *Anna Karenina*: Tolstoy the human being gives place to a spirit of supernatural attributes, 'something occult and fearful, the ever-present shadow of the Infinite . . . a Question silenced by the Inaccessible, a far-away sigh breathed by Fate over Nothingness. . . . I see passing in procession the eternally unknown spirits of Power and Might: they alone have the right to deride mankind; and before them, I bow down' (p. 324). Tolstoy constitutes himself demi-god.

There are other distinctions to be drawn between this Russian colossus and the French pygmies; whereas they labour at purely artistic perfection, Tolstoy, by his very neglect of style, appears to enhance the impression of haphazard life which his work breathes. And there is Tolstoy's predilection for aristocratic heroes, the culminating reason, in the opinion of the Viscount Eugène-Melchior de Vogüé, for his superiority over the French naturalists.

Whether you like it or not, it is the peaks that first attract your gaze as you look round on the world; if you linger in the lower regions, your public will not follow you. . . . You will only be able to keep this public faithful by being obscene, by pandering to its most brutal instincts; we still await the naturalist novel which will be readable while remaining decent [p. 327].

Mindful no doubt of the inflated sales of *Nana*, and of the licentiousness of Huysmans' earlier novels, Vogüé reminds his readers that '*War and Peace* is in the hands of every young Russian girl; *Anna Karenina* unfolds its perilous subject like a manual of morality, without one suggestive painting' (p. 323).

There is no doubt that Vogüé felt Tolstoy ought to be used as a literary model by the French novel-writers of his day. In 1886 he was already quite prepared to draw a parallel between the influence of Walter Scott on French minds in 1820 and that of Tolstoy on

his contemporaries.[1] All the comparisons that Vogüé makes between Tolstoy and the French naturalists tend to one conclusion
only: they are all designed to show how superior a writer Tolstoy
is. But has he that quality of 'Christian charity' or 'social pity'?—
the quality Vogüé never grew tired of emphasizing in his presentation of Gogol, Turgenev, and above all Dostoevsky, and which
distinguished them, in his opinion, from the pundits of the French
realist school. It was this we were to regard as the essential merit
of the Russian novel; it was this that was needed to 'revive' the
French novel. But it was the one quality that Vogüé does not claim
for Tolstoy: for the reason that it was not there. The austerity of
Tolstoy's condemnation of the reprobate sours the milk of human
kindness. This is true particularly of *Anna Karenina*, the abstract
hero of which 'is Duty, opposed to the blandishments of passion'
(p. 317). In this fiercely austere morality, what room is there for
pity of the erring creatures who sin against the canon and are
inevitably crushed?

Tolstoy has no pity for any of his victims. You will never hear in him
the soft notes of compassion which are so frequently to be heard in the
productions of Dickens, Turgenev, and even of realists such as Zola and
Bourget, who never let slip the opportunity of stressing their human
feelings. To Count Tolstoy it may, perhaps, appear strange, but many
of his readers reproach him for being cold, unfeeling, harsh. To have
Anna Karenina throw herself under the train, and not once breathe a
sigh! To follow the death-throes of Ivan Ilyitch—and not let fall a single
tear! This seems so incomprehensible and revolting to many readers
that they are prepared to deny the artistic genius of Count Tolstoy.[2]

This extreme declaration of a twentieth-century Russian critic
exposes the flaw in the essential argument of the *Roman russe*.

Elsewhere in his book Vogüé has all the time been at pains to
point out that the outstanding quality of Gogol, Turgenev, Dostoevsky, the quality that sweetens the harshness of their realism
and raises it to a sublimer plane than had been reached by Flaubert
or Zola, is their implicit sympathy with their characters. In a
harsher age we might use the word 'sentimentalism'; and it is

[1] Letter to A. de Pontmartin, 30 July 1886: 'Je crois qu'il [Tolstoy] a pénétré
les esprits de notre génération aussi profondément que Walter Scott ceux de la
vôtre. Mais il faut attendre quelques années encore pour faire la preuve.'

[2] L. Shestov, *Dobro v uchenii gr. Tolstogo i F. Nietzsche* (St. Petersburg,
1907), p. 10.

beside the point to argue whether Dostoevsky (other than in some of his minor works perhaps) is in fact a sentimentalist: it is sufficient that Vogüé (and others in France at this time) saw him as such.

But to claim that Tolstoy similarly is a sentimentalist is more than Vogüé can honestly do. True, Sarcey had shed tears over Anna's clandestine visit to her child whom the rigours of the law had forbidden her to see: but even Sarcey admits that 'Tolstoy . . . treats her [Anna] with really pitiless cruelty'.[1] Tolstoy never himself sheds tears over the fate of his characters, and Vogüé was too discerning a reader not to be aware of this.

Tolstoy, a naturalist as much as Zola or Maupassant, excelled them merely in being a greater man, a more profound artist; and it is a manifest waste of time to advise young writers to produce works of genius. Was Vogüé mistaken, then, in pressing Tolstoy on the French as a model?

It would be rash to conclude so. Tolstoy had a very definite message for the French, but it was not a literary one.

Tolstoy's novels are all histories of conversions (this is especially true of *Resurrection*, the novel he wrote after Vogüé's essay). All his principal characters, Bezukhov, Prince Andrew, Levin, are, like Tolstoy himself, in perpetual search for an issue from the problems proposed by a materialist interpretation of the universe. They mirror the characteristic revolt of many minds at the end of the century against the scientific theory of evolution based on natural selection, and the unjustifiable extension of this theory from biology into the realms of sociology, economic science, and so forth. The ideas of a universal struggle for life, of the survival of the fittest, were repellent to Tolstoy just as they were to many others in his age: and the notion that Utopia was being attained by the progressive advances of science and technique was absurd.

In Tolstoy's novel the revolt took the form of a 'conversion' to 'doing good'—the rather vague conclusion which is reached by his two heroes, Levin in *Anna Karenina* and Bezukhov in *War and Peace*. Their conclusions were a foreshadowing of what was awaiting Tolstoy himself, and at the time Vogüé was writing, Tolstoy had ceased to use fictitious characters to reflect these problems and was engaged in finding and formulating his own solutions. Vogüé devotes several pages at the end of his chapter to recording Tolstoy's 'crisis' and conversion, and subjects *What I Believe* and *What then*

[1] Sarcey, 'Les Livres', *Nouvelle Revue*, 15 Jan. 1886, p. 403.

should we do? to a somewhat disdainful analysis; repeating the celebrated 'death-bed' letter of Turgenev he summons this 'great writer of the Russian land' to return to the cultivation of his literary gifts. This impatience of Vogüé's is liable to be misleading. He would have been the last to deny that, for any thoughtful novelist, one of the most obvious paths of escape from the impasse of scientific materialism was precisely a return to religious faith of some sort or another. Tolstoy, in resorting to 'mysticism' to resolve the problems that positivism could not touch, was simply the pioneer along the road which certain members of the naturalist school itself would shortly tread. The only difference (but it was a capital one) was that Huysmans and Bourget were reconverted to Catholicism, whereas Tolstoy forged his own evangelist faith—in doing which he was perhaps prompted chiefly by his own insubordinate nature and his perpetual distrust of received ideas. But the difference, for a Catholic like Vogüé, was important. The slighting account of *What I Believe* should not be looked on as a condemnation of ends, but of means. It was Tolstoy's ridicule of organized religion, his personal interpretation of the New Testament, that was unsavoury: not the attempt to break out of the vicious circle of nihilism and find 'the peace that passeth all understanding', the knowledge of God.

It is worth noting that six years later Vogüé appears to have realized his mistake. He admitted then[1] that Tolstoy's teaching, however chimerical it may appear to many, 'is a response to certain urgent demands, in his own country and in the two hemispheres, since people never tire of reading him'. In declaring previously that Tolstoy would lose his power over the minds of Frenchmen by abandoning the novel for didactic writing, Vogüé now fears that he made a gross blunder for which he does penance. Tolstoy's theoretical writings contain exaggerations: but their excuse may be found in the inattentiveness of men to any doctrine unless its conclusions are forced to the point of absurdity.

Broadly speaking, the objections that may be brought against Vogüé's evaluation of Tolstoy fall under two heads. In the first place he was searching, in Tolstoy's literary productions, for a quality conspicuous by its absence, that is, sentimentalism; and, secondly, his Catholic upbringing prevented him from realizing at this stage the immense significance of the system of ethical thought

[1] Vogüé, 'Les Cigognes', *Revue des Deux Mondes*, 15 Feb. 1892.

that Tolstoy was in the process of evolving. Vogüé was looking for Tolstoy's message for French literature; but this message was not to be compared with the message he had for the consciences of Frenchmen, and indeed of men of all nationalities.

Earlier essays on Russian literature had been simply informative. Vogüé's book was polemical. His predecessors had marshalled facts. Vogüé opened a debate which lasted for at least twenty-five years. After 1886, the Russian novelists were not merely the representatives of an exotic and barbarous art, as they had very largely been for Mérimée and the earlier generation of 'orientalists'. They were now a factor in French literature, a source of inspiration perhaps, guides for better or for worse. One was compelled to adopt an attitude, either, with Vogüé, welcoming the breath of idealism with which they imbued the stuffy atmosphere of scientific materialism, or else, with a strong party of traditionalists, deprecating this 'septentriomania' as it polluted the original springs of French art.

Vogüé of course had not dreamt of advocating the Russians as models in every respect. There was much, especially in matters of artistic technique, that shocked the Latin whom he always remained. He limited his comparisons between the two literatures to the plane of the spirit. And the debate was pursued on this plane.

In the fifteen or twenty years that follow the publication of the *Roman russe*, one witnesses a lively altercation on Vogüé's thesis that 'the influence of the great Russian writers will be wholesome for our exhausted art'—an altercation which gained in virulence as the foreign masterpieces became known in ever-widening circles. The debate trailed off only when it became evident that Tolstoy and Dostoevsky had ceased to be the infatuation of a clique, and were in process of becoming a legend for the many. Mastication, in fact, was over, and digestion had started.

III

THE BREAK-THROUGH

Vogüé's articles on Tolstoy and Dostoevsky had sounded as it were the 'tucket' with which, in Elizabethan plays, the arrival of kings is announced. The stage is now filled with the royal characters in person, caracoling with much neighing and clashing of armour. In a passage of his study of Tolstoy for the *Revue des Deux Mondes* (deleted in the final version published in book-form) Vogüé expresses a certain diffidence about praising a bear which is still in Russia. By the time the *Roman russe* was published, if we may exchange our metaphor for Vogüé's, the bear had charged across the frontiers laden with the three ponderous tomes of *War and Peace* and the two volumes of *Anna Karenina*.

It may be that there is no completely adequate means of ascertaining the precise measure of diffusion of an author among his reading public; even were data readily available showing how many copies of a given book were distributed in a given year, one would still be uncertain how far sales could be equated with reading individuals. When a particular author is in fashion, it is likely that a number of purchasers of his works will never open them. Nevertheless, some idea of the stages of the 'invasion' of the Russian novel may be gained by examining the rapidity with which translations and retranslations were made into French.

The earliest recorded translation of Tolstoy into French dates from 1866. Under the title *Nikolinka*, certain pages of an English translation of *Childhood* were put into French and published as 'L'Enfance d'un seigneur russe'. Tolstoy's first appearance in the French language was probably even earlier: we know that *Sevastopol*, written in 1855, so impressed the Tsar at the time of the Crimean War that he ordered a translation to be prepared. It was either this translation or a later one that appeared in *Le Temps*, largely through the good offices of Turgenev, in 1876.[1]

The first translation into French of *War and Peace* was made (in 1879) in Russia also. Princess Irene Paskevitch, who was responsible for this monumental task, had preceded the work by a render-

---

[1] See above, p. 21.

ing of *Family Happiness* in 1877. Her work was anonymous, but received high praise from French reviewers.[1]

Anna Karenina was first published in France in 1885. The translation was anonymous, but according to Sarcey was due to 'a French lady married to a Russian, and whose name is Mme Bohomoletz'.[2]

As for Dostoevsky, two of his novels had appeared in book-form by the time Vogüé published his *Roman russe*: these were *Insulted and Injured* and *Crime and Punishment*, both in 1884. Specimens of Dostoevsky's work had, however, been translated much earlier. Extracts from *Poor Folk* had been given by Philippe Douhaire as far back as 1853 in an anthology entitled *Le Décaméron russe*; while the *Courrier russe* and the *Journal de Saint-Pétersbourg* (two French journals circulating inside Russia) had published translated extracts from *Crime and Punishment* and *A Gentle Soul*[3] in 1866 and 1877 respectively. The latter paper also published, in 1881, Humbert's translation of *Insulted and Injured*, three years before it made its first appearance in France. It is of course rather unlikely that more than a sprinkling of 'orientalists' in France would have been subscribers to these papers.

To sum up then: by the beginning of June 1886 (the crucial point of our history, when the *Roman russe* first appeared in the book-shop windows) there had appeared two translations of novels by Dostoevsky (*Insulted and Injured* and *Crime and Punishment*), and three translations of novels by Tolstoy (*Family Happiness*, *War and Peace*, and *Anna Karenina*). To complete the list, we should add two more books of Tolstoy's which have not been mentioned so far in this chapter: *What I Believe* (translated as *Ma Religion*, in 1884), and *The Cossacks* and *Sevastopol*, issued in one volume in the spring of 1886. In all, then, seven volumes, all of which (save *Family Happiness*) had been published for the first time at Paris at intervals over the preceding twenty-four months.

But after June 1886 the scene changes completely. At the end of

[1] Perhaps a matter of gallantry: the princess signed herself: 'Une Russe'. Vogüé's review appeared in the *Revue des Deux Mondes*, 15 June 1879.

[2] Sarcey, 'Les Livres', *Nouvelle Revue*, 15 Jan. 1886, p. 407.

[3] The latter being published separately in the same year, at St. Petersburg, with the title *La Douce Créature*. A translation was not brought out in France until 1886 (by Halpérine-Kaminsky, who gave his version the Russian title, *Krotkaïa*).

the year Vogüé likened the rush of translations to an invasion, the *revanche* for 1812. The French had set fire to Moscow. The Russians will not burn down Paris—its own inhabitants, Vogüé comments in a wry reference to the events of 1871, can do this without help from outside. The Russians will instead flood Paris with printer's ink! All the summer they have been surreptitiously pullulating, as Vogüé puts it, and have hatched out of every printing-press. In a review of recent publications he mentions seven translations of Tolstoy, four of Dostoevsky, two of Pisemsky, one of Goncharov, and a belated version of Turgenev's *On the Eve.*[1]

Once the flood-gates were opened, the torrent could not be halted. Vogüé had noted at the close of the year 1886 that, as far as Tolstoy was concerned, 'with the exception of a few trifles, all the work of the novelist is to-day translated'; but there remained 'that of the religious and social reformer'.[2] Volumes bearing Tolstoy's name on the title-page continued to pour forth. In 1886 there were seven such books; in 1887, seven again; in 1889, three; in 1890, eight. If, between 1890 and 1900, fewer novelties from Tolstoy's pen were announced, this was because his earlier works had indeed been exhausted. In point of fact one counts thirty-three translations in these ten years, a number due chiefly to Tolstoy's prolific output during this period. His reputation, which by now had spread all over Europe, was such as to ensure an immediate audience abroad for anything he wrote. And in the meantime his great novels were not forgotten: *War and Peace* was reprinted eight times, *Anna Karenina* nine times, between 1886 and 1900.

Dostoevsky was more rapidly exhausted. *The House of the Dead* and *The Possessed* appeared in 1886, *The Idiot* in 1887, *The Brothers Karamazov* in 1888. One may count eleven other translations of minor works between 1886 and 1900. The more recent retranslations of Dostoevsky are at once an indication of the abiding interest he has for the French and a reflection on the inadequacy of the earlier translations—adaptations, quite often, rather than translations—through which, none the less, Dostoevsky first became known in France.

The invasion of the Russian novel, however, was not simply a matter of the naturalization of Tolstoy and Dostoevsky. The flood

[1] Vogüé, 'Les Livres russes en France', *Revue des Deux Mondes,* 15 Dec. 1886.
[2] Ibid., p. 824.

that bore the whales washed up many lesser fish, and a great deal
of very small fry. Here again figures broadly tell the tale. After
1870 and before 1884, there is only a steady trickle of Russian
literary works translated into French: the yearly figures are: 1, 1,
2, 5, 1, 2, 3, 3, 3, 2, 3, 5, 1, 1. The jump in volume between 1884
and 1889 is noticeable: *exclusive* of the works of Tolstoy and
Dostoevsky, the numbers of books translated each year are: 1884,
5; 1885, 4; 1886, 5; 1887, 8; 1888, 10; 1889, 8. And in the next
ten years, until the end of the century, there is little sign of a
slackening in the rate of translations: the figures for these years
(still exclusive of our two chief authors) are: 1, 4, 9, 5, 13, 11, 5, 4,
7, 4.

The novelists whose works were translated include some whose
names rank high among Russian prose-writers of the nineteenth
century. There was in the first place Ivan Goncharov, for whom
Wyzewa broke a lance in 1891, protesting that it was unjust to
bestow so much attention on Tolstoy, Turgenev, and Dostoevsky
while neglecting this highly talented rival of theirs.[1] Actually Goncharov's best-known novel, *Oblomov*, had been translated in 1877,
and in 1886 was reprinted. In the same year his *Precipice* was translated and the French rendering of *A Commonplace Story* appeared
in 1887.

Besides Goncharov there was Pisemsky, the first specimen of
whose work was on sale in Paris in 1881, two more novels following
in 1886. There was Garshin: *Nadezhda Nikolaevna* was translated
in 1888, and in the following year *La Guerre* came out, an 'adaptation' by Halpérine-Kaminsky, Maupassant furnishing an introductory article. In the nineties the French were introduced to Leskov
and Korolenko. With the turn of the century came the first stories
of Gorky and of Chekhov.

The French reception of this literary invasion was, from the very
start, lukewarm except among the most zealous partisans of the
Russian novel. As early as 1886 feeling was strong that the reading
public was being imposed on by these multifarious translations,
especially those of the secondary Russian novelists: for with
Pisemsky, Leskov, Korolenko, came a host of barely remembered
writers, Madame Annenskaya and Madame Zhelikovskaya, D. P.
Muravlin, I. N. Potapenko, B. M. Markevitch, and many others.

[1] Wyzewa, 'Ivan Goncharof', in *Écrivains étrangers*, *2ᵉ série*.

It was the 'golden age' for translators, as one of them (J.-W. Bien-stock) declares rather naïvely in his recollections of the epoch. Teams of translators were formed, partly from students belonging to the Russian colony; three or four translations would be in progress at once, and as the translation of one page was finished by one student, it was whisked off to the printing-press without further ado.[1]

The movement was simply a 'cashing-in' on the success of *War and Peace* and *Crime and Punishment*, and before 1886 was far advanced, Sarcey struck a note of warning. 'We ought really to be careful we are not becoming infatuated, and I fear a sufficiently strict choice is not being made among the works of the Russian novelists. . . . Masterpieces alone seem to me to have the right to what I should like to call the honour of international currency.'[2] At the end of the year Wyzewa prophesied that 'the zeal of Parisian publishers in translating the Russians will doubtless be the principal literary phenomenon of the year 1887, as it was the principal phenomenon of the year that has just gone by'. But he is no less mistrustful than Sarcey, and fears lest 'this colourful invasion of volumes of highly varying merits will occasion a slackening in the sudden enthusiasm of French readers for this literature so copiously revealed'.[3] In less serious vein, Wyzewa tells how the Parisian publishers offered their customers fifty volumes of Tolstoy, promised a hundred of Dostoevsky, and sold them as translations from the Russian, books that had never been heard of in Russia; everything was received with rapture, 'and when several publishers began at the same time to issue the same work, our boulevards re-echoed with hoots of joy'.[4] Nor did it stop at Tolstoy and Dostoevsky: 'we saw descending on us an infinite quantity of oddly named writers. . . . There were even certain Russian novelists who did not exist, but whose genius we were none the less permitted to appreciate thanks to the astuteness of the translators.'[5]

Vogüé himself, about this time, deprecated the way in which

---

[1] See Boutchik, *La Littérature russe en France*, p. 31.
[2] Sarcey, 'Les Livres', *Nouvelle Revue*, 1 Sept. 1886, p. 167.
[3] Wyzewa, *Écrivains étrangers*, 2ᵉ *série*, p. 155.
[4] Ibid., p. 160. This happened, for instance, to Tolstoy's *Childhood* and also to his *Death of Ivan Ilyitch*. Of the latter Vogüé wrote (op. cit., p. 824): 'Écrit par l'auteur au mois de mars de cette année, ce récit est déjà traduit en double à Paris. Juste ciel! c'est une course.'
[5] Wyzewa, ibid., p. 206.

'publishers and translators have profited by the pronounced taste for books from Russia. . . . Russian literature has been boosted like an issue of shares in strong demand. I am afraid there may be a smash.' He already detects in the reading world 'a slight shudder of reaction' which is 'nothing as yet, but it would be as well to take account of the symptom'.[1]

As the years passed, the premonitions of Wyzewa and Vogüé proved well-founded. In a letter to Halpérine-Kaminsky dated 27 August 1892, Vogüé deplores the 'material greed of publishers' which had killed the goose that laid the golden eggs: they had forfeited the confidence of the reading public which sought enlightenment about works of choice, and had no wish to be crushed beneath an avalanche of paltry productions. Leger commented morosely on the wreckage in 1899. 'Many a Russian novel has dashed the hopes which had been founded on it by a speculative fury more commercial than literary in character.' You do not need to rummage long in the second-hand stalls on the banks of the Seine to fish up many a 'shipwreck of Muscovite life in the sixpenny box, or even being remaindered for twopence'.[2]

One of the chief reasons why French publishers pushed so actively translations from the Russian, was that Russia was one of the few important powers which had not been a signatory to the Berne Convention. After 5 September 1887, the permission of the author or of his heirs had to be obtained and royalties had to be paid for translations of books out of most of the other main European languages—English, German, Spanish, Italian. But it continued to be possible for anyone to translate into French any work published in Russia and have it published in France without remitting a penny to the author. This circumstance must have contributed in no small measure to the boom in translations from the Russian in the late eighties and nineties, which was altogether out of proportion to the importance of the literature; it accounts, too, for that curious phenomenon encountered, the same work being translated over and over again and issued by one publishing house after another.

The influence that these lesser Russian novelists may have had on French literature must have been restricted and, compared with that of Tolstoy and Dostoevsky, negligible. Turgenev was the only

[1] Vogüé, op. cit., p. 837.   [2] Leger, *Le Monde slave*, 2e série, p. 145.

possible rival, among their compatriots, that these two had to face in competing for the favour of the French reader; and they rapidly outstripped him in popularity after 1886. True, Taine was still convinced, when the *Roman russe* was published, that Turgenev should be given the palm: 'alongside him, Dostoevsky and Tolstoy appear to me to be ignoramuses of genius, who compose powerful works without knowing their trade';[1] but Taine held this view in the teeth of the majority it seems. In the same year Vogüé comments on 'the unfair reaction which has turned the public away from Turgenev', who has been supplanted in popular estimation by writers far more at variance with French artistic traditions. Vogüé discounts the phenomenon as a mere freak of fashion, and trusts Turgenev will, before long, come into his own again.[2]

But the eclipse continued. In 1894 Wyzewa observed that 'in the recent share-out of fame which we have instituted for the great writers of his race, Turgenev alone, more or less, seems to have lost what the others have won. . . . No one, or hardly anyone, thinks of reading him at the moment.'[3] And, looking back at the end of the century, Brunetière asserts that 'the Russians may prefer Turgenev to Tolstoy and Gogol or Pushkin to both of these, it remains true none the less that it was through Tolstoy and Dostoevsky that the Slav soul entered into communication with European literature'.[4]

It is notorious that a writer's reputation abroad may bear no relation to his standing at home. The poet, like the prophet, may sometimes find himself honoured everywhere save in his own country; but conversely, the laurels on the head of many a native poet wither in a foreign air. One may perhaps venture one or two reasons for the relative obscurity into which Turgenev fell in France when challenged by the triumphs of Tolstoy and Dostoevsky. Turgenev is a stylist and an artist: the other two conspicuously lacked these qualities of purely aesthetic perfection, but in spite of it, or perhaps for that very reason, won resounding successes. Style and 'atmosphere' are the first things lost when an author finds a foreign public: this is not necessarily because the translations deform his thought; but his appeal is to a fund of emotion held in common by the members of one race and culture,

---

[1] Taine, letter to Vogüé, 8 June 1886.
[2] Vogüé, op. cit., p. 834.
[3] Wyzewa, 'Revues russes', *Revue des Deux Mondes*, 15 May 1894, p. 458.
[4] Brunetière, 'La Littérature européenne au xixe siècle', *Revue des Deux Mondes*, 15 Dec. 1899, p. 652.

on which an alien tribe has simply no drawing rights. The Racines, the Keatses, the Turgenevs, the Anatole Frances, must be content for the most part with 'home consumption'; although, perhaps because their art is so intimately bound up with the national spirit, they will often be more dear to their compatriots than the writers whose stock abroad stands as high as it does at home or higher.

At any rate it took little time for Tolstoy's stock to soar in France: once he had gained a footing, he went on from strength to strength. Vogüé had struck an almost diffident note at the beginning of the study of Tolstoy which he inserted in the *Revue des Deux Mondes* in 1884, but little more than a year later, Arvède Barine could laugh at Vogüé's 'timidity', asserting that 'each new translation of a work by the author of *War and Peace* is to-day, in Paris, an event in literature'.[1] In December 1886 Wyzewa affirmed soberly that 'we are as well, if not better, acquainted with Tolstoy's works as with those of our most renowned French novelists'.[2] A good idea of Tolstoy's widespread appeal is conveyed by Romain Rolland's account of the enthusiasm of the 'normaliens' about 1886. 'My fellow-students and I were all very different one from another. In our little group . . . there frequently arose discussions, there were many disagreements; but for several months the love of Tolstoy united us practically all.' And it was not just a students' craze. Rolland recalls his surprise, while on a visit to his home in the provinces, to hear ordinary townsfolk with no special interest in literature, speaking seriously and with emotion about *The Death of Ivan Ilyitch*.[3]

In the nineties Tolstoy may be said to have fairly taken his Western public by storm. He eclipsed other Russian novelists who had laid earlier siege to the attention of the French. 'As soon as I hear his great voice,' says Wyzewa, 'the words of a Gogol and a Turgenev sound like empty chatter.'[4] He invited comparison with the greatest of the earth, and was looked on in France as the national writer of Russia.[5] Even the more frivolous elements of

[1] A. Barine, 'Le Comte Tolstoï', *Revue Bleue*, 5 Dec. 1885, p. 726.

[2] Wyzewa, *Écrivains étrangers*, *2ᵉ série*, p. 168.

[3] Rolland, *Vie de Tolstoï*, p. 2.

[4] Wyzewa, 'Revues russes', *Revue des Deux Mondes*, 15 Oct. 1893, p. 939.

[5] Cf. Z. Wenguerow: 'Le 70ᵉ anniversaire de Tolstoï', *Mercure de France*, Jan. 1899, p. 280: 'Comme c'est le cas avec Shakespeare en Angleterre, avec Goethe en Allemagne, l'œuvre de Tolstoï a dépassé les limites de la critique

French society had discovered Tolstoy and were revelling in *Anna Karenina* for reasons which would have horrified the austere moralist-author.

Our ladies of fashion [wrote one facetious chronicler] affect a taste for Tolstoy's novels. They leave an odd volume lying about their drawing-room, with a book-mark; and the servants whisper: 'Madame is reading Russian!' . . . Oh! how they delight in the marvellous chapters in which Tolstoy dissects for them fibre by fibre the sufferings of a betrayed husband, and explains to them his impotent rage. . . . These chapters are read and re-read, and got by heart; who knows? They may serve a purpose:

Forsan et haec olim meminisse juvabit![1]

The whole-heartedness of the welcome extended to Dostoevsky was tempered by certain misgivings, chiefly on aesthetic grounds. Vogüé had remarked, sourly and a little naïvely, in the *Roman russe*: 'His novels are at last being translated in France, and, what sur- prises me still more, people seem to be reading them with pleasure.'[2] To his friend Pontmartin, however, he had written (31 December 1884): 'I do not believe that he [Dostoevsky] is having the universal success of Tolstoy, but already he has found some fanatics'[3]— while on the occasion of the publication of the first translation of *The Idiot*, he observes that this strange writer, 'barely known through a few translations . . . has been exalted, then denigrated beyond reason'.[4] Dostoevsky's fundamental message, as Vogüé understood it, was becoming well known even among those who had not the patience to read his works: 'a lot has been talked about Dostoevsky in the past year'.[5]

In 1887 'Dostoevsky is beginning to be read and even liked in France'.[6] *Crime and Punishment* had been a revelation: thanks to this one work, Dostoevsky 'took his place among the foreign novelists whose name is familiar to the French public, at least to

esthétique, est devenue un événement de la vie nationale, intimement liée à l'histoire de la terre russe.'

[1] E. Combes, *Profils et types de la littérature russe* (1896), pp. 369–70.

[2] Vogüé, *Le Roman russe*, p. 204.

[3] The context suggests that the reference is to enthusiasts in France, not Russia.

[4] Vogüé, preface to Dostoïevsky, *L'Idiot*, p. i.

[5] Vogüé, preface to Dostoïevsky: *Souvenirs de la maison des morts*, p. ii (the remark should be dated mid-1886).

[6] L. Sichler, *Histoire de la littérature russe*, p. 316.

the lettered public. . . . Even those who could not stomach him, could not refrain from acknowledging his power, and saluting in him one of the most vigorous and original geniuses to whom our century has given birth.'[1] It was felt, however, even by the most zealous of the *slavomanes*, that his hour was yet to strike. Dostoevsky 'will only be truly understood when the rising nerve-storm of our century has reached its apogee'![2]

In 1889 the literary correspondent of the *Revue Bleue* proclaimed that 'the author of *The House of the Dead* has become one of the guides of our time, and rightly so', and made light of his detractors, defenders of an out-moded ideal of beauty. For his renewal of emotionalism the Russian may be pardoned his lack of art.[3] One has to go back to Poe, says Hennequin in the same year, to find a foreign writer who created so strong an impression in France among the more thoughtful sections of the reading public.[4] In the early nineties, ignorance of even the minor characters in Dostoevsky's novels is—ignorance indeed. Octave Mirbeau, inveighing against the injustices of certain pontiffs of literary criticism, exclaims: 'You may see them every day slavering over Flaubert, vomiting on Villiers, bragging they have never heard of Laforgue . . . and mistaking Marmeladov for a minor Russian poet.'[5]

Broadly speaking, then, it may be safely said that the wave of enthusiasm for the Russian novel in 1886 did not recede as suddenly as it had arrived. The terms in which Tolstoy and Dostoevsky are spoken of by contributors to the most widely read French periodicals leave little doubt that, by the end of the ninth decade of the century at any rate, most Frenchmen with any interest in contemporary letters would have had some acquaintance with the more outstanding of the works of the two Russian novelists.

The public, however, believes what it is told, to a discouraging degree. The pronouncements of French critics over these fifteen years are to be regarded both as pointers to the direction in which the current of opinion was flowing, and as controlling factors too: the lock-gates, as it were, that determined the strength of the flow.

[1] R. Frary, 'Le Mouvement littéraire', *Nouvelle Revue*, 1 July 1887, p.122.
[2] É. Halpérine-Kaminsky, '*La Puissance des ténèbres* sur la scène française', *Nouvelle Revue*, 1 Feb. 1888, p. 629.
[3] A. Filon, 'Courrier littéraire', *Revue Bleue*, 9 Nov. 1889, p. 604.
[4] Hennequin, *Écrivains francisés*, p. 163.
[5] J. Huret, *Enquête sur l'évolution littéraire*, p. 213.

Some of these critics were specialists in the study of foreign literatures and of Russian literature in particular; others—the majority
—had no qualifications for undertaking this work save their general
training and aptitude for the treatment of literary questions. It is
only by examining the opinions that these men put on paper that
one can arrive at a conclusion about the general drift of sympathy
(or antipathy) on which the Russian novel was borne.

IV

CONSOLIDATION

THE critical reception of the Russian 'invasion' can be broken down into four phases, each with definable characteristics, and one arising naturally from the other. We have used a military metaphor in speaking of Vogüé's 'assault' on the naturalist citadel, and in applying the term 'break-through' to the period during which, thanks to the rapid multiplication of translations, interest in the Russian novel spread far and wide. We have now arrived at the third stage, that of 'consolidation', which, chronologically speaking, coincided with the 'break-through'; it was a consolidation of critical opinions, Vogüé drawing more or less guarded support for his views from various quarters. The fourth stage, the 'counter-attack', was initiated in 1894 by Jules Lemaître, whose arguments attracted a strong body of traditionalists and nationalists at the very end of the century.

Among the innumerable and mostly ephemeral expressions of opinion about the Russians, a selection has to be made of the most typical and also of the most thoughtful: in the choice made, preference has been given to those writers who had some original development to graft on to Vogüé's conclusions.

On the extreme right wing of literary criticism in the eighties stood Vogüé's old friend and near neighbour, Armand de Pontmartin, whose entry into the world of letters had been made long before, in the years immediately following the triumph of Romanticism in France. Right at the end of his life he wrote two articles about Dostoevsky; the first of these, entitled 'Le Roman russe en France', is to be found in the 7th series of his *Souvenirs d'un vieux critique* (1886), and takes Vogüé's study of Dostoevsky as its point of departure. No doubt Pontmartin was disposed to look with an indulgent eye on the hobby-horse of his young friend Eugène-Melchior; but it is with numerous mental reservations that he offers his pinch of incense at the new altars.

It cost the older man little to grant Vogüé his first point, that there is a world of difference between 'our French realism and the far more powerful realism of the Russian novelists, particularly of

Dostoevsky'. To a Catholic and anti-republican like Pontmartin, any stick would serve for beating Zola. Following Vogüé still, he lays stress on the spirit of charity which pervades all Dostoevsky's works and which (so he says) is totally lacking in the purely physiological studies of the naturalists. Pontmartin emphasizes, even more strenuously than Vogüé, the broad religious streak in Dostoevsky, showing how (in *Crime and Punishment* particularly) the cry of suffering never turns to blasphemy, chastisement is seen as the means to atonement, and atonement the act that calls down forgiveness and redemption. Dostoevsky gives Pontmartin the text for little anti-democratic sallies, and the critic notes with satisfaction how far we are, in the tale of Sonya and Raskolnikov, 'from the idea of revolt, of anti-social strife, on which our novelists and dramatists rely to rehabilitate vice and crime' (p. 296). Truly of Dostoevsky, who was later to become the lodestar of revolutionaries like Charles-Louis Philippe and André Gide, it may be said that he was all things to all men; or, more properly perhaps, that every soul could nest in some bough of this magnificent tree.

In all the foregoing, Pontmartin is in agreement with Vogüé, and pushes his thesis to lengths the author of the *Roman russe* had shrunk from. But the older critic is rather more wary in underwriting Vogüé's main contention about the medicinal value of the Russian novel for the sick French mind. 'Nothing is more interesting', says Pontmartin, 'than this new appearance of Russian literature in French literature. But in my view we should be unwise to regard it as more than a chance occurrence of considerable magnitude' (p. 297). Russian literature deals with emotions, describes social conditions and social maladjustments, evokes aspirations, which are all quite foreign to the French. Pontmartin decidedly does not look to the Russian novel to correct the excesses and impurities of the contemporary novel in his own country. Mere imitation over here of the Russians would simply lead to their faults being exaggerated and their beauties lost. With a fine flourish, Pontmartin perorates:

Nos anémies et nos névroses réclament de bons rosbifs et du bon vin de Bordeaux, et non pas du caviar et de l'eau-de-vie de grain. Lisons, avec une attention profonde, avec une sympathie intelligente et aussi avec une ardente compassion, les récits fébriles, effrayants, magnétiques, saignants sous la hache du bourreau ou le bistouri de l'anatomiste, du malheureux Dostoïevsky; mais ne laissons pas dire que, dans la patrie

de Montaigne et de Racine, de Bossuet et de Molière, de Voltaire et de
Montesquieu, on n'est plus bon qu'à créer ou à copier une littérature
d'épileptiques, de malades, de visionnaires, de possédés, d'assassins, de
filles, de forçats, de monomanes et d'imbéciles [p. 298].

In 1887, probably, or 1888, Pontmartin returned to Dostoevsky
and reviewed with venom his novel *The Gambler* (which perhaps
would have been better left untranslated at least for a few years
longer: Dostoevsky was a most uneven writer). This second article
is contained in the 9th series of the *Souvenirs d'un vieux critique*.
The note of reserve with which Pontmartin had spoken of the
Russian's works in 1886 swells now to an angry roar of exasperation:

> Who will rid us . . . of the Russian novel, of this eternal Tolstoy, of
> that sempiternal Dostoevsky? You believe it's all over. . . . Oh no! After
> the positively last appearance, there are more to follow; and I am inclined
> to suppose a workshop, a factory in the background; and that publishers,
> lured by false hopes of profit, pay wages to hacks to manufacture
> Dostoevskys and Tolstoys' [p. 199].

Here is a reflection of the more sordid aspect of the 'Russian
invasion', on which we touched in our third chapter.

The susceptibilities of the Catholic Pontmartin were touched to
the quick by the ridiculous scene in which the Gambler tells of
the trouble he had to get his passport visaed at the Holy See, and
how he insulted a priest so as to speed the business up. 'And some
people want to sacrifice the French novel to twaddle like this!'
snorts the outraged critic (p. 204). Pontmartin lays his hands on
every weapon he can find, even holding it against Dostoevsky that
he gives his characters unpronounceable names (!) so unlike the
euphonious Rob Roys and Quentin Durwards that had charmed
his youthful ear. The accusations he makes that Dostoevsky is
unoriginal and lacks good sense are somewhat weakened, coming
after such petulance.

Pontmartin explains that he has only lingered over *The Gambler*,
'inferior to the most mediocre of French novels', because he hopes
it will initiate a 'legitimate reaction against the invasion of the
Cossacks in literature. Their success is due only to the surprise of
their assault'. Russian literature, which 'reveals an alliance between
ancient barbarism and a hastily acquired hothouse culture', is the
very worst of remedies to apply to French art in its present state
of excitement and enervation. 'Tolstoy was mad, Dostoevsky was

an epileptic; strange correctives to offer the devotees of Gustave Flaubert, the admirers of Baudelaire, the eccentric and decadent exponents of the naturalist novel!' (pp. 211–12). Besides which, Pontmartin has been assured by one who knows Russia well that these novelists, particularly Dostoevsky, enjoy only a bubble reputation, even in their native country!

If it can be taken that Pontmartin is a fair representative of traditionalist criticism, it is clear that Vogüé will recruit few followers from this camp. He will have to turn to younger and more flexible minds to find disciples who will propagate his message or, at all events, purge it of the errors it contained—not the truths.

One of the acutest and best-informed students of foreign literatures in France, Théodore de Wyzewa, overhauled the principal argument of Vogüé's book within the first six months of its publication, in an article headed 'L'Invasion des Russes dans la littérature française'.[1]

Wyzewa attributed the sagging popularity of the naturalist novel in France to the fact that its exponents restricted themselves to recording physical sensations and neglected the inner (psychological) mechanism of behaviour. Their presentation of life was one-sided, hence their art was unsatisfying. A certain impatience with the naturalist novel ensued, and it was generally thought—but mistakenly, Wyzewa believes—that this impatience arose because of the 'impassiveness' of the naturalist authors. Hence the success of Ohnet's *Maître de Forges* (1882), which was astutely advertised as being dished up with a strong flavour of sentimentalism.

None the less, it was felt still that the remedy was not altogether there. And then Vogüé came on the scene. This critic

was deeply aware of the real, unformulated desire of the French public, the desire that the psychical element in life should be at last restored; and he had likewise realized that the Russian novelists excelled by the attention they paid to the intimate side of life, the part that goes on in the mind. But he proclaimed, in addition, so as to captivate Parisian souls, that these Russian novelists waxed sentimental (s'attendrissaient) over their characters. On that, enthusiasm leapt up [p. 159].

[1] This was the title given when it was reprinted in 1897 in Wyzewa's *Écrivains étrangers*, 2e série. It first appeared, under the rubric 'Les Russes', in the *Revue Indépendante*, Jan. 1887. Our page references are to the book, the periodical being hard to come by.

In point of fact, declares Wyzewa, Vogüé was embroidering on his text. 'The Russian authors—I am speaking of the serious ones—do not practise this sentimentalism. They are prevented from doing so by the theoretical bases of their school and by the special character of their race' (p. 161). The objective of the realist school in Russia is the same as that of the realist schools in all other countries: to photograph the average man in average circumstances. The artist must never allow his lines to be blurred by emotionalism. If a realist novel, French or Russian, gives the impression of being impassioned rather than cold, this can only be because the characters selected for depiction are endowed with passionate natures. The selection of course depends on the individual novelist:

Hence all the confusion of our ideas about the Russian novelists. These writers belong to a race to whom the slightest incidents of life appear tinged with emotion, and if their characters never remain indifferent to the situations through which they pass, this is because, in ordinary life, Russian characters are always easily moved [p. 162].

What Vogüé had made appear to be not much more than a trick of the trade applied externally, Wyzewa attributes to something far deeper, the racial qualities of the Russians.

The Slavs have the peculiar gift of combining a sober and unerring vision of externalities with an incessant emotional interest in them. Hence, in the works of their greatest writers, 'passion does not accompany the story, it blends closely with it: and it is not the passion of the author for his characters, but the passion of the characters themselves, perceived through the passionate soul of an artist' (p. 164). The French find it hard to be detached without falling into indifference: quite the reverse for the Russians.

Wyzewa takes each of the outstanding Russian novelists in turn, as Vogüé had done, but turns the arguments of his colleague upside-down, and emphasizes how 'impassive' these artists really are. Gogol's masterpiece, *Dead Souls*, 'astounds us by the extreme impassiveness of its author' (p. 166). Turgenev, in all his books, 'always avoids becoming emotional over life as he shows it' (p. 167). Can it be said that any one of his characters appeals to him more than another? Turgenev's impassiveness is more strongly marked even than Flaubert's, for Flaubert only affects impassiveness—in reality he is a highly passionate writer, his passion being a furious contempt, which sometimes destroys his impartiality and distorts his picture of reality.

But there is Tolstoy—Tolstoy who appears to realize the ideal of the 'tender-hearted artist'. Each of his novels is an argument in favour of an idea, his characters can be infallibly grouped as sheep or goats, the pages of his novels are encumbered with his own theorizings and personal reflections. Might it not be that he is 'this sentimental novelist that our hearts, sick of impassiveness, yearn after?' (p. 168).

By no means, exclaims Wyzewa. Tolstoy undoubtedly conveys the impression of being more emotional a writer than any other: but only because, more than any other, he is gifted with the ability to project himself into the emotions of his characters. In, for instance, *Childhood* and *The Death of Ivan Ilyitch*, 'the reader is gripped with the delicate joys of childhood, the vague longings, the ungrounded melancholy which pervade the slow-moving hours of eventide, and then by the dreadful fear of death. But these sorrows and pleasures affect the characters of the story, not the author' (pp. 168–9). The intrusion of the author in *War and Peace*, to expound his theories on the workings of history, is exceptional, a matter of faulty construction.

Vogüé's revelation, then, has not been an unmixed blessing in Wyzewa's opinion. Certainly he should be congratulated for having focused the attention of the French on these works of art which fully deserve their reputation. But his revelation, being founded on a fallacious theory of the sentimentalism of the Russians, gave the French a distorted view of the true nature of Russian realist art. It also denied certain Russian authors, who could not be alined with the others, the applause and appreciation to which they were entitled,[1] while it brought others into prominence who might safely have been ignored. Wyzewa is altogether doubtful about the benefits French artists will derive from the revelation. 'They have been given too many new books, too quickly, too much at random. And since they were told to admire in these books qualities which were absent from them—despite the very praiseworthy zealousness of translators—French artists have not objected to pay homage, but have scarcely been able to draw any lessons.' Some French imitators of the Russian novel there may be: but the only lesson they have

---

[1] Wyzewa was perhaps thinking especially of Goncharov. See above, p. 52.

drawn is to throw over the technique of patient personal observation practised with such success by the naturalists: and Wyzewa, without mentioning names, speaks of 'several young writers who M. Zola might have hoped, a few years back, would turn into scrupulous followers' and who now 'strain themselves to adopt a thousand odd attitudes of awkward pity for the cardboard dolls they mass-produce' (p. 174). Tolstoy, Turgenev, and Goncharov deserve, however, a more intelligent reading than that. Their real achievement, according to Wyzewa, is that they have restored the art, which with the naturalists had fallen into abeyance, of putting into prominence the psychological, as well as the mere physiological motives of behaviour; thus they convey a complete picture of the internal workings of the human mind instead of a defective one.

What is the next stage? 'The Russian novel has killed French naturalism without replacing it.' The younger generation of writers in France would be best advised to turn their backs on the Russians, to recollect 'that they have a soul, and that this soul is anything but Russian, but belongs to their own province and country. Then Tolstoy and Goncharov will be able to help them—in some small measure—to release normal ideas and emotions from their souls. And, omitting to wring their hands in front of their readers, they will be able to resume the task of their great forerunners' (p. 175). This is the essential modification Wyzewa introduces to correct Vogüé's presentation of the Russian novel.

The immediate effect of this article was slight. The trend it combated was too strong. Wyzewa does not appear to have returned to the attack: the remainder of his articles on the Russian novelists —which were quite numerous—dealt with the foreign writers on their own merits, not in the repercussions of their works on French literature. But his arguments at this stage, and his final word of advice with its slightly nationalistic ring, were perhaps not entirely forgotten by the leaders of the anti-Russian reaction after 1894.

Émile Hennequin's *Écrivains francisés, études de critique scientifique* was written, as the author himself explains in a preface, to apply a method of literary history directly opposed to that of Taine. Instead of seeking in 'race, milieu, moment' the formative influences on genius, Hennequin set out to account for the development of a nation's thought and spiritual standards by reference to the influence of the great men who have acted as its beacon-lights. Instead of studying works of art on their own artistic merits or on the personal impression the critic receives from them, Hennequin proposed to examine the enthusiasm these works aroused in the mass of their readers, analysing in particular the reasons why this enthusiasm was greater at one epoch than at another, and in one social class rather than in another. He baptized this new method of criticism 'estho-psychology'.

In order to prove that 'these movements, in which the masses congregate around the man who can reveal himself their master, take place without regard to frontiers' (p. vi), Hennequin chose to study exclusively, in the *Écrivains francisés*, cases of foreign influence on French literature and thought. What is significant from the point of view of this present study is that, of the six authors Hennequin selected for the application of his analytical method, three (Turgenev, Dostoevsky, Tolstoy) are Russians.[1]

A concern with moral issues is common to all three. Turgenev stands apart from and above the French realists by his warmth and mellowness, his readiness to smile and be indulgent with the fool and the weakling. The moral elevation of Tolstoy's books derives from the impression he conveys of a certain interdependence existing among his characters; the jagged edges of the individualists dear to French authors are melted away in the glow of fellow-feeling and friendliness—which yet avoids slipping into the musty sentimentality which, says Hennequin, is all too common when a French author is dealing with scenes of family life. Tolstoy's characters are 'kindly by nature, their first impulse is to go affectionately towards their kind, they are instinctively predisposed to be open-hearted and sympathetic, they are inclined, despite social hierarchies and prejudices, to respond to the secret pull of brotherly love which in the last resort compels men to act humanely towards one another' (p. 224).

The ethical loftiness of his novels is not, however, the principle of their fascination. Hennequin honours the great Russian far more for the purely aesthetic qualities of his writing. Hennequin was one of the first to champion the 'complexity' of the Russians which upset many Frenchmen's notions about the unity and simplicity essential to any great work of art. He recognized that this

---

[1] Of the remainder, one is English (Dickens), one German (Heine), and one American (Poe).

complexity or apparent incoherence was in fact an indispensable
appanage of Russian realism.

War and Peace and *Anna Karenina* do not seek to analyse one
particular state, one particular passion, they 'contain life itself', the
whole life of a group of men and women of differing ages. And this
impression of untamed, unshorn life which his novels convey is
achieved by breaking loose from 'the narrow limits of a coherent
and dramatic series of incidents'. Tolstoy realized that the novel,
'if it is required to mirror life in all its interest and importance,
must be, like life itself, complex, many-sided and diffuse': the work
of art may thereby 'lose its polish, lose the artificial concentration
of effects and the sham unity of characters; but it will be able to
rise to the quivering and many-toned variety of real life, to the
point where it can blossom out into the same wealth of contrasts
and subtle developments as nature' (p. 199). *War and Peace* is the
archetype of this all-embracing form of art, and 'almost reaches
the true aim of the realist novel' (p. 211). Hennequin considers
Anna Karenina to be the 'more restricted and more untrue work';
his disapproval deepens for the later didactic fables, while on the
doctrinaire works of more recent years he pours the heaped vials of
his scorn: Tolstoy betrays himself here as a bigot sinking into the
'acute ravings of the craziest lunatics' (p. 230). It was Tolstoy's
misfortune to have thought it necessary to pass judgement on the
phenomena that he observed so keenly, and to banish from his
work those that he decided were evil, while studying with too
marked a sympathy those he believed were good: for reality
'is as rich in corruption as in purity' (p. 234). In other words,
Tolstoy the thinker violates the principles of realism in the
same measure as Tolstoy the artist had enlarged and fortified
them.

Tolstoy's moral optimism had been, in Vogüé's eyes, his finest
ornament, his greatest claim to respect: in Hennequin's analysis,
it is the darkest blemish, the quality least fit for propagation. But
although Tolstoy's fictions 'are not those of an honest thinker',
they could perhaps become—'were they less steeped in kindliness
and informed more by cold justice—the model, the type of the
human epic of the future' (p. 244). They foreshadow 'the future
form the novel will take, when it has become exclusively the historical, social, biographical description of a mass of human beings'
(p. 255). Unfortunately for Hennequin's prognostications, the novel

has still not reduced itself to any one such form, but remains as protean as ever.

It was, however, Dostoevsky who inspired Hennequin with his most exalted phrases. Hennequin, in fact, far more than Vogüé, may be said to have been the first Frenchman who responded fully to the magic of Dostoevsky, and he will remain for twenty years a lone pioneer. His original essay on Dostoevsky appeared in the *Revue Contemporaine* as far back as September 1885 (a matter of nine months after Vogüé's article on this writer was published). Save for certain additions he later made to this original draft, the study is based entirely on the two novels that had at that time been translated into French—*Crime and Punishment* and *Insulted and Injured*.

To begin with, is it possible to regard Dostoevsky as a member of the realist school?—the question Hennequin had raised in connexion with Tolstoy, he brings up afresh with reference to Tolstoy's fellow-novelist. The problem had for long exercised Vogüé, who was loth to divorce the author of *Crime and Punishment* from the companionship of Gogol, Turgenev, and Tolstoy, indisputably realists—if only for the sake of the unity of his book. Vogüé, however, was forced to admit that Dostoevsky's realism is, at best, one-sided. 'He is a traveller who has covered all the earth in his wanderings, and admirably described everything he saw, but who travelled only by night.'[1] He hints that certain of Dostoevsky's scenes seem more fantastic to a Parisian than to a Petersburger: these incredible characters with their wild and whirling words are copied from real life, which in Russia is altogether less sedate than it is in France.[2] No doubt Vogüé's readers were ready to take his word for it.

Dostoevsky must be classified as a realist by anyone reading certain scenes in *The House of the Dead* and in *Crime and Punishment*, which outdo French naturalism in the pitilessness of their 'realism':[3] but Vogüé here is unconsciously confusing realism with mere atrociousness.

For all this, it is evident that this pigeon-holing of Dostoevsky's art did not fully satisfy Vogüé: 'people who insist on classifying writers, will ask if he is a realist or an idealist; this hybrid author

[1] Vogüé, *Le Roman russe*, p. 267.
[2] Id., preface to Dostoïevsky, *L'Idiot*, p. vi.
[3] Id., *Le Roman russe*, pp. 236, 252.

eludes their clutch'.[1] In the preface he wrote for the translation of
The House of the Dead, Vogüé drew the attention of 'students
curious of new literary forms' to this work.

They will feel words fail them, when they try to apply our customary
formulae to the variety of aspects presented by this talented writer. On
first encountering him, they will appeal to all the rules of our literary
catechism to pin down this realist, this impassive, impressionist writer;
they will go on, thinking they have him in their grasp, but Proteus will
have escaped them; his untamed realism will resolve itself into an anxious
quest for the Ideal, his impassiveness will reveal a flame burning within.

This was as far as Vogüé had pursued the matter. His hesitations
are understandable. Dostoevsky presents his reader with an enigmatic mingling of observed reality, which can at times be utterly
compelling (as, for instance, in the description of the double murder
done by Raskolnikov), with scenes which are, viewed from the
standpoint of experience, wildly improbable (such as the account
of the scandalous charity ball given under the auspices of the
governor's wife in *The Possessed*).

Hennequin, whose judgement of Dostoevsky is a great deal more
charitable than Vogüé's and seems to have been reached with very
little reference to his predecessor, develops with much care the
thesis that Dostoevsky is in essence a realist. But, as Zola had said,
no artist imitates reality precisely, what they show is always a
distortion due to their individual temperaments. The distinguishing quality of the realist artist, in Hennequin's view, is that he dis-
figures the vision of the world by making it appear more ugly than
it is, that is, in attributing to it in full measure those qualities which
we are prone to find evil, or else to pity.

Where Dostoevsky was concerned, Hennequin perceived that
the distortion of reality found in his books was not due to his
defective vision, but was a sort of spiritual catharsis, deliberately
undertaken. 'This man is acquainted with reality; certain of his
observations, that, for instance, about the way women drink wine,[2]

---

[1] Vogüé, 'Dostoïevsky', *Revue des Deux Mondes*, 15 Jan. 1885, p. 350. This
sentence was deleted from the final draft in the *Roman russe*.

[2] Hennequin seems to be referring to the scene in *The Possessed*, iii. 7, where
Stefan Trofimovitch offers a glass of wine to a peasant woman, who 'drank it
decorously in three sips, as women do, and, with an expression of intense suffering on her face, handed back the wine-glass'; or, it may be, to the description in
Crime and Punishment, vi. 3, of Katya drinking a glass of wine offered by
Svidrigailov: 'she drank the glass at once, as women drink wine, that is, without
breaking off, in twenty gulps . . .'.

are as precise and as gratuitous as certain detailed findings of French realists. . . . Yet in this art of pure realism which he possesses to such perfection, Dostoevsky is not in his true element.' He uses his gifts of observation and analysis not in order to reproduce life but in order to keep in check his own morbid tendencies —'the excessiveness of his visionary's powers'. Dostoevsky, suppressing his native acuteness of insight, adopts all the juggler's tricks of an 'idealist' novelist, scamping the causal links between events, the motives behind acts. His vision is that of the 'distant and horror-stricken spectator' and he sees life 'from the outside and from afar off, whence it seems incoherent and strange' (pp. 166–7).

Hennequin does his best to acquit Dostoevsky of the charge, which Vogüé and others had made and will make in the future, that he fills his novels with characters that are scarcely ever to be met with in 'real life' outside sanatoria for the mentally sick. His argument is that by exaggeration Dostoevsky seeks—and attains— an acuteness of illusion which more sober analysts miss. All Dostoevsky's characters, at all times, are keyed to fever-pitch: their ideas, thoughts and fancies shoot up and burst like fireworks. But they are *living*—'these beings who, beyond the confines of the commonplace, represent the psychological exception, particularized and intensified in a state bordering on madness, they exhibit all the hesitations, sufferings, mobility and complexity of a creature of flesh and blood' (pp. 174–5).

Just as the truly distinctive quality of Tolstoy's characters is their unexceptional normality, so the salient characteristic of the vast majority of the protagonists of Dostoevsky's novels is their abnormality. They are more petulant (Dunya) or more patient (Sonya); more lustful (Rogozhin) or more chaste (Myshkin); more domineering (Barbara Petrovna) or more abject (Stepan Trofimovitch); more cunning (Smerdyakov) or more stupid (Dmitri), than the inhabitants of the workaday world.[1] Dostoevsky is at home in extremes, without sacrifice of complexity. His characters are stripped only of inessential superficialities; it is because the ordinary observer, through whose eyes a Tolstoy gazed, sees only

[1] In these examples I am developing Hennequin's thought on my own account. His original essay, as has been observed, was based on the reading of only two novels—*Insulted and Injured* and *Crime and Punishment*. One of the most remarkable features of his essay is that the analysis should be so penetrating, built on so narrow a foundation.

these superficialities, that Dostoevsky's picture seems distorted, incredible. Realism's avowed aim was to portray the 'average man'. Dostoevsky painted the unsuspected, but not for that exceptional, 'under-soul' which lurks in the depths of the 'average man'.

In order to discover and bring to light these depths, intelligence, phenomenal powers of observation, or a wide experience of mankind were ineffective, not even essential. It was a matter of intuition.

This is the basis of the broader criticism which André Suarès, just before the War, attempted to apply to Dostoevsky, and which Gide triumphantly achieved in 1923. But the germs of the new criticism are here in Hennequin's suggestive essay. The history of French—and, one might add, European—criticism of Dostoevsky might well have taken an unexpected turn if Hennequin had not been so prematurely cut off (he was drowned while bathing in the Seine, in July 1889, aged only thirty) and had had time to develop his ideas: or even if they had been formulated with greater clarity in the *Écrivains francisés*. Hennequin's writing is oddly tortuous, and his obscurity at times verges on incomprehensibility.

Besides discussing the question of Dostoevsky's realism, Hennequin has some original comment to offer on the Russian's handling of the themes of suffering and compassion. According to him, Dostoevsky's attitude of horror-struck pity for his fellows is due paradoxically to his alienation from them. His nature was under the control of his sensual impressions, his rational faculties were under-developed (perhaps by reason of his epilepsy). There was an enormous lack of proportion between his sensibility and his reasoning powers, the former immense, the latter stunted. Hence the extremity of his compassion for suffering: he lacked, for one thing, the understanding which would have told him that the degree of suffering varies according to the degree to which the sufferer is accustomed to it.

His neo-Christian mysticism was a product of his subnormal intellectual powers and of his detestation of the merciless theory of a universal struggle for existence which dominated the scientific outlook of his time. Like a chess-player in exasperation at being about to lose, upsetting the board with a curse and a violent blow, Dostoevsky escaped from the pitiless conditions of the game and took refuge in blind faith, bowing down, says Hennequin, 'before the very Being in Whom this act of faith invests the responsibility for evils from which He is supposed to be the refuge' (p. 181).

Hennequin deplores this outcome, for the artist declines. 'Incapable of attaining the peace of an ideal philosophy, [Dostoevsky] grew confused and aggrieved, and produced works which are ethical and humanitarian treatises rather than interesting novels' (p. 184). Tolstoy as well as Dostoevsky fell into this snare which awaits the artist blinded by the need to deliver his message. Hennequin enumerates the many excellent qualities of the novel of Tolstoy and Dostoevsky: 'the breadth and depth of their investigations, the freshness of their approach to man, their sincere and lofty art, the serious fervour of the gospel of pity which they propose', and asks whether he is not in the presence of something greater than the ideal implicit in the traditions of 'art for art's sake'. But in the end he sets his face against the Russians, remembering that

the problem of society, of the life of man, cannot be solved by the passionate outbursts of those who decry the intelligence . . . that Truth is pacific, persuades by its presence alone, and has no need of apostles, that only falsehood raises its voice, that works of art should not strive to mislead, that it is enough for them to contain implicitly the precepts of the good life and to show them complied with . . . [p. 184].

What of the effect the new art may be expected to have on French literature and thought? Hennequin attributes to the Russians a dual influence: firstly, a moral one which affected the whole of the more highly educated section of the population and which he believes may possibly lead to social reforms; and, secondly, a technical one which confined itself to literary circles proper. Hennequin makes the remarkable and rather curious statement (pp. 298–9) that only a small number of writers were struck by the moral qualities of the Russians' art, their passionate intensity, their noble fervour, which ensured them their success among the reading public; French artists as a whole preferred to dwell on their technical achievements and idiosyncrasies, such as the extraordinary interest of the narrative, the peculiarity of Dostoevsky's creations, and the analytical prowess displayed by Tolstoy. There will be occasion to put to the test this appreciation of the situation when we come to examine in detail the works of some of the French novelists whose writings seem to have been markedly affected by the Russians.

Hennequin joins with Vogüé in interpreting Turgenev, Tolstoy, and Dostoevsky as artists in whom the emotional outlook predominated over the intellectual or rational: but, being himself a rationalist and an intellectual, he in the end adopts an attitude firmly opposed to this conception of art, and hence to Vogüé's advocacy of the Russians as 'models'. He is hostile without spoiling his case by irreverence; and, reluctantly as it seems, fires the first shots in the 'counter-attack'.

His objections, however, are fundamentally different from those of Lemaître and of Lemaître's followers. He is quite unconcerned with the nationalistic aspect of the question. Lemaître will try to prove that the Russians' 'gospel of pity' was anticipated by French romantics and neo-romantics. Hennequin would maintain that the use of a work of art as a vehicle for such preaching is unacceptable, whether it be Tolstoy or George Sand who is responsible.

V

COUNTER-ATTACK

IT was perhaps in the nature of things that, after the first few
years during which scarcely anyone had anything harsh to say
about the newcomers, a current of reaction should set in. This
happened in the early nineties. The Russian novelists had been
'the fashion' for five or six years: now the fashion had turned against
them; for the next few years Ibsen will be the rage among those
who plume themselves on their international culture. In due course,
it will be the turn of Björnson, then of Strindberg, d'Annunzio,
Chekhov, Shaw, Gorky, Wells. . . .

The reaction, the 'counter-attack', for many of those who trum-
peted it, was, one suspects, simply the manifestation of a desire to
be abreast with the times, to follow the latest fad, and to clear themselves of the charge of being out of date. About 1890, those readers
who had never been particularly taken by the productions of Tolstoy and Dostoevsky were emboldened to proclaim their aversion;
while those who had been only lukewarm in their enthusiasm looked
about for a new hobby-horse. It is significant that in the survey of
the trends of contemporary literature made in 1891 by Jules Huret,
a reporter on the staff of the *Écho de Paris*, scarcely any of the
authors and critics interviewed so much as mentioned the names
of Tolstoy or Dostoevsky: Huret himself comments on this peculiarity in his preface. Certain novelists expressed their wish to see
a halt called to the influence of the Russian novel: thus Paul Bonnetain said he would not be surprised if the literature of the future
turned out to be purely socialist; nor would he be sorry if such
were to be the case. 'After so much pity *à la slave*, a touch of plain
simple justice seems due' (*Enquête sur l'évolution de la littérature*,
p. 247). Bonnetain, incidentally, had been the prime mover in the
launching of the 'manifesto of the Five against *La Terre*' in 1887,
and had thus, at one point, made common cause with Vogüé
vituperating in the introductory chapter of his *Roman russe* against
the 'obscenity of the naturalists'. J.-H. Rosny, whose signature had
also appeared on the manifesto, prophesies 'a reaction against the
evangelical morality introduced by the Slavs, that is, against the

denial of civilization and progress in favour of the idea of renunciation' (p. 233).

The professionals whom Huret interviewed may have been unwilling (perhaps simply out of professional jealousy) to pay lip-
service to Tolstoy and Dostoevsky, but it is significant that certain
of them, in the forecasts they make of the probable development
of the French novel, appear to anticipate a future art which should
incorporate some at least of the more outstanding characteristics of
the Russian novel. One or two of them believe that the consecrated
novel-form is doomed to desuetude. Edmond de Goncourt asserts
that in his view the novel is 'an overworked, down-at-heel form of
art, which has said all it has to say': a new form must be found, and
whoever invents it will count among the leaders of the intellectual
movement of the twentieth century (p. 168). Now Tolstoy in particular, and Dostoevsky scarcely less, had given brilliant examples
of a new novel-form covering immense canvases in minute detail:
and it is impossible not to believe that these triumphs encouraged
Romain Rolland, Marcel Proust, and Georges Duhamel to embark
on the prose epics that are *Jean-Christophe*, *À la recherche du temps
perdu*, and the Salavin and Pasquier novel-cycles.

Joseph Caragüel looks for the same sort of development as Goncourt. He demands a highly analytical novel which should represent
life in its extremest complications. (This is precisely what Dostoevsky had done; many critics, in fact, blamed him for the excessive
complication of his plots.) Caragüel would have the minor art-
forms left to minor writers, while the great men, 'in the wake of
Flaubert, George Eliot, Tolstoy' will aim at 'an aesthetic co-ordina-
tion of the heterogeneous elements of life' (p. 226).

Zola, in his answer, seems almost to define the Russian novel.

The future will belong to the writer or body of writers who fully
understand the spirit of modern society, who, freeing themselves from
too strict a theoretical conception, adopt a more logical, more emotional
attitude to life. I believe in a wider, more complex portraiture of truth,
in a greater vista opened on humanity, in a kind of classical age of
naturalism [p. 173].

The conspiracy of silence about the two Russian novelists in
1890–1 means then little more than that the first fine intoxication
was over: the gilt had been rubbed off the gingerbread. But the
ideas imported with the Russians had struck deep: and in disguised
forms they re-appear. The signs are healthy. *War and Peace, Crime*

and Punishment were not destined merely for the triumph of an hour; their charm was too potent to be attributed merely to their exoticism or to the adroit campaign of a small party of publicists. Imperceptibly their art and their message were seeping down into the very bed-rock of French literature and thought.

A certain reaction against the Russian novel, however, undoubtedly did set in in the nineties, and it is through no mere desire to push a metaphor to the bitter end that we describe it as the counter-attack to Vogüé's offensive of 1883–6. Just as Vogüé was recognized as the pioneer in the introduction of the Russian novel into France, so he was held responsible, by those who deprecated the excessive interest this literature had called forth, for the exaggerations of 'septentriomania'. This term was invented by Jules Lemaître, one of the most respected critics of his day, and colonel of the battalions of the counter-attackers.

Lemaître's attitude of amused scepticism with regard to the Russian novel goes back to the early days of its importation into France. He could never at any time be numbered among the 'Russophiles': 'there is not a ha'porth of the Slav in me' he said of himself. But the fury of enthusiasm which was sweeping Paris kept his raillery within bounds at least until the mid-nineties: by that time opinion was ready for a recession in taste.

In 1888, discussing Tolstoy's *Power of Darkness*, Lemaître suggests that 'these Russians have been rather played up' and that 'people have used their evangelical naturalism to bear rather hardly on the inquisitive, sensual, disdainful type of naturalism peculiar to our novelists'; he asserts that the latter are after all greater artists and that 'their refusal to wax sentimental and to show very obvious marks of pity is perhaps no more than a certain self-restraint or else a fear lest they transgress the limits of what is artistic'. Lemaître feels stirred to defend the writers of his own country 'against these diffuse, disorderly, and mystic Slavs. . . . Lord! anyone can be a mystic if he wants to!'[1]

Dostoevsky's novel filled Lemaître with misgivings. 'In the last few years' he comments in 1888, 'Russia has perhaps caused us to talk a lot of nonsense.' Confronted with Dostoevsky's 'artificial and antithetical' characters, a true Parisian 'wavers between fervent admiration (for he is a trusting soul, greatly attracted to anything

[1] Lemaître, *Impressions de théâtre*, 1ère série, pp. 270–1.

from abroad), and the most irreverent mockery, when he happens to think twice . . .'.[1]

By 1894 Lemaître was no longer hesitating between admiration and mockery. He had made up his mind; and instead of the mild eyebrow-raising of 1888 (when to express disapproval too openly was to court the risk of committing a solecism), Lemaître now bares his teeth. In serried arguments he sets out his reasons for thinking the Russians have been over-valued by their French apologists. Lemaître entitled his article: 'De l'influence récente des littératures du Nord',[2] linking up his objections to the infiltration of the Russian novel with a similar distrust for the success that was being reaped by the works of English and Scandinavian writers. 'Septentriomania' was the name he gave to the excessive enthusiasm with which the French had hailed successively the novels of George Eliot, Dostoevsky, and Tolstoy, the plays of Ibsen, Björnson, Hauptmann, 'du Danois [sic] Auguste Strindberg . . . du Belge Maeterlinck'. Lemaître does not attack the foreign authors themselves on artistic or any other grounds (save perhaps by implication for plagiarism); in fact he has occasionally some highly flattering remarks to make about them in passing. The general drift of his argument is that French zealots are quite deluded in thinking that what they admire in these foreign models is something hitherto absolutely unknown in French literature.

In his discussion of the two Russian novelists, which naturally takes up only a portion of his essay, Lemaître concentrates on refuting two central points in Vogüé's study: the idea, firstly, that the Russians stand above the French in the 'charity' and human sympathy that their work breathes; and, secondly, that Russian realism is constantly escaping into a metaphysical, superhuman atmosphere to which the French never aspire.

Vogüé had cited in illustration of Dostoevsky's sensibility the scene in which Raskolnikov confesses his crime to Sonya; Tolstoy's idealism was manifested nowhere more clearly than in the story of Pierre's conversion by Platon Karataev. Lemaître professes to be greatly astonished that such scenes should have been thought to contain any startling novelties. 'Need I point out', he asks, 'that

---

[1] Lemaître, *Impressions de théâtre, 4e série*, pp. 257–8.
[2] It was inserted in the *Revue des Deux Mondes*, 15 Dec. 1894, and was reproduced in Lemaître, *Les Contemporains, 6e série* (1898).

Victor Hugo and the Romantics had not waited for Dostoevsky and Tolstoy to show us prostitutes who are saints, or beggars and wretches who possess the secret of perfect wisdom and charity?' As for Karataev, the French can surely improve on this figure: the donkey of Victor Hugo's 'Le Crapaud' is just as resigned and just as good-natured, and if anything less intellectually gifted than Tolstoy's celebrated moujik.

From these somewhat specious analogies between the characters and themes of Hugo and those of Tolstoy and Dostoevsky, Lemaître deduces that all the Russians have achieved is to bring together in one form of art the sentimental idealism of the French romantics and the careful observation of the French realists. In any case, Lemaître is by no means willing to concede that the French realist-naturalist school is as devoid of charity as the advocates of the Russians would have one believe, and rushes to the defence of Flaubert whom Vogüé had so badly mauled.

But what of the 'intelligence des dessous, de l'entour de la vie', which Vogüé had said was the second distinctive mark of the Russian realists, claiming that 'their characters brood over the universal mystery, and, for all their appearance of being deeply wrapped up in the drama of the passing moment, they lend an ear to the murmur of abstract ideas.'[1] There is nothing here, in Lemaître's view, that cannot be found in the very writers whom Vogüé castigates most fiercely. Emma Bovary's very soul quivers with a sense of mystery; Charles Bovary, too, in his final remark: 'It's all the fault of fate!'—'What am I saying? Do you imagine that even the imbeciles are unaware of it? Bouvard and Pécuchet . . . but they spend all their time brooding over the universal mystery!'

Lemaître concludes that the only real novelty in the works of the Russians was the exoticism of the form. 'The Northern writers, and therein lies their charm, return us, if you like, the substance of our own literature of forty or fifty years ago, modified, renewed, enriched through having traversed minds which differ noticeably from ours. *En repensant nos pensées, ils nous les découvrent.*'

And there is a certain amount of truth in this observation. Dostoevsky's first work was a translation of a Balzac novel, and he was an impassioned admirer of George Sand. Traces of her writings are evident to the most casual peruser of his books: in *The Brothers*

[1] Vogüé, *Le Roman russe*, p. xlv.

Karamazov, for instance, the relationship between Father Zosima and his disciple Alyosha bear so marked a resemblance to those between Father Alexis and the novice Angel in *Spiridion* that it is hard to believe Dostoevsky was not borrowing from George Sand. But what does this prove? Lemaître would surely not have impugned Molière's originality on the grounds that he quarried for his plots in Plautus, Terence, Lope de Vega, Scarron, Rotrou, and half a dozen other authors?

The critic further acknowledges that the Northern writers have rendered the French the service of proving that realism need not necessarily be irreligious. But the inferiority of French literature in this respect is, in Lemaître's opinion, in a fair way to being made good—and he cites Paul Bourget, Maupassant in his later writings, and Paul Margueritte. It remains to be seen to what extent the qualities of the work of these writers Lemaître names are due precisely to the influence and example of Tolstoy and Dostoevsky.

He ends his essay on a significant note of warning. His literary patriotism is alarmed. French writers, responding to all these currents from abroad, are

the true cosmopolitans, for a cosmopolitan, that is a European literature, must by definition be understandable and held in common by all the nations of Europe, and it can only become so if it is orderly, well-proportioned and lucid; and these are just the qualities which for centuries have been reputed to grace our nation. . . . None the less . . . there is a risk that our characteristic intellectual qualities will end by being weakened; that our genius, by dint of being European, will finish by being less French.

It is this fear in particular that is at the root of the polemics of many of Lemaître's followers, and a hostility towards foreign literary influence, what Lemaître himself calls 'literary chauvinism', becomes very readily a common attitude among the self-appointed guardians of the pure French traditions.

The author of the *Roman russe* lost no time in making his own riposte, which was good-humoured and without acrimony: Vogüé and Lemaître were, after all, colleagues on the staff of the same periodical. The occasion was a discussion of the work of d'Annunzio, from the point of view of Tolstoy's influence on this Italian novelist.[1]

[1] Vogüé, 'La Renaissance latine', *Revue des Deux Mondes*, 1 Jan. 1895.

Vogüé starts by rapping Lemaître gently over the knuckles for the dangerous breadth of his generalizations. 'The literatures of the North have one thing in common—that they did not flourish in the South; but, apart from this geographical consideration, I believe that English literature differs as much from German, and German from Scandinavian or Russian, as Spanish differs from Italian.' As for Lemaître's analogies between the themes and characters of Tolstoy and Dostoevsky on the one hand and those of Hugo, Sand, and Flaubert on the other, Vogüé gives Lemaître the benefit of the doubt and does not take him seriously.

There were several others who dissented from Lemaître: a couple of months after the appearance of 'De l'influence récente des littératures du Nord', André Hallays countered with an article entitled 'De l'influence des littératures étrangères',[1] which was an attempt to reassure the timid souls frightened by the inrush of translations. Hallays pointed out, firstly, that admiration does not necessarily mean imitation; and, secondly, that ideas have no fatherland, and that to argue about where they originated or whether they were acceptable or not to the 'national genius' is futile. In any case, foreign literatures themselves (save in England, wrapped in an intellectual as well as a political 'splendid isolation') are just as susceptible to influences from across their frontiers: the modern age is characterized by a universal fusion of interests. Hallays pleads that this interpenetration of national literatures should be encouraged for the contribution it may make to the growth of political cosmopolitanism and the fostering of peace.

In an essay on 'Le Cosmopolitisme et la littérature nationale',[2] Brunetière endeavoured to answer the burning question raised by the advent of 'literary cosmopolitanism': 'should we congratulate ourselves on this widening of our intellectual horizon, or should we not rather make it the subject of patriotic representations?' He points out with a great deal of justice that those who condemn foreign influence in art 'do not deny that there is "a lot of good" in Tolstoy and Ibsen, but they cannot forgive them for having written "outside France"; and with heavy hearts but stern determination they turn a question of literature into a question of patriotism'. Brunetière argues that, far from representing the French romantic tradition, the Russians and other writers from abroad follow in

---

[1] Inserted in the *Revue de Paris*, 15 Feb. 1895.
[2] Dated Oct. 1894. May be read in Brunetière, *Études critiques, 6ᵉ série*.

the wake of classicism—and by their example show the French how they may extricate themselves from the worst heresies of romanticism: the notion that art could be its own aim, divorced from the service of mankind, and the hyperbolic cultivation of the ego. But if these were precisely the lessons of the French classical writers, 'in the name of what narrow-minded patriotism ought we to reject once more the lesson? . . . What danger do these people think the "French spirit" will incur by becoming once more what it ought never to have stopped being?'

The writer is careful to stress that he is not arguing in favour of an outright imitation, in all respects, of the Northern masterpieces: they are far from ideal specimens of art. But to refuse to profit from the works of foreign novelists or playwrights, 'when they offer us information about ourselves, about our "humanity", which is new because the point of view at which they post themselves is new, or the manners of the society on which they base these observations'—this is to be unfaithful to our own traditions and to past examples: Corneille rifling Spain of the glory of the Cid, Rousseau outdoing Richardson with his *Nouvelle Héloïse*.

Brunetière ends on the same note as had Hallays, and calls up a utopian vision of 'literary cosmopolitanism' smoothing away racial hatreds and ushering in an era of peace.

The comparison Lemaître drew between the writings of the Russians and those of the French romantics may have suggested to André Le Breton the idea of drawing[1] a point by point parallel between the novels of Tolstoy (*Resurrection* in particular), and one of the products of romanticism with which they had many common features: Victor Hugo's *Les Misérables*. Le Breton, by taking Lemaître at his word, answers most effectively the case he had made out against the Russians.

There are certain obvious points of resemblance between *Resurrection* and *Les Misérables*: they are both concerned with the redemption of a fallen woman; both are peopled by convicts, prostitutes, revolutionaries, and the dregs of society, shown to possess many unsuspected virtues; both contain satires of the juridical systems of their respective countries; 'and over all that', adds Le Breton, 'I know not what breath of brotherly love and pity there is, in which everything bathes'. The two novels are so similar in theme that their titles could be interchanged.

[1] In 'La Pitié sociale dans le roman', *Revue des Deux Mondes*, 15 Feb. 1902.

But it is the differences that are significant. Contrast the theatrical scene in which Valjean rises in court and accuses himself, unable to endure that an innocent man should be condemned in his stead, with Nekhlyudov's hesitation in closely similar circumstances. Contrast too Valjean's brusque conversion from evil by Myriel, with the gradual betterment of Katyusha, each successive stage carefully indicated by the author. Which of the two writers, asks Le Breton, is the more convincing?

The difference between Tolstoy's realism and Hugo's romanticism can be studied even more profitably by considering *Les Misérables* alongside *War and Peace*.

The emotion inspired in us by the great scenes of *Les Misérables* is the same as we feel in the theatre, when a play of Shakespeare's or Corneille's is being performed. The emotion we feel at reading Tolstoy's stories is the same as that we feel faced with the incidents of life, in the presence of real suffering, or at the death of a loved one.

One may argue that Tolstoy's 'social pity' is only a refurbishing of Hugo's generous sympathy for the outcast. But whereas Hugo's sentiment is bookish (Le Breton derives it from the writings of Lamennais and Lacordaire, of Saint-Simon and Fourier) and personal (the accidental drowning of his daughter in 1843, Le Breton suggests, was partly responsible for Hugo's frame of mind when writing his novel)—Tolstoy's social pity has roots going far deeper, striking from the national soil. Social pity can be analysed as a combination of Christianity and democracy: and the Russians are at once the most fundamentally Christian people in Europe and the most susceptible to democratic ideas.

On counts of art and thought, then, Tolstoy is, in Le Breton's view, immeasurably superior to the French romantic whom Lemaître would regard as his source.

Lemaître's view-point, of course, had adherents as well as opponents. We have recorded some of the arguments of the latter: the picture now needs to be completed by taking into account the train of disciples Lemaître drew after him.

At the risk of repetition, it is worth emphasizing that Lemaître had not attacked the Russian novel because it was bad art; he merely expressed a difference of opinion with Vogüé regarding the value of the Russian novelists as models for the French. Vogüé had vaunted Tolstoy and Dostoevsky in order to mortify Zola, whose crudity and materialism had revolted his aristocratic and idealistic soul. But at the time Lemaître was writing, the naturalist school was discredited and dispersed. The leading or rising novelists were Bourget, Anatole France, and Barrès; their art (that of the last two at any rate), drew from indigenous sources, and to have preached cosmopolitanism at them would have been incongruous, Brunetière notwithstanding. The literary stage had completely shifted in the interval. What made sense in 1886 made perilous nonsense in 1894 and thereafter.

The close of the century was marked by a sudden and dangerous rise in the political temperature of the French nation. There was the Boulanger fiasco to alarm the parties of the Left and humiliate those of the Right; and there was the Dreyfus case to inflame the latent xenophobia of reactionaries. In 1898 the 'Action Française' was founded, its nominal aim being to maintain intact French traditions and strengthen the feelings of solidarity which link one generation to another: in fact it was a rallying ground for all militant nationalists, army die-hards, and anti-republicans.

Politics and literature are never deeply divorced in France, and the question of Russian influence was made a *casus belli* by the chauvinists. They seized on Lemaître's arguments and used them in their clamours for intellectual tariff walls, although the essay 'De l'influence récente . . .' had not sprung from any irrational and all-embracing aversion to imports from abroad. Towards the extreme end of the century, to hold the notion that French literature could or should owe anything to the Russian novelists was not far off heresy in the eyes of all 'good patriots'. Nothing is odder than this development. Tolstoy and Dostoevsky were ushered into France by a 'young conservative' writing in a periodical of irreproachably right-wing tendencies; fifteen years later, the very same section of opinion regards them with distaste and distrust as literary 'métèques', convinced they are mongrelizing the pure strain of French literature.

One of the first French critics to adopt a markedly hostile attitude to the Russian invasion was Ernest Combes. This man of wit and learning was a teacher at the Collège Stanislas, which is an academic establishment at Paris controlled by the Church but staffed in part by laymen. Combes's *Profils et types de la littérature russe* (1896), an impressionistic commentary on Russian literature from the earliest days, written in a light, ironic tone, bears particularly hardly on the

'Russophilia' of some of his compatriots. He mocks at their enthusiasm, largely the result he says of an optical illusion, a mirage
produced by the distance of Russia from France and the general
inability to read the language (p. 354).

Dostoevsky in particular arouses a fury of disgust so violent that
one suspects affectation. *Poor Folk* is 'more stupid than dirty',
Crime and Punishment 'très convenable . . . aux souteneurs et aux
filles publiques', while *The Brothers Karamazov* preaches moral
irresponsibility (p. 346).

The excessively severe trouncing Combes meted out to Dostoevsky was based mainly on what was taken to be the Russian
novelist's delight in the morbidity of his subjects. Combes, who
was in the first instance a Hellenist, calls attention to the very
different case of the Greek tragedians, who, although they occasionally chose nauseating themes, invariably redeemed

the nastiness of their subject by the nobility of their form. . . . Contemporary novelists, on the contrary, seek to astound . . . and fall into
madness and filth; they pride themselves on peeling the skin off the
conscience of an idiot, and they descend to sifting muck, to showing off
blisters. You will grant me that these novels . . . cannot be very savoury;
what will they be like, when their author is as sick as his heroes? This is
precisely the case with Dostoevsky [p. 342].

Dostoevsky's physical affliction and the record of his distressful
life were held by the French, not without reason, as explaining
(and explaining away) much that seemed irrational in his art. 'We
shall always look on Dostoevsky as the writer with the most unbalanced, original and exceptional talent, or genius if you prefer,
of the present time; the man will have to be explained by his
exceptional pathology.'[1] Combes, of course, is not prepared to
accept the wretchedness of Dostoevsky's existence as an excuse for
the wretchedness of his art.

It is unimportant, I imagine, to the reader, whether Dostoevsky was
subject to wondrous nightmares, whether or not he had visions in the
course of an epileptic fit, if his novels when he wrote them were not
extraordinary and wondrous; and it is going a little too far to conclude
that an author has genius because he suffered greatly in his life.[2]

---

[1] Vogüé, 'Les Livres russes en France', *Revue des Deux Mondes*, 15 Dec. 1886,
p. 833.
[2] Combes, *Profils et types*, pp. 353–4. The psycho-pathological interpretation
of Dostoevsky seems to have been taken up in France in the early twentieth

Another of Combes's grievances against Dostoevsky was that he was not even original, and he elaborated with verve on this theme which Lemaître had brought into prominence.

Ce bric-à-brac ne nous vient pas, il nous revient de Russie! Les vieilles défroques d'Eugène Sue et de V. Hugo nous reviennent rafistolées *grosso modo* avec les jupes frisées de Fleur-de-Marie, d'Esméralda, de Marion Delorme, etc. Sentez, vous reconnaîtrez l'odeur. Le bain de psychologie alambiquée, dans lequel Dostoïevsky et consorts les ont trempées, les a reteintes mais non lavées. La réhabilitation des filles perdues, l'apologie du laid, la béatification des gredins, etc., tous ces trucs, avec lesquels V. Hugo, à sa honte, a si souvent battu monnaie, sont éventés depuis longtemps [p. 350].

This outburst verges on the absurd: it marks, perhaps, the extreme limit of the reaction against Dostoevsky, and has no other value.

There is, however, a grain of truth in Combes's defamations. Dostoevsky had certainly read Eugène Sue, the inventive author of the *Mysteries of Paris* and *The Wandering Jew*, and is not above using some of his tricks to help the functioning of his novels, and especially to intensify their atmosphere. But the fact had already been admitted by Vogüé, who did not let the occasion pass without adding a reflection or two which should have stifled Combes's ill-natured gibes. The influence of Sue is very apparent in *The Idiot*, with its abuse of such devices as chance encounters, sudden inheritances, secret interviews between noblewomen and courtesans, &c. But, according to Vogüé, it is precisely 'by its quaint medley that this book is highly symbolic of the country in which it was written; this country dons our cast-off clothes, which appear all the more grotesque because it wears them with solemn awkwardness, and beneath this masquerade we find a fund of powerful, original and virgin thoughts, characteristic of an unknown race'.[1]

century. In 1903 Dr. Bajenow, a physician from Moscow, delivered a lecture on 'Dostoïevsky et de Maupassant' (published in the *Archives d'Anthropologie criminelle*, Jan. 1904), in which the two writers were viewed from the standpoint of the psychiatrist. A French doctor, Gaston Loygue, published an *Étude médico-psychologique sur Dostoïevsky* in 1904. In 1905 Ossip-Lourier incorporated some of Bajenow's ideas in his *Psychologie des romanciers russes* (in particular the idea that Dostoevsky's novels rank far higher as medical case-books and primers of criminology than as works of art). The following year, in his *Demi-fous et demi-responsables*, Dr. J. Grasset expanded Lourier's thesis still further and declared that the characteristic types depicted by *all* the Russian novelists were 'des demi-fous vivant en liberté hors des asiles', while the authors themselves were 'semi-insane' likewise.   [1] Vogüé, preface to Dostoïevsky, *L'Idiot*, p. vi.

Combes ends by professing to be completely dumbfounded by the admiration of some of his contemporaries for Dostoevsky, saying that he pities those of his imitators who do not realize what they are doing, while as for those who do, he thinks they are gay rascals making their profit out of an unsuspecting public. Combes's violence should not be taken too seriously: it is quite unlikely that his book had any extensive influence in France, and if it has been examined at some length in these pages, it is, once again, because Combes's rhetoric is perhaps not altogether negligible as a symptom of the trend of feeling regarding the Russians at the height of the reaction.

Lemaître's arguments found echoes in other and soberer writers at the close of the century. Thus in 1899 we find Leger commenting sarcastically that people have unearthed in Russian literature 'a mass of novelties: pity which, it seems, had not been already used by Virgil, love of humankind which was unknown to Cicero, charity which you cannot find in the Gospels'.[1] Another writer, like Wyzewa of Polish nationality, K. Waliszewski (who describes himself in the foreword to his *Littérature russe* (1900) as 'an intellectual go-between in two worlds which are both half-foreign to me') voiced Lemaître's opinion in even more outspoken fashion.

What we ourselves have been able to give to Tolstoy's native land, he returns it to us, with some new scraps of tinsel decking our old rags. There is nothing surprising in the fact that we have been at a loss to recognize, under this odd and at times absurd disguise, the noblest fruit of our womb, even this humanitarian sympathy, with the invention of which many of us, forgetful of the 'divine' Sand, have been good enough to credit the Russians. What is really surprising is that some people have been pleased to regard these frightful caricatures as inspiring revelations.[2]

There is no patriotism like that of the immigrant.

We can regard Vogüé's article 'Nationalisme et cosmopolitisme'[3] as the opening speaker's reply to the debate. Vogüé considers the question in its political and economic aspects, endeavouring to discover in which of the two contrary directions the world was

---

[1] Leger, *Russes et Slaves, 3e série*, p. 119.
[2] Waliszewski, *Littérature russe*, p. 394.
[3] Inserted in the *Revue des Deux Mondes*, 1 Feb. 1901.

moving—towards unification or towards fragmentation. Wisely, Vogüé reached no absolute conclusion: midway through the twentieth century the issue is still undecided. But he clearly condemns the more imbecile manifestations of national prejudice, in politics and in art, the 'distrustful patriotism' which tries to erect a spiritual Wall of China ('iron curtain' as the modern phrase has it), 'a fence behind which we are asked to die of consumption in the native purity of our nationhood'. The outcries of these 'defenders of the Latin genius' remind Vogüé of the celebrated letter sent to Madame de Staël by the chief of the Imperial police when she attempted to publish *De l'Allemagne* in France: '. . . Nous n'en sommes pas encore réduits à chercher des modèles dans les peuples que vous admirez. Votre dernier ouvrage n'est point français. . . .' What *is* un-French, in Vogüé's view, 'is the cantankerous narrow-mindedness which can be noticed by everyone who has been observing our society for the past twenty years'; he repeats Brunetière's argument that one is closer to the French genius when one has enough confidence in one's own good health not to be afraid of pestilences which may be wafted in through open windows.

Nothing is more opposed to the national tradition than confinement and dieting; our fathers did not practise abstinence, they did not shrink from foreign foods. They borrowed liberally, from every country, at every age. . . . This fine appetite, and with it this generosity which restores to every nation the riches which were taken from each one of them, but struck now at our mint—these are the very conditions of our normal life: literary, industrial and social.

And Vogüé remembers and repeats, in slightly different words, the passage with which he had concluded the preface of the *Roman russe*:

like everything in existence, literature is an organism that supports itself by nutrition; it has to assimilate ceaselessly foreign elements so as to transform them into its own substance. If the stomach is sound, the assimilation proceeds without danger; if it is too worn, the organism can choose between perishing of inanition or of indigestion. If such were our case, one bowl of Russian broth more or less would not alter our death-sentence.

What was a salutary warning in 1886 had become an indispensable reminder by 1901.[1]

[1] Or even earlier. In an article 'Jean-Jacques Rousseau et le cosmopolitisme

But Vogüé's remarks at this juncture do not constitute the last word in the dispute. Later in the same year Henri Bordeaux announced gravely, in an article entitled 'L'Invasion étrangère dans la littérature française',[1] that if protective measures were not quickly taken,

if the critics, guardians of our artistic treasures, of our traditions, of our culture, do not take up their arms, that is, the pen, there will soon be no French literature left, or at any rate it will be relegated to the back pages of our periodicals, to the cellars of our book-shops, which will calmly continue to display their translations of foreign authors.

Bordeaux gives the example by sounding the alarm and calling on his countrymen to repel 'the invasion that has no cause or reason, is disorderly and tasteless, and brings us every day either secondary and useless works, or specialized ones and others at variance with our nature, the invasion which bids fair to warp our native sensibility and replace our culture by a kind of ill-prepared cosmopolitan education'.

Was this the genuine anxiety it pretended to be, or no more than the concern of a budding novelist faced with unwelcome competition from abroad? Vogüé had spoken of certain young authors 'who had knocked up against piles of foreign novels in the book-shops' and who decided that the integrity of the French genius was threatened on all sides. Bordeaux was willing to admit that certain works of the Russians should be read: but discretion was essential.

In 1902 J. Ernest-Charles comments scornfully on the 'contemporary snobbery which turns us into passionate perusers of every specimen of foreign literature', but explains, to his own satisfaction at least, the curiosity of the French in respect of foreign works of art: for every single one of these works, even the most original of them, bears some testimony to the continuing intellectual supremacy of the French the world over. The article[2] in which

littéraire' (actually a review of J. Texte's book of the same title), which appeared in the *Revue des Deux Mondes*, 1 July 1895, Vogüé had inveighed in closely similar terms against the obtuseness of those who try to fly in the face of the modern tendency towards cosmopolitanism in art: '. . . S'il faut mourir de consomption, peu importe que ce soit en vivant de régime, avec la tisane de la *Dame blanche* et du vaudeville national, ou à la suite des excès que l'on commettra en allant entendre Wagner, Ibsen et les autres "barbares".'

[1] Inserted in *Le Correspondant*, 25 Dec. 1901.
[2] '*L'Adolescent*, par Dostoïevsky', *Revue Bleue*, 20 Sept. 1902.

these remarks occur was written on the occasion of the publication of Dostoevsky's *A Raw Youth*: and Ernest-Charles exercises his ingenuity in tracing French influence in this novel: Balzac is, he thinks, much in evidence; certain scenes appear to have been copied from *Madame Bovary*; the hero is modelled on Stendhal's Julien Sorel.

And so the battle surged backwards and forwards, few fresh arguments being brought up to reinforce either side. It cannot be said that one faction or the other ultimately succeeded in establishing its point of view. In matters of this sort, there can be no question of swaying opinions one way or the other; there will always be a body of thinkers who believe interest and instruction are to be found in the work of great men of every country, just as there will always be a section convinced that works of art in any country must arise as a natural projection of its own past. The discussion may go on till doomsday; but at the end of it all, as at the end of a House of Commons debate, one may be sure that the proportion voting one way or the other will not have altered very much.

VI

THE RUSSIAN NOVEL AND THE
DISINTEGRATION OF NATURALISM
I. MAUPASSANT AND HUYSMANS

THE apostle of the Russian novel in France had in 1886 proclaimed his conviction that the influence of the newly
revealed masterpieces would be 'wholesome' for French art.
The moment has come to consider how deep this influence ran and
in what direction: but first of all, which writers it affected most.

It is common to speak of 'currents of influence'. Literary influence
on a nation-wide scale, however, is better likened to the fall of rain
on some stony plateau. Where the rain falls on bare rock, it will
have no 'influence': the water will perhaps accumulate in pools,
but it will have no life-giving force—it will run away or be dried
up in time by the sun. In patches, however, it will fall on soil, and
will then be able to assist in the germination of seeds and the
nurture of vegetation.

Some creative artists were quite unaffected by the rain-storm
from the East. Either their genius was too original and rebellious
to suggestions from outside, or else they did not take kindly to the
particular message the Russians had for literature. Many other
writers were affected superficially and to no lasting effect: the
theme of a Dostoevsky novel borrowed here, elsewhere a character
modelled on one of Tolstoy's creations, but no real permeation by
the spirit of the Russian novel. A few, finally, responded in a marked
fashion. Of these few, the ones who occupy, as well, a prominent
place in the annals of French fiction are a mere handful. For the
purpose of studying how the chemistry of literary influence works,
a writer whose works have no intrinsic value may very well prove
to be a more instructive subject than some great and original artist
whose natural resources were strong enough to permit him to
dispense with inspiration from abroad.

For this reason the case of Guy de Maupassant may appear to
be an unpromising one—so self-reliant an artist can surely owe
little to external inspiration. Yet it is hard to deny that at a certain
stage in his development, precisely about the time that the Russian

novelists were enjoying their hour of greatest triumph, Maupassant in his novels seems to reflect the same preoccupations as they had; and the close disciple of Flaubert seems to have strayed from the normal naturalist route into a course which on the face of it could have been plotted for him by the author of the *Roman russe*.

Let it be admitted at the outset, however, that there is no abundant evidence that Maupassant was at all strongly impressed by the Russians. In the celebrated preface to *Pierre et Jean* he gives a catalogue of novels designed to prove that nothing is more elastic than the term 'novel'. This list of twenty-five works does not contain one from the pen of a Russian author: in fact it contains only four of foreign origin at all, and these four (*Don Quixote*, *Werther*, *The Elective Affinities*, and *Clarissa Harlowe*) were all what might be called classics, close on a century old or more. All the same it is somewhat surprising that Maupassant did not honour either Turgenev or Tolstoy with a mention, unless one allows for the inevitable tendency of novelists to dissimulate their sources.

For there is no doubt that he was familiar with the works of these two writers at an early stage. Through Flaubert he became personally acquainted with Turgenev, and the acquaintance ripened into a friendship with, on Maupassant's part, a dash of reverence. One of the fruits of this friendship was two articles written by Maupassant about Turgenev: the first, under the title 'L'Inventeur du mot *nihilisme*', appearing in *Le Gaulois*, 21 November 1880, the second, composed after Turgenev's death, appearing in the same paper on 5 September 1883.[1] In the first of these articles Maupassant mentions also Tolstoy specifically as the author of 'that superb book, *War and Peace*'. It seems then that, together with Flaubert, Maupassant was one of the relatively few Frenchmen who read *War and Peace* when it was first translated, and did not need to wait five years until Vogüé expatiated eloquently on its surpassing merits. That Maupassant was not speaking merely from hearsay seems to be proved by a statement by Tolstoy himself. At the beginning of an article on Maupassant published in 1893, Tolstoy explains how he first read a book by the young French short-story writer. Turgenev, who was visiting him in 1881, gave him *La Maison Tellier* with the words: 'Read that when you have a mind

---

[1] Maupassant was preparing a fresh monograph on Turgenev, intended for the *Revue des Deux Mondes*, when he fell ill at the end of 1891. See E. Maynial, *Vie et œuvre de Maupassant*, p. 74.

to. It's by a young French writer—have a look at it, it's not bad;
he knows you and thinks a lot of you.[1]

Turgenev afforded Maupassant his first introduction to Russian
literature. His reading of Tolstoy's greatest book must have aroused
his curiosity and may well have prompted him to read the other
works of this author as they were translated. There was enough in
common between Maupassant and Tolstoy for them to be able to
appreciate each other's books with understanding. Tolstoy thought
very highly of *Une Vie*, though he disapproved of the episode of
the priest advising Jeanne how to have a second child; and it is
altogether likely that Maupassant would have found great pleasure
in reading *Family Happiness* with its somewhat similar theme, even
though he might have squirmed at the moralizing tone the author
adopts in parts. These are necessarily suppositions: but surprisingly
little seems to be known about Maupassant's reading, and his
correspondence, or such of it as has so far been published, throws
little light on his likes and dislikes among contemporary writers.

By the end of 1886, the critical year of the Russian invasion,
Maupassant had published a dozen volumes of short stories and
two novels. His reputation was established and his vein recognized.
And yet in his third novel, *Mont-Oriol*, which had been written
for the most part in 1886 and was published in 1887, he appears to
turn his back on the style of writing which had brought him a noisy
renown. The 'pitiless' disciple of the Master of Rouen introduces
curious new notes of sympathy; his characters are more gracefully
resigned to the disappointments of life than they are in *Une Vie*;
they are less blatantly self-seeking and pleasure-loving than in
Bel-Ami.

There were many reasons why Maupassant should have softened
down the tones of his earlier style. Unlike Flaubert, he was not a
literary hermit, though he had a great respect for his art; it may be
that the change of atmosphere in *Mont-Oriol* was a concession to
the new demands of literary fashion. This is certainly the construction put on it by his editor, Havard, who rejoiced at the 'new note'
and declared that 'this book will bring us twenty to twenty-five
thousand new readers, for it will appeal to the most timorous of
middle-class souls whom your earlier productions persistently

[1] See E. Halpérine-Kaminsky, *Tolstoï—Dumas—Zola—Guy de Maupassant*
(1896), pp. 95–6. My italics.

scared away'.[1] But in so far as the fashion of emotionalism in the novel had been to a great extent set by the Russian novelists, their influence may be considered to be in play here.

It may be again that Maupassant felt the naturalist vein was running dry, and he wanted to explore a new path. Or else purely physiological factors may have been at the root of the change: Maupassant was ageing, and the first symptoms of the ultimate decay in his mental faculties may be apparent in this unwillingness to look on life with the cynical grin of his youth.

But within the body of the novel there are, as it were, distant echoes of Tolstoy, and it is not improbable that a recent reading of those of his works which were translated in 1885–6 had some influence on certain scenes in *Mont-Oriol*.

It is more especially in the second part of the novel that these touches are evident. The first part bears more clearly the mark of Flaubert, and of Balzac too, and of the gayer Maupassant of the earlier stories: there is the comedy of the rivalry of the three doctors for the rich patients at this expanding spa; the humour extracted from the antics of the patients, slavishly following the doctors' prescriptions, and suffering agonies of indigestion because the hotel serves them the wrong sort of food; the manœuvres of the wily peasant Oriol and the astute Jewish business-man Andermatt, each trying to double-cross the other. Typical of the old-style Maupassant is the comedy of Andermatt beaming on Christiane when she becomes pregnant, and attributing the happy event to the properties of the waters instead of to the ardours of his wife's lover. All this betokens no change in Maupassant's manner, and the courtship of Christiane by Paul, conducted with tenderness and imagination and without a trace of brutality, if it has few precedents in Maupassant's writings, cannot be related to the influence of the Russians.

The second part, however, has the elements of a double tragedy; and it is a tragedy of *renunciation*, pitched on a low key, the kind of tragedy that Tolstoy was so fond of: in *War and Peace*, with Sonya courted and then abandoned by Nicolas Rostov, and Princess Marie finding her husband-to-be making love to the French governess; in *Anna Karenina*, with Kitty jilted by her suitor Vronsky. Maupassant had, of course, played on the chord of man's fickleness before: in *Bel-Ami*, for instance, Georges Duroy abandons his

---

[1] See A. Lumbroso, *Souvenirs sur Maupassant*, p. 417.

mistress, Mme Walter, in order to marry her daughter and pocket the dowry. But Mme Walter, when she realizes how she has been betrayed, gives way to an almost bestial transport. In describing the more piteous woe of Charlotte, and in inventing the splendid mute reproach of Christiane at the end of *Mont-Oriol*, Maupassant is obviously being more true to the example of Tolstoy than to his earlier self. Charlotte reacts exactly like Kitty, Christiane is a kindred soul to Sonya, and neither has any affinities with the jealous matron of *Bel-Ami*.

This second part of *Mont-Oriol* is a story of sentiment; it revolves around the theme of love, but the springs of this love are not sensual attraction, but sympathy and compassion. Paul's love for Christiane is killed when he sees her deformed by pregnancy, for he is 'of the race of lovers, not of the race of fathers'. But he turns to Charlotte, not because he is fascinated by her physically, but because he sees her burst into tears when she realizes that her suitor (Christiane's brother), a mere dowry-hunter, has forsaken her for her better-provided sister. Paul is 'stirred to the depths of his heart by this girl's first disillusion'. Later he is 'overcome afresh by this deep pity, by this anguish of the heart . . . overwhelmed with compassion and tenderness'. In other words he feels for her exactly what the hero of *War and Peace*, Pierre Bezukhov, feels for Natasha after she has realized that the man she loved, Anatole Kuragin, is a worthless scoundrel and has abandoned her. When he talks to Natasha 'a feeling of pity never experienced before overwhelmed Pierre's soul. . . . She started to cry again, and an even stronger feeling of pity, tenderness and love took possession of Pierre. He felt the tears trickling down under his spectacles and hoped they would not be noticed.' Paul, in Maupassant's novel, is moved, more by pity than anything else, to agree to marry Charlotte, and in Tolstoy's book, Pierre cries: 'If I were not myself, but the most handsome, cleverest and best man in the world, and were free, I would this very moment ask on my knees for your hand and love.' And he rushes away, 'checking the tears of tenderness and happiness', says Tolstoy, 'that were sticking in his throat'.

The function of the suffering of Maupassant's heroine, again, seems to be essentially Russian in nature. In Tolstoy and Dostoevsky suffering is the key that opens the communicating doors between souls: it works not otherwise in *Mont-Oriol*. The mental anguish Christiane has to endure, instead of embittering her,

widens her scale of emotions, gives her feelings of solidarity and
sympathy with creatures until then outside her ken. A donkey she
sees dying by the roadside, instead of arousing disgust (for it is a
disgusting sight, and Maupassant was still enough the naturalist
to make us feel that), prompts her to evoke its past life, the carefree
happiness of the colt, then the interminable labours and hardships
of its existence, the enfeeblement of age, and death at last, a
deliverance. 'Christiane, for the first time, realized the wretchedness of creatures in bondage.' Further down the road she passes
the ragged family who had owned the donkey, and who are now
pulling their cart themselves. Christiane reflects on their poverty,
'and new ideas welled up from the depths of her stricken soul. She
glimpsed the misery of the poor.'

Suffering, in Tolstoy, performs exactly the same operation of
opening the sufferer's eyes to the huge ocean of pain that has always
surged around him among creatures of a lower social or organic
development than himself—pain to which he had been blind in the
period of his contentment. This characteristic of the Russian novel
had been stressed by Vogüé, who attributed it to a Buddhist strain
understandable in Orientals, which, 'in its desperate efforts to
broaden yet further the charity of the Gospels, has soaked the
Russian genius in a wild tenderness for nature, for the humblest
of its creatures, for all disinherited and suffering souls'.[1] As an
illustration of the way in which, in Tolstoy's books, suffering en-
larges for the sufferer the frontiers of his sympathy, one may recall
the picture of Bezukhov, enduring all the privations of captivity
and under the constant fear of death, who forgets his past existence
and the caprices with which he used to beguile the tedium of being
a millionaire prince: during that disastrous retreat his deepest
sympathies were for Karataev, the most earthy of peasants, and a
little nameless 'blue-grey dog with a long body and short bandy
legs'.

A further function of suffering in the Russian novel is to purify
and ennoble the character of the sufferer. In the novels of Maupassant's purely naturalist period, the sufferings of a woman betrayed
or neglected by husband or lover have no obviously redeeming
effect. The successive blows dealt to Jeanne (in *Une Vie*) by knowledge of her husband's faithlessness and by his horrible death,
seem to teach her nothing. She brings up her son foolishly, and

[1] Vogüé, *Le Roman russe*, p. 344.

allows him to squander their fortune. She is entirely passive under the unhappiness of which her own weakness is the chief cause: far from growing in moral stature, she shrivels like a leaf in the furnace.

Christiane, however, is tempered by suffering: she emerges an altogether stronger character. Her words to Paul, after she has passed through the mental anguish of disillusionment and humiliation and the physical agonies of childbirth, are an eloquent comment on her moral progress. 'Those are difficult times to live through. But, when you have suffered like that, you feel yourself strong till the end of your days.' This change in attitude in Maupassant must be attributed either to a revolution in his own thinking or to the influence of the Russian novel: perhaps in part to both. Tolstoy's heroines are never diminished by their trials: from Katya, in *Family Happiness*, whose suffering is of no very painful nature, to Dolly in *Anna Karenina*, at grips with a faithless and spendthrift husband, they are all invariably matured by disillusionment, never soured or broken.

In one important respect, however, Maupassant's conclusions on the value of suffering differ from Tolstoy's. In the latter's books suffering has a unifying effect, drawing men closer together. But Christiane, in her agony, is conscious rather of a greater isolation from her fellows: 'She realized that men walk side by side, through every event, and that nothing ever really rivets two beings together. . . . She saw clearly that no one has ever succeeded, and no one ever will succeed in breaking down this invisible barrier which in life sets human beings as far asunder as the stars in the sky.' This conception of man's isolation is peculiar to Maupassant. The pessimism of Tolstoy derived from a conviction that man cannot develop as an individual, intellectually and spiritually, without paying the price in unhappiness. The recipe for happiness was the abnegation of individualism. But for Maupassant there was no recipe for happiness.

Isolation in suffering is the key-note of all Maupassant's succeeding novels. But there is one emotion that can bridge the gulf between two suffering creatures, and that is pity. The relief that is afforded to one's own pain by dwelling on the misery of others is an emotion which the self-centred heroes and heroines of the French naturalist novel could never experience. When Emma Bovary turns to the priest for spiritual comfort, Bournisien

H

comically misunderstands her and cannot be persuaded that she is not suffering from some purely physical ailment. Flaubert's characters are all hermetically sealed, incapable, seemingly, of disinterested outpourings of sympathy or affection. But Tolstoy's characters cling to each other by innumerable strands of sympathy, pity, love, and affection. The hall-mark of the Russian novel, according to Vogüé, was the sympathy the author felt for his characters and they for each other.

Maupassant's fourth novel, *Pierre et Jean* (1888), is drenched with this pity, a pity which recks not of deserts but is the natural manifestation of minds unwarped by self-seeking. The situation owes much to that of *Hamlet*, Mme Roland playing Gertrude to Pierre's Prince of Denmark: a son, learning of a fault in his mother's past life, loses his respect for her, loses his faith in womankind, and avenges himself on her in a hundred subtle ways. He torments her in spite of himself,

and he himself suffered as much as she! He suffered terribly in loving her no more, in respecting her no more and in torturing her. When he had inflamed the bleeding wound he had gashed open in the heart of the woman and the mother, when he felt how wretched and desperate she was, he went off alone through the town, so racked by remorse, *so bruised by pity*, so distressed at having thus crushed her beneath the contempt he, her son, showed her, that he would have liked to throw himself into the sea and drown himself to be at peace.

Jean, his brother, learning the shameful secret in his turn, displays a different sort of pity—for his is a different nature, and besides, he is the fruit of his mother's guilty liaison, and he has not Pierre's reason for feeling indignation at his father's betrayal. 'And his heart, his guileless heart, was torn by pity. *He* was no judge, not even a merciful judge, he was a man full of weakness and a son full of tenderness.'

In the end Pierre decides to leave and signs on as a ship's doctor. His filial affection is poisoned and he is made wretched out of the new sense of homelessness he now feels. But the sight of creatures more wretched than himself lightens his heart of a load by inspiring it with pity—the same pity that had invaded Christiane's heart at the sight of the ragged nomads and their dying donkey in a moment when she felt most harassed, the same pity that had moved Bezukhov, among the driven and famished prisoners, when his own fortunes were at their lowest ebb. On his ship Pierre wanders into the hold where a troop of emigrants, filthy, ragged, are crowded together.

Et, songeant au travail passé, au travail perdu, à la lutte acharnée, reprise chaque jour en vain, à l'énergie dépensée par ces gueux, qui allaient recommencer encore, sans savoir où, cette existence d'abominable misère, le docteur eut envie de leur crier: 'Mais foutez-vous donc à l'eau avec vos femelles et vos petits!' Et son cœur fut tellement étreint par la pitié qu'il s'en alla, ne pouvant supporter leur vue.

The impression made on Maupassant by Tolstoy seems to have receded by the time he wrote *Fort comme la mort* (1889), though he is far from turning back to his old style; as Hugues Le Roux remarked, in reviewing the book for *Le Temps*,[1] 'the novelist's indifference is breached. Pity for mankind has filtered into him through some minute wound which quickly closes up. Will this trickle of tears dry up? or will it grow and burst forth in a torrent?' This 'minute wound' may have been scratched by the Russians: but one cannot be too sure. The Russians may have merely infected it, and the wound—the susceptibility to pity—may have always been present in Maupassant but kept in check until his reading of Tolstoy showed him that great art need not necessarily be un-emotional. Personal experiences, too, and growing ill health, may have played their part. A private letter, dating from 1890, seems to show that Maupassant felt, at this stage, nothing of the non-chalant and cynical attitude to life which seems to have inspired his earlier stories. He writes:

I have so many aching spots in my head that the slightest ferment of ideas makes me want to cry out. Why? Why? Dumas would say I have a weak stomach. I rather think my poor heart, proud but shrinking, is the trouble—a human heart, this old human heart people laugh about, but which gets excited and hurts—and I feel it in my head too, I have the soul of the Latins which is worn out. And then there are days when I don't feel like that, but when I suffer all the same, for I am a hyper-sensitive type [*je suis de la famille des écorchés*]. But all that, I don't talk about it, I don't show it, I hide it very well, I think. There is not the slightest doubt that everyone thinks I am one of the most indifferent people in the world.[2]

[1] *Le Temps*, 15 June 1889.
[2] See R. Dumesnil, *Chroniques, études, correspondance de Guy de Maupassant*, p. 384.

A personal note seems to sound in *Fort comme la mort*, which is the study of the pangs of an ageing man who conceives a love, 'stronger than death', for a young girl. It is linked to the parallel study of the despair of an ageing woman who feels her charms waning and her power to hold her lover relaxing. Maupassant has treated the theme with extraordinary delicacy, and none of the brutality which it might have called forth in a writer following strictly the traditions of naturalism. The suffering is on a moral and spiritual, not on a material plane: but it springs all the same from more self-centred motives than the sufferings of, shall we say, Levin in *Anna Karenina*, when he thinks Kitty loves Vronsky more than she loves him. It can evoke no pity but self-pity in the sufferer himself: for his only confidant, the woman with whom he has had a life-long liaison and whose daughter has inspired this disastrous passion, feels naturally as much jealousy as pity.

By the time he wrote his last novel, *Notre Cœur* (1890), Maupassant had passed right out of the orbit of Russian influence, and there is little in this odd story that can be attributed with any fairness to his reading of Tolstoy.[1] It is a curious and rather trivial instance of the vagaries of passion. André Mariolle finds every satisfaction in his mistress, a society hostess, except warm love and true attachment: so he contracts another engagement, with a servant-girl who adores him, and achieves peace of mind (or so one is led to suppose), in dividing his life henceforth between Élisabeth, who is devoted to him, and Michèle to whom he is devoted.

It is clear that there can be no breath of idealism about this tale. Generally speaking it must be admitted that one of the changes which the themes of suffering and pity underwent when they were transposed from the Russian to the French novel was that they became based on a far narrower platform. Men and women in the books of Tolstoy and Dostoevsky suffer a cosmic ache: they suffer in the search for the fulfilment of their destiny or else (particularly in Dostoevsky) because of the humiliations put on their spirit by indignities of a social or material order. In the books even of those French authors most strongly affected by the Russians, suffering is usually the suffering of the cheated senses, exalted, perhaps, to

---

[1] The suggestion has, however, been made that Maupassant modelled Michèle de Burne on the heroine of Turgenev's novel, *Smoke*. See A. Albalat, 'L'Amour honnête dans le roman', *Nouvelle Revue*, 1 May 1894, p. 157.

a high level, but rooted nearly always in some amorous deception. Consequently suffering is more egoistic: it is no longer 'the suffering of all humanity' but the suffering of the baffled lover. And since such suffering is egoistic, it is less likely to compel pity. As Maupassant wrote of the hero of *Notre Cœur* when he seduces his maid Élisabeth: 'The thought never crossed his mind that he should send the girl away, preserve her from the danger from which he had suffered so cruelly himself, and have pity on her more than [Michèle] had had pity on him, *car aucune compassion ne se mêle jamais aux victoires sentimentales.*'

There are then, as this investigation has shown, good grounds for supposing that Maupassant's novel passed through a phase in which the influence of Tolstoy made itself definitely felt. But the phase was confined to the years in which the Russian novel was at the height of its popularity in France, and the influence decreased thereafter. It was never at any stage a major factor in the genesis of his novels but, as far as it goes, it provides some illustration of the extent to which Vogüé's prophecies came true when he announced that the naturalist novel (of which Maupassant had been among the three or four original and most powerful exponents), was due for extinction or radical transformation under the pressure of the Russian examples.

Another writer, connected with the naturalist school, whose work at one stage fell under the influence of the Russian novel, was Joris-Karl Huysmans. Like Maupassant, he began about the mid-eighties to break away from the doctrines which had led him to associate with other members of the Group of Médan. His apostasy went deeper than Maupassant's. In his literary evolution, Maupassant gives the impression of describing a full circle, his last novel, *Notre Cœur*, being as devoid of ethical argument as his first, *Une Vie*. Huysmans moved steadily away from the earthy and cynical naturalism of his earlier style (typified in *Les Sœurs Vatard*, 1879, *En ménage*, 1881, &c.) towards the lofty spiritualism of his later works (*La Cathédrale*, 1898, *L'Oblat*, 1903, *Les Foules de Lourdes*, 1906). It was only in part a literary development, since Huysmans's gradual conversion to Catholicism is fully reflected in the changing spirit of his work. The two currents, aesthetic and religious, are inextricably mingled, and Huysmans was attracted to Catholicism,

like a second Chateaubriand, as much by its promise to the artist
and lover of beauty in him as by its spiritual appeal to the world-
weary penitent.

While it would be unwise to suggest that his conversion was anything but the main driving force behind this literary evolution, other
factors contributing to the metamorphosis cannot be neglected:
and among them is the influence of Dostoevsky. This influence
was temporary and limited—more limited perhaps than the influence of Tolstoy on Maupassant which has just been discussed. It
can be studied properly in one novel only: *Là-bas*, published in
1891, a book which is a monument to one of the unhealthy by-
products of the Catholic urge—Satanism, religion inverted. Huysmans's preceding works of fiction were for the most part composed
before Dostoevsky became known in France:[1] and the latter works
were suffused with the spirit of Catholicism, altogether at variance
with the philosophy of the anti-Catholic Russian master.

In the very first pages of *Là-bas*, mention is made of Dostoevsky.
Durtal, the hero of the novel, a self-portrait who recurs in other
books of Huysmans's, is trying to guess which way the cat of French
fiction will jump next—and his considered opinion is that the cat
has run its head into a noose. His premiss is that the novel must
be rescued at all costs from materialism (naturalism), the devotees
of which were henceforth doomed either to sterility or to a jejune
recopying of the masterpieces of their elders. And yet, outside
naturalism, what was there? Durtal enumerates the unattractive
alternatives: 'the volcanic inventions of the Romantics', the 'woolly
works of a Cherbuliez or a Feuillet', or the 'tear-stained little
stories of a Theuriet or a Sand'. And Durtal-Huysmans sketches
out his ideal, which is to

keep the truthfulness of the document, the precision as to detail, the
firm, sinewy language of realism, but at the same time to sink shafts into
the soul [*se faire puisatier d'âme*], and not try to explain away mystery as
an infirmity of the senses; the novel, if that were possible, should divide
itself automatically into two parts, soldered together none the less or

---

[1] The exceptions being *Un Dilemme* (1887), a short story in the manner of
Boule de Suif, in which a heartless and avaricious lawyer bullies to death the
mistress of his dead grandson, fearing the scandal she may cause and the claims
she may have on his estate; and *En rade* (1887), a novel set in the brutalized
country-side of *La Terre*, in which Huysmans varies the usual naturalist pattern
only to the extent of describing several of the hero's night-dreams.

rather blended, as they are in real life, that of the soul and that of the body; the novel should concern itself with their interaction, their clashes, their harmonizing. In short, one should follow the high road so firmly marked out by Zola, but it would be needful also to trace in the air a parallel path, another road, to attain what goes beyond and follows after, to create, in a word, a spiritual naturalism; that would be something uncommonly fine, uncommonly full-blooded and strong.

It is no far cry from this 'spiritual naturalism' of Huysmans's to the 'mystical realism' which had been Vogüé's definition of the art of Dostoevsky. Huysmans admits as much, grudgingly. At the moment, he says, no one has attempted anything on these lines: 'At the most one could cite, as approaching this concept, Dostoevsky.' And he adds: 'Et encore est-il bien moins un réaliste surélevé qu'un socialiste évangélique, cet exorable Russe!'

An unjust remark, but one which shows at once why Huysmans never experienced more than a passing interest in Dostoevsky. The Russian writer offended both his religious and political instincts: evangelical might describe Dostoevsky, if the term signifies merely one who has greater faith in his own interpretation of scriptural passages than in that of an organized religion; socialist, in the narrow and party sense, Dostoevsky, in spite of his part in the Petrashevsky conspiracy, probably never was, but it is understandable that Huysmans should call him so. The obvious preference that Dostoevsky gives in his books to the under-privileged individual, the fact that his most unsympathetic characters are usually well-born or well-to-do (Valkovsky in *Insulted and Injured*, Svidrigailov in *Crime and Punishment*, Fyodor Pavlovitch in *The Brothers Karamazov*), betrays or seems to betray a concern for the wrongs of the downtrodden quite foreign to the artist in Huysmans.

The 'spiritual naturalism' which Huysmans can detect—to a limited extent—in Dostoevsky but nowhere else in contemporary literature, is best exemplified, as Durtal's further ruminations indicate, in certain works of pictorial art: and he instances in particular Grünewald's 'Crucifixion'.

Reading Huysmans's description of this painting one is compellingly reminded of the mysterious picture that hangs in Rogozhin's house. The parallel between the passages in *The Idiot* which deal with this canvas and the passage in *Là-bas* seems close enough to be more than a fortuitous resemblance. In the Russian novel the picture is a reproduction of a 'Descent from the Cross' attributed by Myshkin to Hans Holbein. Rogozhin draws Myshkin's attention to it at the end of a conversation the two have had, chiefly about Nastasya Filippovna. Dostoevsky does not, on this occasion, describe it other than to mention its subject and to record the Prince's exclamation: 'But this picture is enough to make some men lose their faith!' and Rogozhin's 'unexpected' rejoinder: 'That it can!'

The picture is mentioned again farther on in the novel when we learn more about it, this time from the lips of Ippolit, who was also struck by the canvas during a visit to Rogozhin's house. The chief and most striking characteristic is the stark realism of the artist. 'Painters', says Ippolit, 'are accustomed to represent the Christ, both on the Cross and in His descent from the Cross, always with a trace of extraordinary beauty in His face: they seek to preserve Him this beauty even in the most fearful torments. But in Rogozhin's picture there is no question of beauty.' And Huysmans says of Grünewald's picture:

Ah! in this Calvary, blood-bespattered and blurred by tears, how far one has moved from those meek-and-mild Golgothas which, since the Renaissance, the Church has adopted! This Christ with lock-jaw was not the Christ of the Rich, the Adonis of Galilea, the robust fop, the handsome lad with the auburn locks and the well-combed beard, with the dull, horsey features, whom the faithful have worshipped for the past four hundred years. Here was . . . the Christ of the first centuries of the Church, the vulgar Christ, ugly because he shouldered the sins of the world and in humility took on the most abject of shapes.

Both Dostoevsky and Huysmans summon up the vision of what has gone before the crucifixion, and both in similar terms: 'It can clearly be seen', writes the first, 'that this is the corpse of a Man Who has endured endless torments even before crucifixion, wounds, torture, Who was beaten by the guards, beaten by the people, when He was carrying the Cross and sank beneath its weight, and finally endured the pangs of crucifixion.' And in the other picture Christ, says Huysmans, 'had accepted that His Divinity should be as it were suspended, from the time He was struck and beaten with rods, insulted and spat upon, receiving all these lesser incursions of suffering, up to when He endured the fearsome torments of an endless death-agony'. And in both books there is a strongly realistic description of the actual figure of the Christ—although Huysmans goes into much greater and horrific detail and describes not only the head (to which Dostoevsky's pencil confines itself), but covers every part and member of the battered, bleeding, and suppurating body. Here is the relevant passage in *The Idiot*:

The face is painted with pitiless realism;[1] there is nothing here but nature, and so indeed must be the corpse of a man, whoever he is, after such tortures. . . . In the picture this face is fearfully gashed by blows, puffy, with dreadful, swollen and bloody weals, the eyes wide open, the pupils dilated; the great staring whites of the eyes shine with a kind of deathly, glassy reflection.

The details differ in Huysmans's description (but it is, after all, a different picture he is describing); but a similar attention is given to repulsive particulars.

The head appeared, tumultuous and enormous; encircled by a dis-ordered crown of thorns it hung, exhausted, one haggard eye barely open, in which a look of suffering and fright still quivered; the coun-tenance was ridgy, the brow callow, the cheeks sunken; all the distorted features wept, while the gaping mouth grinned with its jaws contracted by atrocious tetanous spasms.

And Huysmans concludes: 'never yet had naturalism escaped into such subjects . . . Grünewald was the most frantic of the realists'.

Huysmans is not by any means copying Dostoevsky: it seems likely that the memory of this passage he read in *The Idiot* com-bined with his memory of the Grünewald picture, and prompted him to analyse a 'realist' pictorial treatment of a sacred theme while his mind was still running on Dostoevsky, whose name had been invoked a page or so back. That is as far as it is safe to go. The *functions* of the two pictures are widely different. Dostoevsky (or Ippolit) uses the picture to emphasize the indignity of suffering death: as an intending suicide, Ippolit wishes to leap into the arms of death instead of passively awaiting its cold embrace. Huysmans (or Durtal) sees his picture as a symbol of what all art should strive for—brutal sincerity linked to a transcendent awareness of the Divine.

---

[1] 'Le visage est peint avec un réalisme impitoyable'—as Derély translated. The words of Dostoevsky are 'litso ne poshchazheno niskol'ko', i.e. 'the face is not spared in the slightest' (no concession being made to sentiment).

This ideal he attempted to realize in *Là-bas* by juxtaposing two plots. The primary, contemporary plot deals with Durtal's every-day life, his friendships with Carhaix, a campanologist, with Des Hermies, a man of letters like himself, and his liaison with Mme Chantelouve. The secondary plot is the history of Gilles de Rais, which Durtal is engaged on writing. It is an atrocious piece of fifteenth-century cruelty and witchcraft: Gilles de Rais tried to sell himself to the devil for wealth and power, committed unspeak-able crimes, and ended by giving himself up to the civil power, making a complete public confession, and accepting the sentence imposed by the ecclesiastical court.

This story, picked up and continued at intervals throughout the book, delighted Huysmans because it showed so clearly at least one element of the Middle Ages which set it far and away above the modern period in his view. The men of the Middle Ages appealed to him, just as did Grünewald's picture, for their incredible blend-ing of crude bloodthirstiness with an instinctive and unfeigned religious feeling. By contrast, the moderns, pedestrian, hypocritical, are neither vehemently bestial nor sublimely aspiring, but wallow in a slough of disheartening mediocrity, ashamed of the body, ashamed of the soul.

This idea is part of Huysmans's personal and peculiar outlook on life. Dostoevsky's *Idiot*, however, seems to have provided him with the particular form in which he chose to clothe the idea.

During the course of an evening spent with a numerous company in Prince Myshkin's country-house, Lebedev (one of the buffoons in whose mouths Dostoevsky so frequently puts ideas of consider-able profundity), tells, in his long-winded and declamatory fashion, an anecdote. He is illustrating a notion he has that the modern railway system was predicted, and condemned, in the Apocalypse. Railways (symbolizing modern technical progress) may contribute to the material happiness of mankind, but unrelated to a moral principle of action, they may cause more harm than good. He then comes to his anecdote. It is set in the twelfth century, a time of great famines, in which resort was occasionally had to cannibalism. 'One such parasite, approaching old age, declared of his own accord, and without any compulsion, that in the course of his long life, dogged by hunger, he had slain and eaten personally in the deepest secret sixty monks and a few lay children—half a dozen, not more.' The point of this preposterous story (which Lebedev insists is authentic), is, as the teller emphasizes, that, affronting all the tortures and penalties that awaited him, the man went and denounced himself, while he could have kept his secret or done private penance.

Here is the answer to the problem! There must have been something stronger than fire or stake, or even a habit engrained over twenty years. There must have been an idea stronger than all miseries, famines, tortures, plague and leprosy, and all the hell which men would never have endured without the unifying ideas which guide their hearts and renew the sources of life! Now show me anything to compare with that force in our age of vices and railways!

Gilles de Rais does not eat children, but he tortures, violates, and kills them; and he commits sacrilege, just as had the 'parasite' of Lebedev's anecdote. Also, he ends by giving himself up, though he was under no necessity to do this. Like Lebedev, Durtal scents here a great riddle: he suggests Gilles's will might have been undermined by debauchery, or else the idea of the punishment awaiting him might have exerted a morbid fascination. But the whole tenor of *Là-bas* is that the Middle Ages (Huysmans speaks of the 'white splendour' of the Middle Ages shining in the court-room in which Gilles makes his horrible confession) was shot through and through with an *idea* which has faded now—and this idea is surely no different from the one of which Lebedev spoke.

The contrast between the medieval and the modern age comes up for discussion again, at a later stage, in *The Idiot*. Ippolit, in conversation with Myshkin, contrasts himself, shuddering and prevaricating in the face of death, with a stoic of another age like Stepan Glebov, the lover of Peter the Great's first wife, who 'stayed fifteen hours impaled on a stake and died with extraordinary firmness'. And Myshkin, consoling Ippolit, replies: 'The men of those days (I swear that has always struck me) did not in the least resemble those of to-day, our nature is altogether different from theirs. . . .' This passage may be put alongside the comments of Des Hermies in *Là-bas*:

It is quite certain that the nerves quiver in this century, more easily than of old, at the slightest shock. Look at the details the newspapers give about the execution of criminals sentenced to death: they show us that the executioner works timidly, that he is on the point of fainting, that his nerves are jangling when he beheads a man. What a sorry state! Compare him with the sturdy torturers of the old days. . . . They would quarter you, give you the strappado, roast you, sprinkle you with burning oil, keeping an unmoved face, steady nerves, unwrung by all your shrieks and groans. . . .

Huysmans was a writer with ideas rather than invention. His themes, and above all his style, are his own, but the fictional trappings are usually thin or unoriginal. Dostoevsky's influence on his writing does not seem to spread beyond these fictional elements. Huysmans used one or two anecdotes and odds and ends of narrative which he found in the Russian, but twisted them to his own ends. Thus Myshkin, who admits that modern man is a different creature from medieval man, believes that the difference can be interpreted to the credit of the former; Huysmans, on the other hand, admires the feudal executioner more than the modern hangman. And we have seen how Huysmans's discussion of Grünewald's picture ends in a salvo of applause for the genius of the painter, whereas Dostoevsky notes sombrely that Holbein's picture would rob a man of his belief in God. The truth is that Huysmans and Dostoevsky had essentially very little in common: the former, for all his lifelong search for spiritual quietude, found ultimately in the Catholic religion, is through and through an artist, an aesthete; Dostoevsky is a metaphysician with an artist's temperament.

VII

THE RUSSIAN NOVEL AND THE
DISINTEGRATION OF NATURALISM
II. PAUL MARGUERITTE

LOOKING back in 1894 on the first impact, eight or ten years
previously, of the Russian novel on French literature, Gaston
Deschamps compared it to a breath of pure air which pene-
trated miraculously into the oppressive atmosphere of a gaol. 'In
1886 we were shut up, without escape, without light, not too
wretched, very stupefied, in the strongholds of naturalism. Enormous blocks, *l'Assommoir*, *Nana*, had been rolled against the door
by M. Émile Zola. Other workmen had stopped up the windows
with dirty linen, old papers, mortar and clay.' The breath of pure
air, blowing off the steppes of Russia, 'gave us the strength to roll
away the stone from the sepulchre'.

From that moment the ranks of the naturalists were thrown into
a certain disarray. Deschamps may well be intending an allusion to
the two authors whose reactions to the Russian novel formed the
subject of our preceding chapter, when he remarks that 'certain
old companions of Médan denied their master and covered themselves with ridicule by fits of frantic idealism'. Younger writers
were better able to receive the message.

A vague disquiet began to ferment among young men of letters. The
hostile, ironical, mocking observations of the French realists repelled us.
Dostoevsky, Tolstoy are realists too; but they do not believe that 'the
wide world is wholly contained in a petticoat or a pantaloon'. They do
not remain impassive, once they have observed the truth and described
it; they do not cut themselves off in coteries, far from the darkened and
suffering masses.[1]

Paul Margueritte was a member of this younger generation,
whose response to the Russians was far more eager than that of
their elders, and who followed in their wake with much more
serious intent. He began his career, dutifully, by enlisting in the
regiment of the naturalists. His first novel (*Tous quatre*, 1884),

[1] Deschamps, *La Vie et les livres*, Ière série, pp. 212–14.

followed the prevailing vogue. In 1885, however, he was one of the
five young authors who signed the 'manifesto against [Zola's] *La
Terre*', in which the excesses of the master of the naturalist school
were repudiated. Thereafter Margueritte's novel detached itself
more and more from the naturalist tradition and became the vehicle
for ideas and sentiments drawn directly from the books of Tolstoy
and Dostoevsky or at any rate strongly affected by their spirit. A
study of Margueritte's first five novels, written in the half-dozen or
so years in which Tolstoy and Dostoevsky were flooding a 'seller's
market', should bring out amply the scope and direction of this
influence. They are not necessarily his best novels; but from our
special view-point, coming as they do at a time when his reading
of the Russian masters was freshest in the author's mind, they
are the most illuminating.

In 1886, Margueritte published *Jours d'épreuve*. The book is
pitched in a quiet key and describes how a couple pass through
'days'—and years—'of trial', and win through in the end to a richer
and fuller life. Such a pattern was greatly favoured by Tolstoy. It
is visible in the way he follows Pierre Bezukhov from the dissipa-
tions of his youth, through the indignity of his first marriage and
the fiery ordeals of the burning of Moscow and the retreat, to the
dawn of a new manhood, with its greater sense of responsibility
and direction. In the same book Tolstoy shows Natasha, at the
beginning, an irresponsible thirteen-year-old, shedding her frivolity,
wilfulness (and also some of her charm) in her passage through life,
and finishing as a model housewife and a devoted mother. In *Anna
Karenina* there is the history of the development of Levin; and
Family Happiness is a story devoted entirely to the analysis of the
successive stages in the evolution of a girl who looks for she knows
not what from life, but, under the guidance of an older and sagacious
husband, ends by realizing that happiness lies not in the search for
pleasure but in living unto others—within her family circle.

Margueritte's hero, André, comes from an impoverished line of
aristocrats. The tedium of his life, cooped up all day as he is in a
government office, following a monotonous routine for a derisory
salary, preys on his mind to such an extent that he decides to take
his life. The attempt failing, by a chance, he regards the incident
as a providential sign and puts away such thoughts for the future.
The example of a colleague, who, though poor, rears a large family

and finds satisfaction in these homely joys, gives him the idea of
marrying in his turn. He chooses a bride, most unromantically,
from a photograph album.

Within a very short time the misery of respectable indigence
beleaguers the couple. The birth of a child adds to their burdens.
Their first comfortable installation is abandoned for lodgings in a
poorer quarter, and they finally move into the suburbs. For a time
André loses his post. His romantic aspirations are gradually sloughed
away, he is forced to adopt a humbler, but healthier attitude to life.

The fine soaring dreams, passions as one reads of them in novels, this
deceptive ideal courageously sacrificed when he married, were still
plaguing André. He thought of the clashes of love and jealousy, kid-
nappings, adultery, tragic suffering and passion. All that, he would never
savour it! But was it not illusive? and had he not chosen the better part,
down-to-earth happiness, the bare happiness of the resigned, but a sure
happiness?

The book shows how this conviction grows stronger and stronger
in André, and in Toinette too. A conversation between husband
and wife repeats very docilely the lessons of Tolstoyism as Margueritte might have read them in *What I Believe*. As regards the
existence of God, André is sceptic: 'An unknown force has animated
matter, but matter may very well have existed from all eternity'.
Religions are man-made, and prayers to God cannot deflect the
course of Nature. 'Why do we live?' asks Toinette. 'We live, and
that is enough', replies her catechist. 'The solution of the mystery
escapes us, but an ordinary mind, set in the midst of nature and
human society, can understand that we have a duty to fulfil.' And
this duty is 'to live according to the ideas of good and justice which
are innate in us, and which education develops'.

All this is, of course, hackneyed enough, but it may well have
received current reinforcements from Margueritte's reading of
Tolstoy, for instance of Levin's meditations at the end of *Anna
Karenina*: 'I, and millions of men, peasants and sages, in the past
and the present, we are in agreement on one point: and that is, that
we should live for "the Good". The only knowledge that I and all
men possess that is clear, beyond all doubt, absolute, is here.'

In any case, whether this doctrine was inspired by Tolstoy
directly or not, the notion of including in a novel a bald statement
of metaphysical beliefs such as this (for André does not stop there,
but goes on to preach to his wife his ideas about the after-life, the

reason for the presence of evil in the world, &c.) was something new in the French novel, at least since the dawn of realism. Tolstoy on numerous occasions makes use of this procedure, usually judged inartistic by the French since it involved a mixture of the 'genres', and one critic after another in France was struck by Tolstoy's 'error in forever trying to insist, by abstract reasoning, on ideas which he has the gift of bringing to life by plastic expression'.[1] But the influence of the Russians on French writers was not confined to what their drawing-room critics considered the most praise-worthy features of their art.

Toinette undergoes a similar sort of evolution, and after years of a drab struggle for existence,

she was visited no more by these vague aspirations, this dream of a boundless romantic happiness. Of the books of adventure and love she had devoured in a rage, nothing remained but the weariness of them. Gradually, under the influence of André's words and actions, Toinette's mind emerged from chaos and became ordered. Already vigorous ideas were ripening in her: knowledge of her duties and feeling for her family; emotions new to her, which bade fair to spring up with the strength of virgin plants.

Toinette has passed through exactly the same stages as the heroine of *Family Happiness* who had begun married life with similar exalted expectations and is taught, by a few bitter lessons of experience, to abandon them. Katya ends her confessions, which make up Tolstoy's short novel, with the words:

the old [romantic] feeling stayed among those sweet memories to which there is no returning, and a new feeling of love for my children and for the father of my children marked the start of a new existence differently happy, and which I am still enjoying, convinced that the reality of happi-ness is in the home and among the unsullied joys of family life. . . .

In transposing *Family Happiness* Margueritte has taken the emphasis from the study of the wife's development and laid it on that of the man; and he has also chosen his heroine from a class too harassed by material want to be greatly tempted (as Katya was) by the solicitations with which high society was supposed to surround a beautiful woman. Katya, it may be said, was an Emma Bovary who was saved through not being married to a doting imbecile; and Toinette is another Emma who never met the satanic Lheureux

[1] Vogüé, *Le Roman russe*, p. 315.

and whose moments of revolt fortunately peter out in want of
opportunity. Once she meets a possible seducer, André's cousin,
an adventurer who might have played the part of Rodolphe; but as
chance would have it she is pregnant, and his glance is without
interest. Once, while she is in the country, a passing horseman casts
an approving eye over her, making her heart beat faster—but she
never sees him again. Both Tolstoy's novel and the novel of Paul
Margueritte eschew, in the interests of edification, the pitiless logic
of Flaubert.

In his next book Margueritte returned to the perennial novel
theme—extra-marital love. Set in the author's native Algeria, *Pascal
Géfosse* (1887) is an episode in the life of a cynical and remorseless pleasure-hunter, another Bel-Ami with, as his aim, the satisfaction of his senses rather than the attainment of worldly ambition.
Such a character has virtually no prototype in the novels of Tolstoy
or Dostoevsky. There are, however, one or two possible reminiscences of *Anna Karenina* in the book. Louise, who is Pascal's
victim, when her absent husband is praised before her in Pascal's
hearing, is ill at ease. 'For the first time, she thought of her husband
with a kind of shame, and shame in front of the other man.' Anna,
when she returns from St. Petersburg to Moscow, barely conscious
of the first vague stirrings of love for Vronsky, is repelled by the
sight of her husband coming to meet her at the station. 'A dis-
agreeable thought oppressed her heart when she saw his stubborn,
weary look. She felt that she had expected to find him different.
Not only was she dissatisfied with herself, but she confessed to a
certain feeling of hypocrisy in her relations with her husband.'
When Pascal wins her, Louise feels nothing but horror and
remorse; there is no trace of the mingled joy and self-satisfaction
that accompanies Emma Bovary's first lapse.

Perdue, perdue, irrévocablement perdue, par sa faute, sa très grande
faute! Et plus elle descendait au fond d'elle-même, mieux elle comprenait
tout ce que sa chute avait d'irréparable; jadis, dans un monument,
descendant les étroites spirales d'un invisible escalier, en de froides et
gluantes ténèbres, elle avait eu le vertige d'une chute qui ne s'arrêterait
jamais, et en était restée, en sortant, tout étourdie, au soleil. C'était la
même sensation d'angoisse et d'horreur physique qu'elle traversait. . . .
Sa chair cuisait encore de l'inexprimable violation, de cette souillure
sans joie. Après, il s'était jeté à ses pieds, suppliant et tendre, répétant

de ces mots qui font pardonner. Qu'avait-il besoin de pardon? Elle
s'accusait seule.

A naturalist writer, studiously ignoring the spiritual repercussions
of physical acts, would have discounted the sense of sin which here
inspires Louise's tumultuous thoughts.

Tolstoy attributed to Anna the very same sense of sin, of shame,
of horror, when she became an adulteress. Less the starkness of the
French novelist's phrasing, the two scenes are so very similar that
it is scarcely conceivable Margueritte should have written this page
without having in the back of his mind the passage in *Anna
Karenina*. Anna is so humiliated she all but falls to the ground. She
cries out

'May God forgive me!' . . . She felt she was a sinner and a criminal,
that nothing remained for her except to crouch down and beg for forgiveness. As she looked at him she felt her humiliation physically, and she
could say nothing more. But he felt exactly as a murderer feels staring
at the body of his victim. Their victim was their love, the first epoch of
their love. There was something horrible and contemptible in the thought
of the price they had paid for this terrible shame. Their shame in the
presence of their spiritual nakedness, choked her, brought him pain.

Pascal leaves Louise with little repining and few twinges of conscience; and the hero of *Amants*, Margueritte's next novel (also set
in Algeria), is quite as consummate a villain. Living with a pious
and long-suffering wife, he seduces an unmarried girl, who kills
herself when she becomes pregnant. But the Prince d'Ancine is less
detestable than Pascal Géfosse: and the book ends in a storm of
tears, repentance, and pity such as seldom fell on the arid expanses
of naturalist production.

The Prince looked down at his wife wearing mourning for the woman
he once loved, he saw his child, so frail and innocent, and thought of the
other babe that was killed with its mother; he thought of that rare,
charming Frédérique . . . and was overcome by an immense tenderness,
an infinite pity for human suffering, and in a movement of despair which
enveloped Frédérique, his wife, his child and himself, he kissed pale
little Alyette [his daughter] and great tears began to fill his eyes. And
his wife, her two hands on his shoulders, wept copiously, like him, for
her own sorrows: the irreparable fatality of life, happiness forever
forfeit.

Such downpours as these were of more regular occurrence in an

Eastern clime: it was a wind from the steppes, to use Deschamps's
phrase, that had blown them over the metallic Algerian sky. Francisque Sarcey had defied anyone to read *Anna Karenina* dry-eyed:
no doubt he was equally moved by *Amants*. The reinforcement of
the *fin-de-siècle* drift towards sentimentalism in France was one
of the least admirable effects of the influence of the Russian
novel.

The weak-willed, seductive, and sentimental Prince is, however,
fortunately an accessory figure in *Amants*. The central character is
Frédérique. Although in the end she takes her own life, she knows
that she is in any case gradually perishing of an incurable disease.
Margueritte makes much of her morbid state of mind, and by many
a touch it is evident that Tolstoy—and in particular his story *The
Death of Ivan Ilyitch*—is an important source. In both books the
obsession with death is the nodal point.

For Frédérique, 'gradually, from the depths of her conscience,
from the dark corner of her brain where it crouched fearsomely,
the unformulated *idea*, the silent, black idea, slowly raised itself in
the shadows; and she saw, she felt, she recognized the abominable
and hallucinatory presence of the invisible monster: DEATH'.
More graphically than Margueritte, Tolstoy gives a direct reproduction of the spectral dance of Ivan Ilyitch's thoughts: but the
condemned man feels exactly the same horror as the dreadful truth
dawns on him.

'Yes', he tells himself, 'life was there, and now it is leaving me; leaving
me, and I can't stop it going. . . . Yes, why cheat myself? Isn't it obvious
for everyone except myself, that I am dying, that it is only a question of
weeks, of days . . . less than that, perhaps. It was daylight before, now
it is night. I was here, now I am bound for some other place! Where? . . .'
He felt his blood freeze, he caught his breath. He heard only the beating
of his heart. 'I shall be no more, but then, what will there be? There
will be nothing. Where shall I be, when I am no more? . . . Would it be
Death? . . . No, I can't bear it!'

Ivan Ilyitch remembers a syllogism learnt at school: 'X is a man;
all men are mortal; therefore X is mortal.' He realizes he has never
believed it to be true of himself, however true it was for X.
Frédérique tells herself she is menaced not by 'the abstract death
which strikes all men, but by a living death determined in time,
localized in space'.

For both Tolstoy's hero and Margueritte's heroine the obsession of death becomes overwhelming, driving out every other preoccupation. It accompanies Ivan Ilyitch to the court-room when he is exercising his functions as a judge, and to the card-table where he is playing a rubber of whist: everywhere it prevents him from working or enjoying himself. He invents elaborate 'screens' to hide the thought from him as long as possible, but the slightest reference to his illness on the part of some other member of his family he interprets as an allusion to his approaching death, and the temporary good humour he was enjoying gives place to blackest brooding. And Frédérique is in like case.

All day long, the *idea*, in the thousand and one forms of an ingenious torture, obsessed her: it ate with her, went for walks with her, mingled in her conversations which it poisoned, everything became an allusion for Frédérique, forbidding her to make plans for the future, isolating her in the midst of healthy people with their lives before them.

The Death of Ivan Ilyitch must have made a powerful impression on Margueritte, for we find echoes of it not only in *Amants* but in his next novel too, *La Force des choses* (1890). In this story a death occurs in the very first chapters, that of the mistress of the hero, Pierre Jorieu. His cousin, Henri, who has left her in a critical condition, is absorbed in reflections on the subject of death which bear the closest of resemblances to certain ideas in the mind of Ivan Ilyitch while he is on the point of death.

Why then, [Henri tells himself] to die, that's nothing. What is frightful, is the suffering, the physical pain, the sorrow of those who love you; but death, death itself, the thing we fear, the black, horrible idea, does not exist. . . . It exists only in our imagination. You feel nothing. You disappear for everyone else and for yourself. There is no death!

And Ivan meditates: ' "And death, where is it?" He looked for his habitual fear of death and did not find it. "Where is it? What is death?" He felt no more fear, for there was no more death. Instead of death, there was light.' And Ivan's last thought is: 'That's the end of death! It exists no more.'

There are other passages in *La Force des choses* over which the shadow of Tolstoy is projected. Paul Margueritte, in depicting General Jorieu, his hero's father, no doubt drew to a large extent on his memories of his own father, General Auguste Margueritte, who served with distinction under the Second Empire in Mexico

and North Africa and was killed in 1870 on the field of battle. But
it may be also that the fictional character owes something to Tolstoy's representation of the old Prince Bolkonsky, Andrew's father,
in *War and Peace*. Both Margueritte's creation and Tolstoy's were,
in their time, fine soldiers, and are eating out their hearts in enforced
idleness; and both of them have a fine contempt for the commanders
at present in charge of their countries' armies. Both are monastically
severe in their habits, and impose the same rigorous style of living
on their family circle. Jorieu spends his leisure hours 'gardening,
digging and watering the ground, fencing with a fencing-master,
learning the geography of the globe down to the smallest detail, or
solving mathematical problems'. General-in-Chief Bolkonsky oc-
cupies his time 'writing his memoirs, solving problems in higher
mathematics, turning snuff-boxes on a lathe, working in the garden,
or superintending the building that was always in progress on his
estate'. Each of the old men has a daughter: and Annette is as self-
effacing and as timorously dutiful as Princess Mary. She is not
personally attractive, but Henri, seeing her, is touched by 'her
modest attitude and something sweet and good in her face': this is
precisely the impression that Mary, who also lacks the ordinary
feminine graces, makes on those who meet her.

In one respect, however, the two old soldiers seem to separate.
Jorieu is an ardent Catholic, practising the faith of his ancestors.
Bolkonsky is a free-thinker, convinced that all evil has but two
roots—idleness and superstition. But the difference is only on the
surface. To be an atheist in the Russia of Alexander I was to be
old-fashioned: such opinions were more current in the rationalist
century which had just ended; while to make public profession of
belief in the teaching of the Church was an equally old-fashioned
attitude in the society of the young Third Republic into which old
Jorieu had survived.

There is no lack, in *La Force des choses*, of the notes of tenderness
and pity which were invariably associated in France with the Russian novel. At the funeral of his beloved, Pierre is led to forget his
own sorrow in a vast swelling of pity for all creation.

He felt pity not only for his wife, for his son and for himself, but for
all those he saw around him labouring under the spur of necessity:
workmen carrying their tools, crossing-sweepers, needy employees,
servant-girls, prostitutes and even the emaciated cab-horses. It seemed
to him that all these creatures, all these men and women had sorrows

just as he had, and they ceased to be strangers to him, they became his brothers and sisters in suffering.

And he wins a new wife less by his personal qualities than by stirring her through a simple recital of his sufferings. 'She was sorry for him, she suffered with him, she experienced in all its keen, piercing charm the magnetic contact of sorrow . . . she felt herself over-whelmed by a deep, unconquerable affection for Pierre, by an immense pity for him, for his child, for herself.'

It may not be possible to lay one's finger on isolated pages in novels by Tolstoy or Dostoevsky which provided the germ of passages such as these: but it is clear that they owe nothing to the type of writing that had been in favour among the French naturalist novelists, and that their whole spirit derives from the foreign masters.

Victor Charbonnel wrote (in 1896), that 'Tolstoï a la religion de la grande souffrance humaine, et Paul Margueritte a la religion de l'humble et douce souffrance bourgeoise'.[1] To none of the French writer's works could this remark be more aptly applied than to *Ma Grande* (1891). Margueritte here analyses the jealousy which an elder sister, who has devoted her life to caring for her brother, feels for his wife when he marries. The three are unwise enough to attempt living together in the same house. 'Then, each day brought, for all their good intentions, its little pin-prick, its involuntary clash, all those things which disguise themselves under hasty concessions, polite smiles, but which gradually accumulate, become barbed and wound.' Margueritte comments: 'To give an idea of this kind of suffering is not easy, for one would have to descend to details, to all the trivial events of daily life, things to which men scarcely pay any attention, but which women know so well: all women will understand.' The second half of the book is taken up by a long and painful account of these 'pin-pricks': disputes about servants, about the cooking, the resentment of the elder woman who realizes her brother has so many intellectual interests she cannot share but in which his wife partakes: there are no great vicissitudes, it is the unpretentious study of everyday life, and Tolstoy had given many examples of this fine and difficult art. There is no real hatred, no passionate rancour: and the married couple feel

[1] Charbonnel, 'Les Mystiques dans la littérature présente', *Mercure de France*, Jan. 1896, p. 18.

pity and not enmity towards this redoubtable third party. But they can find no way of melting her harsh mistrustfulness which she condemns in herself in her moments of lucidity. In the end, like Ivan Ilyitch, like Prince Andrew, like Nicholas Levin, she is softened and transfigured at the touch of death, and reconciles herself with the young woman she had persecuted.

The first half of *Ma Grande* is given over to Noël's courtship of Sonia. It is indicative of Margueritte's intentions that he chooses the hovel of some impoverished peasants as the setting for the first meeting of the lovers, who thus discover at the start a common bond in their sympathy for suffering humanity. On another occasion their conversation is interrupted by a beggar asking for alms. Noël points out to Sonia the picturesqueness of the supplicant, and she, admitting she had been struck by it too, blames herself. 'Is it not wrong to forget the wretchedness of the man and to see merely the artistic, theatrical side? We are too inured to the afflictions of others: our egoism is hardened; another's suffering seems to us quite natural.' She adds that, when a child, she wanted to give all her possessions to the poor and to turn beggar, asking for alms on the high-road. This might be described as a typically Russian impulse. In *War and Peace* Mary Bolkonsky says: 'If I were asked what I desire most on earth, it would be to be poorer than the poorest beggar.' And by continually associating with the illiterate pilgrims who wandered over Russia at that time she is strongly moved to abandon her home, princess though she is, and join their company—going so far as to get ready a complete pilgrim's costume for herself. 'To leave family, home, and all the cares of worldly welfare, in order without clinging to anything to wander in hempen rags from place to place under an assumed name, doing no one any harm but praying for all—for those who drive one away as well as for those who protect one: higher than that life and truth there is no life and truth!'

Sonia is Russian herself, so that there is nothing inappropriate in the thought that Margueritte here puts into her head. Did Margueritte have any opportunity for studying the Russian individual at first-hand? At any rate it is probable his conception of the Russian 'type' was partly built up out of literary reminiscences. Sonia's mother, Mme Tratkoff, in particular, is a creature with the same lovable but exasperating, domineering but sentimental disposition as that with which Dostoevsky delights to endow the mothers of marriageable daughters that are met with in his novels: Pulkheriya Aleksandrovna, Dunya's mother, in *Crime and Punishment*; Mme Epantchin, the mother of the irrepressible Aglae, in *The Idiot*; Mme Khokhlakov, Lise's mother, in *The Brothers Karamazov*.

Sonia herself has nothing of the passionate impetuosity which seems to be the dominating characteristic of young girls in Russian novels: she is balanced, has self-restraint; her cosmopolitan existence has served merely to mature her mind. Margueritte sets her up as the champion of the new Russian novel in a literary discussion she has with Noël. She blames the French novel (that is, the novels of the 'so-called idealist writers'—for she cannot pronounce on the works of realist writers 'since mothers do not allow their daughters to read them')—she blames the French novel for the excessive and unwarranted importance it gives to the subject of love.

Is it not to fall wilfully into falsehood [she asks] to make of love the knot and centre of every plot, while it must be, I imagine, so infrequent and above all so discreet a sentiment, almost wordless in its joys and sorrows. . . . What I like in Dickens, in Tolstoy [she continues], is that love does not intrude more than it should; their novels are filled with all the other things that make up daily life—work, ambition, art, family affections, nature, the lesser pleasures of routine, and all the rest.

Her favourite reading is 'books that paint life in its true colours, and which teach us not to expect too much of it'.

One may view this as Margueritte's own *confessio fidei* in novel-writing. What he appreciated in other writers and what he strove to reproduce himself, were the qualities of truthful reporting, and the lesson, usually driven home by implication, that not too much must be looked for from life. These are, beyond dispute, two invariable qualities of Tolstoy's work. All his books are characterized by a delicate and never-failing sincerity, and they all tend to the tacit conclusion that only those who bow to circumstances, who fit themselves to the exigencies of life, will find happiness or survive at all: thus the humdrum Levin is contented, at the end of *Anna Karenina*, while the brilliant Vronsky goes off to seek death in battle as an escape from his tormented imagination. These were the two chief bequests Tolstoy made to Margueritte. In *Jours d'épreuve* especially, in *La Force des choses*, and in *Ma Grande*, he excels in depicting life at its humblest, in its least inspiring moods, showing how the gradual attrition of circumstance rounds off and shapes a man or a woman's character; and in all his books the same moral is pointed: do not ask too much of life, learn to renounce, look for more solid satisfactions than the attainment of your own selfish desires. If one adds in the ever-present sense of pity in Margueritte's books, a pity which extends beyond one's dearest friends in sorrow and extends to the whole of poor, suffering humanity, a pity evidently distilled from Dostoevsky's works no less than from Tolstoy's, then the inventory of what Margueritte chiefly borrowed from the Russians is complete. It is clear that he had brought back a very full wallet from his excursions into virgin territory.

VIII

THE RUSSIAN NOVEL AND THE DISINTEGRATION OF NATURALISM
III. PAUL BOURGET

PAUL Bourget had this in common with Paul Margueritte, and, as we shall see, with Édouard Rod, that he began his literary career as a staunch adherent of the naturalist school. It is true that among his first writings is to be found an article, 'Le Roman réaliste et le roman piétiste', in which the naturalists are soundly rated: too much importance should not be attached to this, however, since the article was a contribution to the *Revue des Deux Mondes*,[1] and the young author was, one supposes, obliged to toe the line. But some time in the later seventies, Bourget had the courage to refuse the very enviable post of literary critic on the staff of the same periodical,[2] because he felt he would have to do violence to the ties of sympathy that linked him to the naturalists. A letter to Zola,[3] written after the publication of *L'Assommoir* in 1877, attests how strong these ties were: he was on terms of friendship with the leader of the school and with his lieutenant, Guy de Maupassant.

And yet when, in 1885, Bourget's first novel was published, it was immediately evident that the last thing the author had in mind to do was to follow tamely in the wake of the great naturalist novelists who, all through his youth, had been waging their noisy and precariously successful battle. There are various reasons why this should have been. Bourget did not embark on novel-writing as an unfledged penman. He was already in his early thirties; the first work of his to be published, a volume of poetry, had appeared ten years earlier; as a literary critic, he was well known and respected; he had travelled (to Italy and to Great Britain on several occasions), and was in some degree acquainted with other literatures besides that of his native country. His was a mature and an inquiring spirit, well aware that there existed other horizons

[1] It was inserted on 15 July 1873.
[2] Brunetière was appointed instead.
[3] Published in the *Mercure de France*, 15 May 1931, p. 61.

than the French one. His mind was excessively susceptible to literary influences;[1] and when, in 1883, he met Eugène-Melchior de Vogüé, brimful of the Russian realist novelists he was to 'reveal' to the public at large a little later, it is hardly surprising that Bourget should have listened intently and stored up the other man's words.

Nearly thirty years later, Bourget could remember in detail the conversation during that first meeting.[2] Vogüé talked about the 'thinness' of contemporary naturalism, the poverty of its inner life, and the narrowness of its intellectual horizon; he threw out the names of Tolstoy and Dostoevsky as instances of novelists endowed with a moral breadth which contrasted favourably with the current tendencies of French literature.

This was probably the earliest occasion on which Bourget heard tell of Tolstoy and Dostoevsky. His first opportunity to judge the Russian novel had been in his reading of Turgenev, whom he had met in person, and whose works he admired sufficiently to make them the subject of one of the chapters of his *Nouveaux essais de psychologie contemporaine*.[3] It was only a couple of months after writing this study, and with his own analysis of Turgenev's work fresh in his mind, that Bourget set to work on his first novel, *Cruelle énigme*: it would have been surprising if the book had borne no traces of the influence of the Russian author.

Cruelle énigme has other inspirational sources: in the first place Alfred de Musset.[4] The story of the moral breakdown of an un-spoilt boy when he realizes that his first idealized mistress is cor-rupt, seems to be an elaboration of the early part of the *Confession d'un enfant du siècle*. In its excessively tragic conclusion, however, *Cruelle énigme* bears the imprint of Turgenev's melancholy as Bourget himself had delineated it in his essay. He had picked out Turgenev's pessimism as a characteristic quality of his work. The

[1] L. J. Austin (*Paul Bourget, sa vie et son œuvre jusqu'en 1889* (1940), p. 67) says of Bourget that he was 'un *homme à maîtres* comme il y en a eu peu dans la littérature française. . . . On peut même dire que le drame de ses débuts dans les lettres est celui du disciple qui s'efforce de se dégager de l'emprise de ses maîtres.'

[2] He related it in an article 'E.-M. de Vogüé', *Revue des Deux Mondes*, 15 Jan. 1912, p. 253.

[3] It had appeared in the first instance in the *Nouvelle Revue*, 15 May 1884.

[4] Whose poetry Bourget had read at school with immense enthusiasm. See A. Feuillerat, *Paul Bourget, histoire d'un esprit sous la Troisième République* (1937), p. 12.

acuity of his perceptive senses meant that Turgenev based his art on observation rather than imagination or intuition: and such an art is bound, in Bourget's view, to be pessimistic. A man blind to what is going on around him does not find it hard to be sanguine; but great powers of observation lead to disappointment at the contrast between man's ambitions and his efforts, between his pretentions and his inner poverty. So with Turgenev: all his novels 'end on an overwhelmingly depressing note. The usual subject of these stories is the abortion of a hope, and no one is better able to strike an irresistible note of melancholy from the contrast between the illusion which fades and reality which asserts itself.'

The hero of *Cruelle énigme* breaks with his mistress when he knows she has been unfaithful to him. His illusions are shattered, and he is physically prostrated. He returns, however, to their erstwhile trysting-place, and, finding her there, upbraids her bitterly: 'I no longer believe in anything, I no longer hope for anything, I no longer love anything, and the fault is yours.' Yet after this outburst, he succumbs to her once more: this is the true tragedy, as the novelist would have us see it. 'His dream was over. He had loved this woman with the sublimest of loves; she held him now by the darkest and least noble side of his nature. Something had been killed in his moral being, something he would never find again.'

The words Bourget used to characterize Turgenev's novel apply with equal force to his own. It is, no less than the Russian's novels, 'the story of the abortion of a hope'; it ends on 'an overwhelmingly depressing note'; and the same 'irresistible note of melancholy' is struck from the 'contrast between the illusion which fades and reality which asserts itself'.

Bourget's second novel is at once the complement and the antithesis of the first. The theme is similar, but it is now the lover who is impure and who tempts the woman to her first fault. The dominant note at the end is optimistic, not pessimistic as previously.

Crime d'amour was written between October 1885 and January 1886. It is unlikely that Bourget failed to read and be impressed by the novels of Tolstoy and Dostoevsky—*Insulted and Injured, Crime and Punishment, War and Peace, Anna Karenina*—which were appearing in French translation over this period. His curiosity had already been whetted by his reading of Turgenev's novels, and had been further stimulated by his personal contacts with Vogüé and doubtless also by reading Vogüé's articles on Tolstoy and Dostoevsky. It is in *Crime d'amour* more than in any other novel that the influence of the Russians on Bourget can be most clearly seen. In particular, Dostoevsky's ideas about the 'religion of suffering' find here a momentary convert.

Bourget does not, however, rewrite any of the Russian novels, giving them merely a French setting. His hero is a typically French product of an era of materialist thought; he has nothing in him of the passionate turpitude of the men of pleasure of Dostoevsky's books, a Valkovsky, a Svidrigailov; nor is he a libertine out of weakness of character, as Tolstoy's Pierre Bezukhov or Oblonsky. His debauchery has its roots in a precocious experience of pleasure, and in the contempt for human life which the events of the war and the Commune have instilled in him. His disillusionment is above all intellectual. The tragedy of *Crime d'amour* hinges on Armand's cynical refusal to believe that Hélène is not as loose-living as himself, that she has been in fact entirely faithful to her husband before he seduced her. His experience of women suggests to him that she has had a previous liaison with a M. de Varades, and in his own mind he treats her protestations of purity as graceful fibs. The first rupture occurs when his attitude becomes clear to Hélène. In despair, she actually surrenders herself to de Varades, then goes to Armand and by confessing this fault proves to him her former innocence.

The interest of the book lies in the moral revolution that these events precipitate in Armand's own mind. Bourget sets himself to answer a problem in ethical psychology, and follows the train of thought in Armand as he attempts, by arguing along the old materialist lines, to justify his conduct to himself; in exactly the same way Dostoevsky listens to Raskolnikov's thought-processes as he endeavours to justify himself for another crime—more brutal, more directly in the path of the law's vengeance, but just as calculated and no more tragic: *Crime and Punishment*, in Vogüé's words, was a purely psychological drama, residing 'entirely in the combat between the man and his idea'.[1]

The reasoning of the two heroes differs only by the feverish incoherence of the one and the relatively sober dialectics of the other: their conclusions are precisely the same. Raskolnikov is hurried along the path of crime, as it seems to him, by a power

[1] Vogüé, *Le Roman russe*, p. 247.

beyond his control: from the moment the idea is planted in his mind, by a conversation he overhears by chance in a tap-house, to the moment when through another coincidence he learns that his intended victim will be alone in her flat at a given hour. Armand similarly doubts whether he has been a free agent in the affair, and strives to acquit himself of responsibility by maintaining that everything that had occurred was inevitable, given the circumstances that moulded his character.

The same arguments, the same issue. Raskolnikov finds that all his abstract self-defence crumbles before the vision of the old woman's head split open by his axe. And Armand ponders: 'Good and evil, remorse, conscience, freedom—so many unreal phantoms, disembodied shadows! But one reality which could not be gainsaid was the loss of a soul, and the fact that a fearful fate had made him the instrument of this loss.'

Raskolnikov turns for relief to Sonya, who reads to him from the Gospels and persuades him to make public confession of his deed. Armand is not yet ready to accept all the implications of religious faith, but his meditations on the existence of unhappiness draw him to conclude that ' "we should yield to the feelings of pity this unhappiness awakes in us".—When the young man turned down this new road of pity, he felt, not absolute relief from his remorse, but a kind of desperate tenderness which was dew on his heart at last.' So Raskolnikov feels the surge of new life when he performs an act of pity and succour, bringing Marmeladov home after he has been run over in the streets and leaving twenty-five roubles—almost all he has—with the widow.

Feeling now only pity for Hélène, Armand returns to Paris to see her: he finds her wasted away with sickness. He asks her forgiveness, but she has nothing to forgive, nothing to reproach him for. 'It is this suffering that has saved me, it was in the light of suffering that I judged my life. . . . By what I suffered, I realized what suffering I had caused and what wrongs I had done to those about me.' As Natasha tells Vanya in *Insulted and Injured*: 'It is necessary somehow to win by fresh suffering our future happiness, to earn it by some new torments: everything is purified by suffering.'

Hélène begs Armand never again to trample mercilessly on a woman's heart; and Armand's conversion to the 'religion of human suffering' (Vogüé's cliché to denote Dostoevsky's spiritual message) is complete.

Having seen all the wreckage that can be wrought by selfish and suspicious unfairness, he felt the supreme virtue of pity. It was by taking pity on her lover's remorse and on her husband's love, out of pity for her son's future, that Hélène had stopped herself on the fatal path.... Thus the means of salvation he had not been able to derive from weak reason and which religious dogmas had not afforded, since he was not a believer, these means he discovered in the virtue of charity which dispenses with all proofs and all revelations—but is it not the supreme, the abiding revelation?—And he felt that something had come to life within him, something which would always provide him with reasons for being and doing: the religion of human suffering.

The influence of Dostoevsky's masterpiece *Crime and Punishment* can be seen too in Bourget's third novel, *André Cornélis* (1886), which bears, as a device, the text: 'Thou shalt not kill.' Bourget's thesis is that a murder, however well justified in popular sentiment on the strongest grounds of offence, is inadmissible: it will take subtle toll of the murderer even if he is persuaded in his rational being that the moral prohibitions of religion are invalid. This is absolutely the thesis of *Crime and Punishment*.[1]

Raskolnikov has persuaded himself, by specious argument about the good he will do to the human race in eliminating the obnoxious money-lender, that his crime will be justified, will in fact not be a crime at all. But some invisible moral power that he has outraged makes itself obscurely felt after the deed is done. So with André. Termonde has done away with André's father in order to marry his mother (the situation is that of *Hamlet*, and André's irresolute conduct and self-upbraiding is a repetition of the mental vacillations of Shakespeare's Dane). André's whole life has been consumed by the idea of a righteous vengeance, but he has to arrange it so as not to arouse his mother's suspicions—she loves her second husband more than she had loved her first. In their final catastrophic encounter, André proposes to his step-father that he should commit suicide: the latter refuses, challenging André to put the irrefutable evidence in his mother's hands. This he dare not do, and, in a fit of rage, stabs Termonde, whose last act is to write a note saying he has taken his own life—he is suffering from a mortal disease which would in any case have carried him off within six months.

---

[1] The comparison between the two novels imposed itself immediately on the minds of Bourget's readers. See Brunetière's remarks in the *Revue des Deux Mondes*, 1 Mar. 1887, p. 203.

André is left with the secret of his vengeance locked up in his own heart, and the closing passage of the book indicates his despair as he realizes that his mother will never cease to love Termonde.

The theme of *Crime and Punishment* is the remorse of a murderer and the peace of mind he finds at the end by confessing his crime and atoning for it. In *André Cornélis* the remorse of Termonde is, for the most part, only guessed at by André; his own remorse does not fully emerge until the end. The conversations he has with Termonde will recall to anyone who has read *Crime and Punishment* the sessions Porfiry has with Raskolnikov, save that André is trying to get his step-father to betray himself, the latter maintaining his sang-froid: whereas Raskolnikov seeks out Porfiry deliberately in order to play with fire. André decides to have, with Termonde, 'a conversation full of *nuances* and *sous-entendus*, in which each word should be like a finger pressing on the sorest places of his thought'. In the first interview he talks to him of a pretended visit he has made to the *juge d'instruction* who was concerned with the investigation of Cornélis's death—asks him whether, if he wanted to commit a murder, he would do it by an accomplice (Termonde had actually paid his scapegrace brother to kill André's father)—asks him whether he believes in remorse, &c. This cat-and-mouse game is repeated again and again, with the anomalous situation that André is a more nervous cat than his mouse. Both of them, like any character of Dostoevsky's, use narcotics to calm their nerves.

Of the 'religion of suffering' there is hardly a trace. But if this newly imported system is ineffective, the old religion affords no relief either. André cannot believe in a Deity whose commandment *Thou shalt not kill* applies even to a son whose father has been murdered. He feels no remorse—Raskolnikov feels no remorse—he feels only humiliation at being in debt to Termonde for his final generous act in giving the murder the appearance of a suicide —Raskolnikov feels equal humiliation for having bungled the robbery after he had perpetrated the murder.

Outside the Christian religion, it would seem, there can be no solution for André's agony. The 'religion of human suffering' is already discredited, too pale and unsatisfying. The call for a return to Catholicism grows ever stronger in Bourget's ensuing books.

Over *Mensonges* (written a twelvemonth after *André Cornélis*) broods once more the figure of Musset, with whom the hero, René

de Vincy, has more than a physical likeness: his attitude towards
women is idealistic, he has poetic gifts—the book opens with a
description of a new verse drama René has written, after the style
of *La Nuit vénitienne*. *Mensonges* is yet another *Confession d'un
enfant du siècle*, written by a severer moralist, who is more uncompromising in his treatment of women of the world and who adds,
in the last chapter, as it were a didactic codicil.

The direct influence of individual Russian novels is scarcely
apparent in this book: but the trace of Tolstoy is visible in the
violent denunciation of the 'high life' of Paris, luxurious, corrupt
and corrupting, and in the juxtaposed picture of René's family
circle, honest, humble folk, with narrow outlook and restricted
interests: his sister Émilie who worships him, her overworked,
absent-minded husband the school-teacher, and René's first love,
the unassuming, slighted Rosalie. Bourget may have had in mind
the contrast drawn in *Anna Karenina* between the wealthy but
shameful—and unhappy—establishment of Vronsky and Anna,
and the humdrum but—save for occasional money worries—contented existences of Dolly and Kitty.

In so far, however, as the Russian novel undertook to 'teach a
lesson', to arrive at a definite moral conclusion on the points at
issue (and this was, as we have seen, generally believed in France
to be one of its main characteristics), then *Mensonges*, and all the
novels Bourget subsequently wrote, can be said to have been struck
from the Russian mint. It was Tolstoy's practice, with one heavy
blow in the concluding pages, to hammer home the didactic nail on
which he had been tapping throughout the novel: thus his ideas
of Fate, the workings of history, the importance of the Russian
masses, &c., hinted at and illustrated throughout *War and Peace*,
are crystallized in an exhaustive statement in the Second Epilogue;
in *Anna Karenina* Levin receives, right at the end of the book, the
answer (which is Tolstoy's answer) to the question that had been
harassing him: according to what principles, in the name of what
Power, should a man's life be ordered? In *Mensonges*, in the same
way, Bourget tacked on his 'moral message' after the action of the
book had ceased. It is René's uncle, the abbé Tacomet, until then
the slightest of figures, who is made the mouthpiece, and his words
show Bourget to be nearer the Catholic solution than in any previous book. The abbé is possessed with the idea: 'reconstituer
l'âme française par le christianisme'. He had encouraged his

nephew's talent in the hope that he would use it to the greater glory of God. He engages René's friend Claude, another writer, in a discussion about the mission of the artist. Claude's idea is that the devotees of art must 'inoculate themselves' with all human passions in order to be able to reproduce their essence.

It is true, René very nearly went under [he had attempted suicide when he heard that his idolized mistress was the kept woman of an ageing millionaire], but now, when he writes about love, about jealousy, about the treachery of women, a few spots of his blood will cling to his sentences, red blood, blood that has pulsed through an artery, not just ink poured out of the inkwells of other writers. And there will be one more fine page to add to the literary patrimony of this France which you accuse us of forgetting. We serve her after our fashion.

The priest replies: Blessed are the poor in spirit; and who shall say that the authors of *Werther* and *Rolla* are not responsible for the suicides which have occurred among their readers? 'The wounds of the soul require to be touched only by those whose touch brings relief, and this sort of pitiless, uncharitable dilettantism of human misery, which I know so well, horrifies me.' No one will ever say more than Christ has said on the subject of suffering. Claude is not convinced; but he leaves the abbé with the words: 'You are a righteous man, Sir, that is ever the finest and the surest talent!...'

If Bourget's inmost thoughts find a faithful interpreter in the good abbé, it may be said that with *Mensonges* he turns away once and for all from the dispassionate portrayal of human misery, and is now as thoroughly convinced as Tolstoy himself that the artist must assume a 'moral mission' or should be rejected as a useless member of society. But Bourget's own 'moral mission' will be, more and more, to point out the solutions that Catholicism would urge to certain situations arising from certain tendencies in behaviour.

Le Disciple (1889) was the most eloquent and best conceived denunciation Bourget composed of the dangers of materialist science, when its investigations are uncontrolled and unsanctified by the moral principles deriving from Catholicism. The unwitting villain is Adrien Sixte, inoffensive in deed, but whose dangerously atheistic thought is a formidable corrupter of youth. The novel tells how a horrifying catastrophe, issuing directly from the application of his teaching by an over-zealous disciple, awakens him to the realization of his overriding guilt in the tragedy. He spends a night of vigil over the dead body of his disciple-victim, and watches the bereaved mother praying: 'And for the first time, feeling his thought to be powerless to sustain him, this analyst in whom logic had almost destroyed loving-kindness, bowed himself down and abased himself before the inscrutable mystery of Destiny.' The words of the Lord's Prayer come to his mind, and though he does not utter them, his spirit is turned towards the Heavenly Father whom he had all his life derided, and tears stand in his eyes.[1]

The 'disciple', Robert Greslou, proud, ambitious, who sacrifices his better principles and his very life to the pursuit of an idea, might have come out of one of Dostoevsky's books. Like Raskolnikov once more, he starts with the same confident belief in the superiority of his intellectual prowess over the commonly accepted notions of right and wrong. The calamity he brings down on himself and others hardly disillusions him, so closely does he cling to his idea. He is like Erkel in *The Possessed*, of whom Dostoevsky wrote: 'He was filled with hero-worship for Pyotr Stepanovitch, whom he had only lately met. If he had met a monster of iniquity who had incited him to found a band of brigands on the pretext of some romantic and socialistic object, and as a test had bidden him rob and murder the first peasant he met, he would certainly have obeyed and done it. He had an invalid mother to whom he sent half of his scanty pay—and how she must have kissed that poor little flaxen head, how she must have trembled and prayed over it!' Erkel is the coolest murderer of them all, when it comes to assassinating Shatov at Pyotr Stepanovitch's behest.

Bourget himself wrote of *Le Disciple* that it marked the passage from a purely analytical to a moralizing art, going as far as to say: 'après avoir analysé les maladies morales il est *du devoir* de l'écrivain d'indiquer le remède'.[2] And in the preface to the *Physiologie de l'amour moderne*, which appeared at the same time as *Le Disciple*, Bourget stated that 'the first and last rule for a writer worthy of holding a pen is to be a moralist'. He explains that he does not mean the writer should preach, but that he should 'show life as it is, with the inner lessons of secret atonement which are everywhere buried in it. To render visible, as if tangible, the sorrows of sin,

[1] According to an earlier plan, Sixte was intended to be actually converted and shown at prayer.
[2] *Gazette de France*, 17 June 1896.

the infinite bitterness of evil, the pangs of vice, that is the moralist's task.' Such didacticism by implication would not have been far from Tolstoy's method; but as time went on Bourget grew more and more disposed merely to harness his novel to the chariot of Catholic teaching, to range himself emphatically and unmistakably on the side of the angels.

We may safely omit consideration of the successive books in which this trend is exemplified, and pass on to one written in 1902, *L'Étape*, as fair an example as any of the *roman à thèse* as it finally flowered under Bourget's cultivation. It represents the ultimate stage of an evolution which may well have had its origin in that first conversation with Vogüé in which the diplomat-critic complained of the 'moral thinness' of the contemporary French novel and announced as his ideal the raising of its spiritual level.

Bourget made *L'Étape* a vessel for all the consecrated ideals of the extreme Catholic and conservative he had become. The novel is an inventory of the calamities which overtake a family of which the head has fallen into a twofold error: he has forsaken his own class (the peasantry) in order to enter another (the bourgeois intellectual); and he has raised his offspring without religious training. Bourget spares one of the sons—Jean Monneron—whose eyes are opened by the succession of catastrophes which alight on his family, and who reacts into embracing Catholicism.

Jean has been involved in the founding of an 'université populaire' which Bourget chooses to have called the 'Union-Tolstoï'. This allows him a sally against the Russian, which incidentally shows how violently Bourget (as, indeed, might be expected) condemned the work of evangelical propaganda to which Tolstoy had latterly devoted himself. The 'Union-Tolstoï' degenerates into an unseemly pandemonium when a priest is invited to address its members. 'The chastisement of the great Russian writer, who had fallen, beguiled by his pride, to being a criminal preacher of anarchy in his own land and beyond its boundaries, lay in this simple fact that his name, made illustrious by pages worthy of Balzac, could be taken to designate assemblies of this sort.'

L'Étape was dedicated to Vogüé. The letter he wrote to Bourget in acknowledgement has been published,[1] and it is interesting to note that Vogüé reproached his friend gently for the over-simplifications in the picture he had drawn. 'You paint the world like a

---

[1] In the *Revue des Deux Mondes*, 1 Jan. 1924. The letter is dated 9 Mar. 1902.

good sound Italian Primitive: on the right of the Father, the elect, all good Catholics and legitimists; on His left, the accursed, all republicans and free-thinkers. I believe that an impartial study of the facts ruins your painting.' But the 'spirituality' of the book evokes Vogüé's complete approval.

I gain the impression, in reading you, that I am following the painful work of a great surgeon, operating on this same flesh and blood which others exhibit to us with the intention, concealed more or less carefully, of captivating us by the animal attraction that emanates from the flesh. It is the essential dividing-line that I once tried to establish between the Russian novelists at their best and almost all French novelists; I do not take back a single word. With you, this time, as with them, the obvious *intention* places the writer on a higher platform, facing his rivals who remain in the stalls of a small theatre. You may with impunity handle the harshest, crudest and most daring reality, because you handle it like a surgeon, and even like a father confessor.

This tribute from the original apostle of the Russian novel is of prime interest. Vogüé's usual felicitous phrasing, imperfectly as we have translated it, brings out the essential contribution made by the Russians to Bourget's art: it was turned, thanks to them in no small measure, towards the solving of moral or metaphysical problems, and away from the mere observation of physical phenomena which had largely contented the foregoing naturalist school. The new art was based on interpretation, and supplied an explicit commentary on the novelist's reconstruction of reality. Bourget's error—one into which the Russian writers never, or scarcely ever, fell—was to allow the commentary itself to gain the upper hand, and instead of deducing the law from the series of observed phenomena, to distort these phenomena so as to fit them in with preconceived laws which were to him the sacrosanct articles of religious and political faith.

IX

THE RUSSIAN NOVEL AND THE DISINTEGRATION OF NATURALISM
IV. ÉDOUARD ROD

ÉDOUARD ROD had probably more to do with the acclimatization of the Russian novel in France than anyone else except Eugène-Melchior de Vogüé. Certainly he was among the first to point out the importance of the new literature. His reviews of the Russian novels as they appeared in translation in 1885 and 1886 could not have hoped to attract the same attention as those of Vogüé, Arvède Barine, or Sarcey; for Rod was writing in the *Revue Contemporaine*, a short-lived venture which had nothing like the circulation of the *Revue des Deux Mondes*, the *Revue Bleue*, or the *Nouvelle Revue*. The mere fact that he undertook such work suggests, however, that he must have been strongly impressed by the novels at a first reading.

Among the factors that made for this early attachment to the Russian novel must be counted the circumstance that Rod was born in Switzerland, a country which for centuries has had the reputation of being a meeting-ground for ideas coming from all quarters of Europe; and he studied at Bonn University as well as at Lausanne before he settled in Paris in 1878. Being thus versed, since his youth, in non-French cultures, Rod was in advance well-disposed towards the 'literary cosmopolitanism' which Brunetière later preached; he, at least, would never be likely to see in the Russian novel a 'threat to the integrity of the French genius'. Once in Paris he fell, like Bourget, Maupassant, and many other young writers, under the spell of the ageing Turgenev, and in 1883 walked in his funeral procession. Strong ties of friendship linked him to Émile Hennequin, the author of the *Écrivains francisés* and perhaps, after Vogüé, the most gifted of the early apologists of the Russian novel.

Rod took over the editorship of the *Revue Contemporaine* in 1885, with Hennequin and Wyzewa on his staff. The periodical had a strong cosmopolitan slant, and took a keen interest in current German, Italian, and also Russian literature. In its pages Hennequin published the essay on Dostoevsky which later found its place in his *Écrivains francisés*; while Wyzewa furnished the translation of a story of Tolstoy's[1] besides contributing reviews of Russian novels that were coming out over this period.

The *Revue Contemporaine* foundered; but Rod continued his self-allotted task of proselytizing for the Russian novel. Not, however, in France. Hoping for a chair in the Faculty of Letters at Geneva University, he returned from Paris to his native Switzerland in 1886 and embarked on a series of lectures on the Russian novelists. There appears to have survived no record of what he said; but if his lectures created little stir (Rod was a diffident speaker), they appear to have succeeded in their immediate object, for he obtained the post he solicited.

Rod was a novelist as well as being a student of ideas and literary history: he put his name to over forty volumes of fiction before his death in 1911. In the course of this meritorious career, Rod adopted many models and imitated many masters. He was a writer without any outstanding creative gifts, and almost wholly lacking in any real originality. For this very reason the passage of the Russian novel left a deep mark on his work. Among the generation of the naturalists, he was perhaps the novelist who owed the most to Tolstoy and Dostoevsky.

For he began, in the early eighties, as a dutiful disciple and fervent admirer of Zola, writing the prostitute's life-history which was almost *de rigueur* for a self-respecting naturalist at this time (*Palmyre Veulard*, 1881). Then followed a series of novels and short stories which secured for their author a certain reputation under Zola's wing but gained no startling successes. Written, all of them, before the Russian novelists 'arrived', they need not hold our attention here. It is with *La Course à la mort* (1885) that Russian influence is visible for the first time.

The book, which is barely held together by the thinnest of plots, is a variation on the theme that all things are purposeless since all are doomed to ultimate extinction. The whole range of human activities—social, artistic, emotional—are passed under review in this light. This exaggeratedly sombre pessimism owes far more to Schopenhauer than to the Russian novelists, whom Rod in any

[1] 'Le Cierge', *Revue Contemporaine*, 25 Feb. 1886.

case was only just discovering: a discovery symbolized, perhaps, by a dream related by the hero of *La Course à la mort*, the setting of which is Russia, 'a country I do not know, but towards which a secret urge draws me'. But there are in *La Course à la mort* hints that Dostoevsky's 'religion of suffering' may provide the key to the riddle of the inordinate amount of pain there is in the world. Romantic melancholy, the sadness of a Werther or a René, is out of fashion, for modern man is not so exclusively self-centred in his unhappiness.

What are our own poor sorrows! Our breast heaves with the sighs of all human creatures. . . . Our hearts are filled with emotions not our own: we have read too many secrets in too many sorrowing eyes. And we long to read farther still, we long to penetrate into every soul, to share for one moment their anguish, we long to identify ourselves with those unknown brothers of ours whose misery is not our misery but belongs to us notwithstanding. That is why we understand so well the far-away voice that calls to us: 'Bow yourselves before the suffering of all humanity.'

The far-away voice was, of course, that of Raskolnikov in *Crime and Punishment*, and the words are an exact quotation of Dostoevsky.

Had Rod read Goncharov's novel *Oblomov*, translated into French in 1877? There is a certain similarity between the discontented lethargy of Goncharov's hero and that of the hero of *La Course à la mort*; and both books end in hymns of praise to the joys of a purely vegetative and inert existence.

In his next novel, *Tatiana Lëïlof*, Rod modelled himself on Turgenev. The plot is based on a story of Turgenev's, *Clara Militch*, which is mentioned by Vogüé in the pages of the *Roman russe*.[1] A young Russian girl is compelled to leave her country by the chance of her father's bankruptcy, follows her lover, a Frenchman, who had been tutor to her brothers, to Paris, becomes an actress, and, after various adventures, takes her life on the stage. In describing Tatiana's childhood, Rod drew on his imagination to sketch some fanciful pictures of Russian life, and when the scene shifts to Paris we meet a band of Russian nihilist students who are rather less make-believe. In the development of Rod's novel, however, *Tatiana Lëïlof* on the whole represents a regression towards the naturalism from which, under the influence of Schopenhauer,

---

[1] See Vogüé, *Le Roman russe*, p. 131.

Wagner, and the Russians the author was beginning to shake himself free.

His most candid acknowledgement of indebtedness to Tolstoy and Dostoevsky is to be found in Rod's next novel, *Le Sens de la vie* (1889). Tolstoy himself scented a disciple when he read the book and, with unusual effusiveness, wrote back complimenting the young author warmly. Certain passages he had read aloud over and over in the presence of friends, and he thanked Rod for having procured him 'one of the most pleasant sensations I know: that of meeting an unlooked-for companion in the path I am following'.[1]

The book related the experiences of another egoist who discovers the Russian novels, is overwhelmed with admiration for them, tries to order his life according to their precepts, and ends by realizing that their demands are pitched too high. This history will repay study, for there is every likelihood that Rod's hero undergoes the same spiritual development as his creator during the critical years of the revelation of Tolstoy and Dostoevsky.

The egoist we are invited to observe in *Le Sens de la vie* differs from the one in *La Course à la mort* in that his is an energetic, ambitious egoism. He is just married, and the gentle invasion of his wife's personality gradually releases him from the painful sense of spiritual solitude which had formerly preyed on him. At the same time, however, he acquires a new sense of responsibility, which will not allow him to look on life any more as something which can, at any moment, be thrown off as a useless burden.

At this stage 'an agonizing question raises itself—the question: How and for what reason does life make itself acceptable?' There is no lack of possible answers, but none is truly satisfactory. He is offered religious faith (so Tolstoy in the early stages of his crisis attempted unsuccessfully to convince himself that salvation lay in humbly accepting the teachings of the Church). Faith certainly explains everything, but it is an attitude of mind one possesses or does not possess as the case may be, but which one cannot hope to acquire by an effort of the will. Belief in the progress of the species, the optimism of the eighteenth-century rationalists, is inacceptable since it is evident that in the end this civilization will crumble as others have before it. There is love for humanity, but the term is

---

[1] Letter dated 23 Feb. 1889, reprinted in the *Nouvelle Revue* and quoted by Ch. Beuchat, *Édouard Rod et le cosmopolitisme* (1930), pp. 275–6.

too vague, it 'includes those I detest as well as those I love, the hateful Chinese, and the Russians for whom I feel a sympathy which incidentally has no precise cause'.

Finally there is Pity. 'The Russian novelists, about whom there has been such an uproar, and whose books I have scarcely read yet, have invented the "religion of human suffering".' But he fears that this is just another empty phrase. Certainly he is moved by another's suffering, and will relieve it provided the cost to him is not too great. 'So that I am not more inaccessible to pity than another, for that is how I have always seen it practised, those are the real rites of the "religion of human suffering". But is it enough to make a man accept life and love it? Perhaps it could be for a Christ, in whom this emotion grows to the extent of absorbing all his thoughts and all the strength of his being, but not for an ordinary man.' Pushed to this point, Pity—like Faith—cannot be acquired, but must be the gift of a special grace.

Life, however, bears our philosopher along: with the birth of a child come new responsibilities, new reasons for loving and hating life. Then comes the revelation, like a clap of thunder.

I have just read, one after the other, *Insulted and Injured*, *Crime and Punishment*, *War and Peace*, *Anna Karenina*—and they have left me trembling all over. It is more than the revelation of an unknown world: it is a clarion-call to our slumbering consciences. I think of the great voices of the early Christian preachers, thundering in the basilicas and pursuing with their anathemas the last priests of the pagan gods. . . . Here we see an unexpected dawn rising in the North, here are youthful voices, resounding from afar, which diagnose the ills we suffer from and give us the remedy; here is a new tongue which repeats to us the old lesson forgotten for so long: 'Love one another!' . . . This sincerity triumphs over all our falsehoods; the most sceptical are spell-bound, the most indifferent weep, and we are suddenly invaded by a sublime concern for problems we had in a more cowardly moment refused to face.

Probably nowhere else might be read a more fervid expression of the enthusiasms generated by the first impact of the Russian novel in France on those minds that were prepared to respond; and in this passage Rod touches on all the essential factors in the appeal made by Tolstoy and Dostoevsky: their lofty moral tone, which accorded so well with the inner feelings of those who were repelled by Taine's dictum about virtue and vice being just two chemical by-products like sugar and vitriol; their message of universal love, which found so lively a response in a generation tried in war and fearful of social and international strife in years to come; their example of a serious art which imposed itself alike on creative and critical spirits whom the idle dilettantism of the age had sickened; and above all, the 'renascence of wonder' (as a contemporary English novelist called it), the reminder that the physical world is only one aspect of the universe, the rejection of the uncompromising materialism which had informed the naturalist novel of Zola and his immediate followers.

The BEYOND, that had been forgotten, is resuscitated; the portals of mystery are opened anew, and once more men feel sure that, beyond the useless facts that scientists proclaim, farther than the deceptive promises of justice and happiness that politicians dangle, higher than the joys that artists contrive for our eyes, our spirits and our ears, there lie great open spaces where we would do well to plant our bruised feet, the infinite spaces of a dream which action can make true, of Faith and of Charity.

The Russian novelists invite mankind to a realization of the Golden Age, nothing less.

But almost immediately the mood changes, the distrust of the hardened sceptic threatens to shatter the dream.

Is it a real rebirth of our hearts, or a fleeting excitement? Is there a sincere religion in the making, or is it just a new form in which our dilettante habits will find themselves at home? Are the caravans to bear *us* away to the Unknown, or shall we stay, like gaping bystanders, watching the great-hearted ones set off on this journey? This is the secret that to-morrow will reveal. We are old, we are tired, already we have marched aimlessly for so long and poured out our sweat to no purpose! . . . Will this breath of kindness that wafts over us produce anything other than the useless projects such as old men make and forget? . . . For myself, I admire, I hesitate, and, *if I love him who loves*, I am not sure I should have the strength myself to love.

An opportunity for altruistic love occurs when his first child is born. At the beginning he looked on it with a kind of dread and without love; but as the baby grows his interest in it increases, and he tells himself he has been too self-centred. When the child falls ill and comes to within an ace of death, he realizes that his love for her is genuine, and his love of life itself is strengthened at the same time. His affection for the child finally converts him to the new ideal—to sow contentment around one, 'to make happy, within the narrow limits of what is possible, the poor creatures whose fate is linked to ours'. Everything else we achieve will perish surely: this alone will be spared annihilation.

Has the last word to everything been found when one has been able to lose oneself in the affection one pours out to those to whom one has given life? Is it possible that loving resolves all problems, and that our stricken hearts and our inquiring spirits are alike satisfied with this trifling thing, a family, to find calm and peace?

Rod may have discovered it was so, for his part: but Tolstoy had discovered it before him, and perhaps helped him to discover it. The chosen heroes and heroines of *Family Happiness*, *War and Peace*, and *Anna Karenina*, Katya, Bezukhov, Natasha and Nicholas Rostov, Marie Bolkonsky, Levin and Kitty, all end by finding happiness and contentment in family life, serenely watching their children grow up around them. The Tolstoyan 'moral' of *Le Sens de la vie* is, in fact, exactly the same as that of Paul Margueritte's *Jours d'épreuve*, written three years before: the two books are but different buds from the same stem of influence.

Faith in the ideal of the family is, however, only one part of Tolstoyism: a greater place is taken by the doctrine of social pity, where Tolstoy is on common ground with Dostoevsky. Rod's hero realizes that pity is hypocrisy unless it is active; that charity exacts a complete sacrifice of one's possessions, of one's time, one's energies, in toiling to bring about a new and more just society. And since the fruits of one's efforts will in all probability never be seen, one needs faith—and faith is beyond his ken, as ever.

Impossible to conceive of Pity without Love, without Faith; impossible to love without believing; and if you believe in Humanity, in Goodness, in Truth, in Justice—do not all these absolutes imply the supreme Absolute, God? . . . Yes, men would seem to need apostles; if one loves them and wishes to do them good, one must turn apostle.

He attempts, but fails lamentably. During a holiday he spends in the Alps he is troubled by his incapacity to enter into the lives of the mountain-dwellers. Back in Paris he attends a workers' political rally and is discouraged by the virulence of their hatreds. He would like to tell them: 'The social reforms which lure you on are a mirage; you must look beyond laws, statutes, and constitutions to find the new kingdom where you will meet with happiness, and there is only one way to bring it about—Love. . . .' This is pure Tolstoyism in its social implications, and Rod later expounded it in his essay on Tolstoy in 1891: 'The word of Christ, who bids us turn our left cheek to him who has smitten us on our right cheek, must be taken at its strict face-value. Alone, absolute obedience to this command can bring men back, as individuals and as a society, to the path of salvation.'[1]

When his housekeeper dies, the hero of *Le Sens de la vie* realizes he has seldom felt anything but indifference towards her, in spite of her years of faithful service. In engaging a new one, he allows himself to be guided by his charitable instincts rather than by practical considerations: so he takes an orphan straight from a home. In a short while he decides he will have to be rid of her: she is clumsy and incompetent. 'This first experiment shows me what my humanitarian dreams were worth. No, I have not the makings of a philanthropist . . . all my good impulses will always be swamped by my indifference.'

These two experiences—the public meeting and the dismissal of the maid—open his eyes to his inability to put into practice the ideals the Russians preach. He feels no more compassion for men in suffering than he feels at the sight of an animal in pain, and the emotion is of the same nature. He is only roused by another's misfortune if it is of a kind that he can imagine overwhelming himself, as when he reads of a theatre being burnt down. 'But when I pity creatures whose sufferings are permanent and cannot be bettered, the miners in their pits, the workers who cannot find work, it is without any *de facto* participation in what they suffer, it is with the help of an effort of comprehension, by an act of will-power: to warm my heart I have to reason.'

The idealism of Dostoevsky is not so much illusory as inaccessible: 'Certainly, I must admit it, the Russian novels have led me astray and have caused me to take some steps along a path which is not my own.' Recapitulating his spiritual experiences, he concludes: 'When I observed the strength of the emotions aroused in me by Tolstoy and Dostoevsky, I told myself that it would be wonderful to feel pity as they feel it, and I sought after it, and I treated myself with the particular spiritual stimulants which might have produced it; it did not come.' And little wonder, for the 'religion of human suffering' is no more within my reach than any

---

[1] Rod, *Idées morales du temps présent*, pp. 250–1.

other, and we are debarred from it for just the same reasons: we can impose it on ourselves by reasoning and put it into practice—like people who go to church 'for form's sake' though they do not believe—but we cannot know it in its life-giving and healthful essence. Like those lay theologians who are not able to see anything in Christianity but the dogma, we find in ourselves only the theory of pity.

The difference, says Rod (for we may be sure it was his own conviction that dictated this page), is clear if you open any one of the French novels that the Russians have inspired.

The overflowing torrent, with its noble waves, its troubled, melancholy water—our writers have filtered and canalized it for day-to-day consumption. Their pity is machine-made—sometimes with a reliable trade-mark—but at bottom indifferent, with a heart-breaking indifference, and sadly sterile; coldly they hold forth about the sorrows of men whom they prudently and disdainfully keep at a safe distance. It is the pity of the Pharisee, who passes by the wounded traveller with his eyes shut. It is the pity of the curious dilettante, who wants to know what pity is like for the sake of knowing it or because he thinks it a fine emotion, and who juggles with it as with any other toy—art, love, vice or virtue. . . .

Rod's *alter ego* decides once more—a genuine pity for humanity being beyond his capabilities—that, for him, the only path to salvation lies in restricting his philanthropy and self-abnegation to his family circle. In this little domain he could be happy—were it not for the fear of death, irrevocable and ineluctable, that poisons such simple joys.

It is on this glance back to *La Course à la mort* that Rod ends *Le Sens de la vie*. His hero is seen in church, striving to clutch at faith by an act of will, and murmuring the Lord's Prayer—'with the lips, alas, with the lips alone'. The scene is not unlike that with which Bourget closed *Le Disciple*, with this difference: that the prayer that trembles on the lips of Sixte has risen from his heart, in Rod's book it has descended from the brain. We may expect Sixte to become a convert to Catholicism; Rod's hero, probably never. The difference in the upbringing of the two authors is almost certainly at the bottom of this divergence. Although Bourget's father was an agnostic, his mother was pious, and his early training was Catholic; Bourget did no more than return to the fold. But Rod's childhood was spent in a Protestant country and in an atmosphere of hostility to the more mystical aspects of religion.

Consequently he was less disposed to find peace of mind in purely confessional solutions of the problems that beset him.

Although it gives us a complete account of a mind deeply affected by the ideas of Dostoevsky and Tolstoy, *Le Sens de la vie* did not exhaust consideration of the problems the Russians had raised in Rod's mind. If they never really converted him, their influence on his thought is of capital importance; and traces of this influence occur in several other of the works subsequent to *Le Sens de la vie*. It was not Rod's practice, as it was Bourget's, to lead his readers to a decisive conclusion regarding any of the questions he treated: he preferred a verdict of non-proven. If very many of the novels of his post-naturalist period may be called 'novels of ideas', very few, if any, of them were 'novels with a thesis'. Rod was not a man with convictions, and he veers about and contradicts in one novel the tentative conclusions he may have reached in the previous one.

Les Trois Cœurs, which followed *Le Sens de la vie* in 1890, is inspired by the verse from the *Imitation of Jesus Christ*: 'As soon as a man seeks himself, love is stifled within him.' We are shown a family man who, this time finding no satisfaction in his family circle, wilfully goes outside it and breaks it up in order to quench his thirst for emotional novelties. Under the stress of suffering— his child is carried off by an illness—he ultimately returns to a regular life. *La Course à la mort*, *Le Sens de la vie*, and *Les Trois Cœurs* are three books each with an egoist as the hero. The first follows Schopenhauer and sinks his ego in the contemplation of its dissolution. The second follows Tolstoy and expands his ego to embrace his wife and children, having failed to expand it with Dostoevsky to embrace all humanity. The third, a romantic or a Rousseauist, follows his ego until it leads him to the brink of destruction.

This new book owes little to the Russians. The preface, in which Rod attempts 'un petit examen de conscience littéraire', has perhaps more to say than the novel. It is quite clear that Rod, by this time (November 1889), has turned his back on Zola. Naturalism

was, in its essence, self-satisfied, very limited, materialist, more curious of social forms than of characters, of the substance than of the soul; while we [that is, Rod and the younger novelists who had begun their career magnetized by Zola] were—and went on becoming more and more so—unsatisfied, full of yearning for the infinite, idealists, neglecting social forms and looking always, among his surroundings, for the essential man.

Rod proceeds to enumerate the reasons for this trend. Apart from the inner necessity of such a development, there were many external influences, all coming from abroad. Rod particularizes Wagner's music, Schopenhauer's philosophy, pre-Raphaelite painting, English poetry, and 'above all, the Russian novel, which has these characteristics [of the aforementioned types of art] but softened them down, corrected them of their artificiality and doubly enhanced them by a strain of popular poetry and by the youthful spirit of their authors'.

At the end of the preface to *Les Trois Cœurs*, Rod paid tribute to Vogüé and Paul Bourget, calling them, respectively, 'inspired' and 'wonderfully intelligent' interpreters of the Russian novel. In a chapter of his *Idées morales du temps présent* (1892), Rod deals in detail with Vogüé's reading of the Russian novelists, showing its significance in itself and the range and depth of its influence on the mind of the age.

The most interesting of these pages are those in which Rod replies to certain charges which good believers had made against Vogüé's religion—'too vague, too independent of the Deity', and against his 'pity, the object of which at times seems intangible'; his critics want to know what is to be understood by this 'religion of human suffering' he extracts from the pages of Dostoevsky. Rod defends Vogüé by arguing that Faith and Pity, even if they have no object or person round which to crystallize, are among the finest of the soul's adornments; if only as a spur to action and to heroism they are needful, 'even if there were no God to Whom they are pleasing, even if there did not exist unhappy spirits, whose sufferings are certainly alleviated by sympathy' (p. 284).

What will be the transformation wrought by convictions such as Vogüé's when applied to literature? They are, as Rod points out, pragmatic, not academic: he who cherishes them cannot but envisage a practical and active mission for the man of letters. Vogüé gives no quarter to the writer who insulates himself from the common people, who disdains their limited intellects and their insensibility to the more delicate aesthetic pleasures.

It is likely that Rod sympathized up to a certain point with this rejection of the doctrine of 'art for art's sake'. At the most he could tolerate it when, as in *Mademoiselle de Maupin* or *Thaïs* (or, we may

add, in *Salammbô* or *Hérodias*), its arena remained remote or fan-
tasmagoric; but when, with the same detachment and indifference,
its exponents set out to dissect our real, contemporary, and living
souls, then they deserve censure. Such subjects, Rod thinks, ought
only to be treated by 'philanthropic' artists. Modern life and
modern distress should be gazed on only with the clear and kindly
eye of a Tolstoy, or through the troubled and tear-blinded vision
of a Dostoevsky.

After setting up a semi-barbarous literature in opposition to the most
brilliant portion of our native literature, we look to the man of letters to
be a kind of captain of souls, a lay prophet, who gazes into the future
with a steady eye, who knows, like a good pilot, where the port lies, and
what turn of the wheel is needed to steer for it. . . . Literature is no
longer a profession exercised more or less successfully, it is a mission one
fulfils according to one's powers (pp. 287–8).

The humble and downtrodden, on whom after all depends ultimately the advancement of the race, require guides of ripe intelligence, firm judgement, and compelling voice.

Rod is not so bold as to predict what will come of this cry for a
more popularly rooted and didactic art: it may well prove to be a
cry in the wilderness. But he fancies all the same he can discern
the beginnings of a new and powerful literary movement based on
Vogüé's teaching. If some have accepted these ideas only because
of the charm of their novelty, in other minds they have awakened
deeper echoes. Vogüé's doctrines 'seem to be in great favour among
the young student population, over whom he wields an undeniable
influence. . . .' Something is decidedly in the air, something new,
having little in common with ideas current in the last half century;
what it is precisely, it would need a bold man to say. And Rod
concludes with the prudent forecast: 'perhaps only a few years will
elapse before the new shoots spring up, and perhaps the men of
our generation will be drawn themselves along the current of a
literature differing from top to bottom from that in which they
began writing' (p. 289).

These are the words of a man who was already finding his vein,
as a novelist, in producing didactic fiction after the Russian manner.
Rod's Protestantism was at home in the reaffirmation of moral
values, which is what he chiefly saw in Tolstoy and Dostoevsky.
He was a little over-bold, however, in suggesting that a revolution
was about to break out which would alter the whole face of French

literature. He was miscalculating the strength of the centuries-old tradition in France that the cult of aesthetic beauty has nothing in the world to do with the establishment and propagation of moral values; and he was not reckoning with the extremely powerful conservative forces which were gathering ready to discredit and destroy the new influence.

X

THE RUSSIAN NOVEL AND THE DISINTEGRATION OF NATURALISM

V. CHARLES-LOUIS PHILIPPE

IF we look for a characteristic common to every author whose susceptibilities to Russian influence have been thus far remarked on, we are likely to find this in their social loyalties: they all shared in the mental outlook and habits of mind of the middle classes. Not one of them at any rate was consciously and militantly a member of the non-propertied classes, and this fact accounts for much in their attitude to the foreign literature. It explains in a large measure the condescension that so frequently tinges their appreciation of Dostoevsky. An ex-convict, who sues for our sympathy on behalf of the outcasts of society, prostitutes, drunkards, and penniless, neurotic students, should not be permitted to recruit among the French ruling classes too fanatic or too numerous a retinue of disciples. His 'religion of suffering humanity' may be admitted as a passing fad; a well-bred author like Bourget may be allowed to introduce the notion into one or other of his novels; but that is as far as it should go. In a France consolidating its overseas Empire and girding itself for the ultimate *revanche*, there was no real room for so debilitating a doctrine as that of Dostoevsky. And in any case it was un-French.

Charles-Louis Philippe[1] is, however, no bourgeois. On the contrary, he was consumed by a violent hatred for the bourgeoisie, a

---

[1] Since in this chapter it is not intended to examine Philippe's works in the strict order of their appearance, it may be appropriate at the outset to list them chronologically. His first published work was *Quatre histoires de pauvre amour* (1897), of which the component stories had appeared in *L'Art jeune*, a Brussels paper, and *L'Enclos* between Aug. 1896 and May 1897. The succeeding books were: *La Bonne Madeleine et la pauvre Marie* (1898); *La Mère et l'enfant*, of which a shortened version was first published in 1900, the complete book not appearing until 1911; *Bubu-de-Montparnasse* (1901); *Le Père Perdrix* (1903); *Marie Donadieu* (1904); *Croquignole* (1906). *Charles Blanchard* (unfinished) was published posthumously in 1913. Three collections of short stories were also published posthumously: *Dans la petite ville* (1910); *Contes du Matin* (1916); *Chroniques du Canard sauvage* (1923).

hatred which he exhaled incessantly in his correspondence and his novels. Like François Villon, he was 'de povre et de petite extrace'. He never forgot, he never wished to forget, his proletarian origins. The remarks he makes about Claude Buy, one of the characters of his novel *Croquignole*, apply equally to himself. 'His father, his mother, and all his ancestry, they all had blackened hands, grey faces, and the shoulders of workers which have grown massive so as to lean more heavily on the tools they were compelled to use; and farther back still, from the very day when it was said "in the sweat of thy brow shalt thou eat thy bread", the obscure multitude of the poor, whose son he was, bore him company, toiling, drop of sweat by drop of sweat, through days when no one laughed, though there rang in their ears the laughter of the rich which proves that laughter can exist. . . .' For such a man, literature would not have the same meaning as for the cultivated child of comfortably situated parents, and literary models would be required for different purposes, to answer different questions and satisfy different aspirations. In particular, he will pay less attention, in others and in himself, to the way a thought is expressed, and much more attention to the value and potentialities of the thought itself. It is clear that such a man will not, as did many bourgeois men of letters soaked in their humanities at school, recoil before the Russians' violation of accepted laws of aesthetics, and in straining after the shadow miss the substance.

Also, Charles-Louis Philippe belongs to a different generation from that of other writers in whom we have examined the impact and influence of the Russian novel. Maupassant and Huysmans were authors with an established reputation when the Russians made their irruption into French literature. Paul Margueritte, Bourget, Rod made their entry almost simultaneously with the translations of Tolstoy and Dostoevsky. Born in 1874, Philippe was still a boy when *War and Peace, Crime and Punishment* and the other masterpieces were winning readers by the thousands in Paris. By the time his schooling was completed the Russian novels had been in the book-stalls for many years; the outlandish names of their authors and of the characters that peopled them had grown almost commonplace; the ideas and emotions they had introduced among the French were no longer novel and were settling down, after the preliminary effervescence, into the deeper reaches of the national consciousness.

When did Philippe make his own personal discovery of the Russians? The question cannot be answered with absolute certainty. Philippe's upbringing was anything but bookish. He was born into a family of village artisans, and his education at the lycée to which he won a scholarship was strictly practical, mathematics being the mainstay of the curriculum.[1] The careful grounding in the classics of antiquity and of France, which had been enjoyed by the majority of his fellow men of letters, was missed by Philippe. His early explorations of the literary heritage of his country were quite unguided and unsystematic. A school-friend, Marcel Ray, who has left some account of Philippe's first literary enthusiasms, notes:

we possessed few books and read indiscriminately everything that fell into our hands. . . . The real masters of his early youth were Théodore de Banville and Catulle Mendès. One does not choose one's masters; Philippe took those he found. . . . Later, when he had need of them, he was quite able to discover Dickens, Dostoevsky, and Thomas Hardy. But about 1893 he was not yet seeking the deeper meaning of life.[2]

If reliance can be placed in Marcel Ray's memory, Dostoevsky must still have been a closed book to Philippe in 1893; but the same witness informs us that wherever Philippe lived in Paris, 'at the Hôtel de Chartres, rue du Dôme—No. 62, rue St. Dominique —No. 8, rue des Mauvais Garçons, he always had a portrait of Dostoevsky in front of him'.[3] Now Philippe was lodging at 62, rue St. Dominique between June and November 1896.[4] We do not know when he was living at the Hôtel de Chartres, but it may be inferred that this was during his first short stay in Paris, from January to May 1894, 'in a room at 6 francs a week'.[5]

Philippe, then, on Marcel Ray's testimony, was ignorant of Dostoevsky in 1893; but during the first half of 1896 certainly, perhaps as early as 1894, he was sufficiently impressed by the Russian master to hang his portrait on the wall of his room. The cult was extended to Tolstoy, whose portrait was hung 'beside that of Dostoevsky, a little below it',[6] while at some stage Dickens was added to the gallery.[7]

[1] Philippe in a letter to H. Vandeputte, 13 Dec. 1896. Philippe's letters to this friend were published in the *Nouvelle Revue Française* between Nov. 1910 and May 1911, and have been collected and published in *Lettres de jeunesse*, 1911.
[2] Ray, 'L'Enfance et la jeunesse de Charles-Louis Philippe', *Nouvelle Revue Française*, 15 Feb. 1910, pp. 173–5.
[3] Ibid., p. 170.   [4] Ibid., pp. 188–9.
[5] Ibid., p. 186.   [6] Ibid., p. 193.
[7] R. Gignoux, 'Dans l'Île de Saint Louis', ibid., p. 205.

It may be safely assumed, then, that Philippe was liable to be influenced by the Russian novel from when he first started writing prose fiction. It will, accordingly, be legitimate to examine all his works from the point of view of this possible influence.

Further, at the time he published his first book, the Russian novelists had passed the apex of their initial popularity in France; in fact, as has already been recorded, a certain reaction against them was already in progress among an important section of Parisian literary critics. There is, therefore, no question that Philippe could have thought of courting favour among his readers by deliberately injecting his works with shots of Slav sentiment. An opportunist manœuvre of this kind, which may perhaps account for certain scenes in Bourget's *Crime d'amour* or Rod's *Le Sens de la vie*, would, in any case, be unthinkable in Charles-Louis Philippe, after all a far more conscientious and serious artist than these two. His borrowings from the Russians were quite disinterested, almost it may be said unconscious. He did not cut pieces from the mantle of Dostoevsky and stitch them together in some new and fanciful dress; he threw the mantle about his shoulders and in this garb strode the streets and scanned the dwellers of his native Cérilly or of Paris, the city of his adoption.

There was a certain indigenous soil in the art of Charles-Louis Philippe which, although richly fertilized by Dostoevsky and others, never altered its substance. His writing can be analysed as a balanced mixture of native and foreign strains.

He was among the most faithful disciples of the Flaubert-Goncourt dogma of documentation. In *Bubu-de-Montparnasse*, for instance, there was a minimum of invention. The idea of the story came to him as a direct result of his friendship with a prostitute in Paris, and he thereupon 'began to amass documents. But, good heavens above!' he ejaculates a little naïvely,

what a time it takes, and what a lot of work it means! Books on sociology, on political economy, statistics, I am going to plough through all that. I shall have to find out what wages women are paid. Better still, my heroine will be a florist. I must learn what they do in flower-shops! I can be observed stopping in front of shop-windows in the streets, examining the flowers to see how it's all done.[1]

[1] Letter to Vandeputte, 4 Dec. 1898. See also letters dated 15 Feb. and 7 Mar. 1899.

Flaubert himself, in the throes of composing *Bouvard et Pécuchet*, writes letters in much the same style. But not only the material facts—the incidents, even the most surprising of them, and nearly all the characters in *Bubu-de-Montparnasse* were directly reproduced from real life.[1]

Philippe was the most personal of realists, who saw life with his own eyes, felt it in his own skin, and wrote of it from his own heart; the words are dictated by his own imagination and he never seeks to stifle the emotions that are kindled by the incidents he observes. 'The artist', he wrote, 'is a good workman who harkens to himself, and, in his corner, in the candour of his soul, writes down what he hears. I make no distinction between the expert village cobbler who makes clogs as he dreams them, and the writer who tells of life as he sees it.'[2]

Charles-Louis Philippe never used another writer's books as a hunting-ground for themes or characters. Of what he read, the spirit alone left its mark upon his mind: the fictional inventions, the tricks of another author's composition, never seem to have impressed him. In his literary judgements he records only whether the poet or novelist he has been reading struck, or failed to strike, a sympathetic chord; and for his own writing he 'tells of life as he sees it'.

A novelist like Paul Bourget might 'take up with' the Russians in obedience to the caprice of fashion, for he writes for 'society', that is, for a limited group of moneyed idlers, who feel nothing deeply and will flit from one source of emotional thrills to another: but Philippe, and those of his stamp, have a different conception of their functions as artists. Illuminating is the description he gives of his meeting with a bourgeois author.

I felt myself superior to him, even in matters of art, because he is slightly snobbish, and, as such, full of the passing fashions of the hour. You and I are simpler, we have a more intense inner life, and it is our character which will dictate our books to us, and it is our emotion which will swell them, will make them strong and fine because they will be human, eternally.[3]

He was everything that the followers of 'art for art' were not. Now

---

[1] See his letter to Vandeputte, 29 Mar. 1901.
[2] Letter to Vandeputte, 9 Feb. 1897.
[3] Letter to Vandeputte, 18 Dec. 1897.

Vogüé had in his time fulminated against the 'art for art' school. But Vogüé's professed disdain of the 'cultivated artist', one suspects, did not run very deep. Himself a dilettante of dilettantes, leaping from one focal point of interest to another in history, literature, politics, art, is it certain he would not have frowned at hearing this young writer proclaim that

it is necessary not to know too many things, or else you must have a phenomenally powerful intellect. Anatole France is delicious, he knows everything, he is a learned man, one might even say: but for that very reason he represents the culminating point of the literature of the nineteenth century. Now we need barbarians. We need to have lived very close to God without having studied him in books, we need a vision of natural life, we need strength, we need fury even. The time for softness and dilettantism is over. We are at the dawn of the age of passion.

Philippe himself may not emerge as a great writer, but he is certain he belongs to a race being born, he will be 'at least one of the very many minor prophets who, a short while before His coming, foretold the Christ and were already preaching his doctrine'. And, without transition, Philippe goes on to discuss rapturously Dostoevsky's *Idiot* which he had just read. 'That is the work of a barbarian.'[1]

From all this it emerges that a search for what might be called the 'direct influence' of the Russians in Philippe's writings will be fruitless. He will not reproduce situations or human types drawn from their works, the style of his writing will be unaffected by theirs. Their influence on him can only be indirect. His mind will work on their ideas, their message, their philosophy. He will 'process' their novels, subject them to profound chemical transformations, and their trace in his books will be apparent only to a reader able to distil the emotional perfume of his writing and compare it with that of the writings of Dostoevsky and perhaps Tolstoy.

A further point that arises is that Philippe's attitude to the Russians was more advanced, more revolutionary altogether than that of the middle-class critics and writers, Vogüé, Bourget, Lemaître. He looks forward to Suarès and Gide more than he looks back to these others. Taine saw Dostoevsky, as Voltaire saw Shakespeare, a 'barbarian of genius'. Philippe saw him as a barbarian too, but the word is stripped of its pejorative implications. A barbarian in his

[1] Letter to Vandeputte, 18 Dec. 1897.

crudity, in his ignorance of the *kalokagathon*: the 'density' of *The Idiot* he mentions as a positive virtue; and his passionate interest in human questions, his characters who 'are at once simple and complex', deserved panegyrics, in Philippe's estimation, not depreciation. Dostoevsky was a writer in whom he recognized a brother, because he wrote from his own heart, in a universe curtained off from the innumerable, ever-veering gusts of literary fashions and aesthetic doctrines.

It would be paradoxical to speak of Dostoevsky's influence on Philippe if Philippe's genetic power was absolutely spontaneous; but, apart from the fact that anything read with enthusiasm inevitably and imperceptibly strikes roots in the imagination of the reader, Dostoevsky did Philippe an immense service in providing him with a monumental replica of himself. Philippe rediscovered himself and found reaffirmation of himself in discovering Dostoevsky, just as did his friend André Gide, whose remark, in his monograph on Philippe, is very apposite at this juncture: 'The strong have never feared what the weak call influences: for the strong, these are never anything but incitements. Philippe never fell under, never accepted any influences but those which he felt revealed to him by his own native strength.'[1]

Philippe's compassion for the downtrodden and the oppressed existed doubtless before he picked up *The House of the Dead* or *Insulted and Injured*: how could it be otherwise, since he himself belonged to that class, by his origins firstly and by his temperament secondly? (For such a class constitutes a spiritual grouping as well as a social one, and the Gospel phrase 'the poor ye have always with you' is not invalidated by eras of social justice, full employment, and equalized wealth.) Philippe was not 'converted' by Dostoevsky: such conversions are notoriously short-lived. He practised 'social pity', he was an ardent devotee of 'the religion of human suffering', before ever he read the Russian novelists.

The truth of this becomes plain when one observes the forms which this pity takes in Philippe: they are not exactly coincidental with those it takes either in Tolstoy or Dostoevsky, and this betrays their independent origin. Dostoevsky has described the misery of the poor, of the neglected in many a novel and many a story; it is

[1] Gide, *Charles-Louis Philippe: conférence prononcée . . . le 5 novembre 1910* (1911), p. 19.

scarcely necessary to quote instances, but some of the most striking
that occur to one are the histories of Nelly (in *Insulted and Injured*),
of the Marmeladov family (in *Crime and Punishment*), of the Gorsh-
kov family (in *Poor Folk*), and the short tale *The Christmas Tree*.
These scenes of wretchedness and destitution are graphically
depicted by Dostoevsky, and the note of commiseration is unmistakable: but there is never the slightest attempt to trace them
back, even impliedly, to their possible roots in social maladjust-
ment. Such a trend would have been dangerous for Dostoevsky
himself, no doubt, and would have made it impossible for him to
publish in Russia; be that as it may, in his works as they stand,
social pity is unaccompanied by express advocacy of social reform.

Philippe, while he never enrolled himself in any social-revolu-
tionary movement, was in close contact with the group led by
Louis Lumet, who directed between 1895 and 1898 a socialist
review, *L'Enclos*. (It was in *L'Enclos* that Philippe's first book,
Quatre histoires de pauvre amour, appeared in 1897.) Lumet headed
a motley collection of socialists, syndicalists, and artists 'who had
in common a revolutionary fervour and the desire to found a "social
art"'.[1] The ideas of these people struck many an echo in Philippe's
works and in his correspondence. In January 1895 he wrote to
Marcel Ray:

I am filled with unbelievable hates, and a revolutionary mania. Oh,
to see the pavements running with blood some stormy evening, when
heads will be broken! And to grind them down, the social monsters, to
lift up their nothingness so that it falls the harder! Altruistic struggle,
that's my ambition. Prepare the masses to formulate their claims, all
of them—and build them up into ideas—then, having condensed all
suffering, and all wasted powers, to hurl them like rocks against the
old ship of society that bears us. We, the younger generation, have
duties in this respect. We must brandish our intellects, and sharpen
the blade of our love for the poor. And we must infiltrate into the
working classes, and live their lives, close to them, and see their desires,
and be their instrument.

This is the ardour of a young man, but the passage of time brought
little alteration in his state of mind. At the turn of the century he
writes:

If one day I grow rich, I feel I would not have the right to live in

---

[1] M. Ray, art. cit., p. 190.

luxury and pleasure. If I did I would be the first to blame myself.
I should lose the right to talk to a workman and call him 'brother'. . . .
There is only one system: to give away one's possessions to the poor, as,
they say, Tolstoy has done. Otherwise you are only a dog barking for
no reason.[1]

Tolstoy, indeed, is nearer to Philippe than Dostoevsky in his conception of social pity and his attitude to social evils. Dostoevsky,
who wrote *The Possessed* to illustrate the iniquity and nullity of
social revolutionary movements, would surely never have subscribed to such outbursts. So true is it that an identical emotion—
in this instance, pity for the suffering—can lead to diametrically
opposed conclusions, depending on the point of view. Dostoevsky's
predominating concern was in the relations of the individual to the
Absolute: Philippe's, in that of the individual to his fellows. In all
his writings, Philippe imitated Dostoevsky's virtuosity in stimulat-
ing the flow of men's pity for their kind, but he canalized this flood,
as the Russian had refrained from doing, to make it turn the
dynamos of class strife. Examples of this difference in the novels
are not hard to come by.

Bubu's cynical adoption of his shameful profession is attributed
directly to the existence of a rich and self-seeking class—the bourgeoisie. 'He had worked to begin with, then he had realised that
the workers who toil and suffer are dupes. He became a *souteneur*
because he lived in a society full of rich men who are strong-armed
and who create certain professions. They want women for their
money. So, of course, there have to be *souteneurs* to give them
women.' When Bubu comes to wrest Berthe from the hands of
Pierre who has persuaded her to abandon her old trade, Philippe
comments, as she walks out of the room submissively: 'She left to
go out into a world where individual charity is powerless because
lust and money are stronger, because those who work evil are
ruthless and because prostitutes are branded from the outset like
passive animals herded to the communal meadow.' Dostoevsky
never stopped to wonder whether Raskolnikov's 'act of personal
charity', when he gives Sonya almost all the money he has to help
her support her step-mother's family after her father's death, was
'powerless' or not. All he is concerned to do is to show how this
act liberated Raskolnikov for a time from his moody preoccupation
with his crime and set free an upsurge of new life. The Russian

[1] Letter to Vandeputte, 27 Nov. 1899.

regards the gesture from the individual view-point only, not from the social view-point.

Of all Philippe's books, *Le Père Perdrix* reflects most vividly the author's obsession with the division and clash between rich and poor, from the very first pages with their sarcastic description of the little town's social hierarchy—the poor workers, the well-to-do workers, the republican bourgeoisie, the reactionary bourgeoisie. The meanness of the municipal authorities stops Perdrix his pittance from the poor relief because he was deemed to have been unduly extravagant in celebrating a reunion of his family. The irony of the proceedings is that the prime mover is the doctor, Monsieur Edmond, who has grown disgustingly fat through self-indulgence. Perdrix picks up some odd ha'pence by wheeling the gouty doctor about in his invalid chair: the passage symbolizes the oppression of the poor by the rich, for in doing this work Perdrix contracts a disease of the leg, which the doctor contemptuously refuses to treat.

Philippe's treatment of the theme of suffering is in one respect then radically different from Dostoevsky's. At the same time Dostoevsky, in many other respects, sounds deeper notes than Philippe, and it could never be maintained that he was not a writer of much vaster appeal, and who dealt with many more lasting problems, than his French disciple. All Philippe's heroes, without any exception, are replicas cast from the same mould—they are all recruited from the ranks of the poorly endowed, in material wealth, but also in spiritual vigour and in will-power: that is, if one takes Pierre Hardy (in *Bubu-de-Montparnasse*), Jean Bousset (in *Le Père Perdrix* and *Marie Donadieu*) and Claude Buy (in *Croquignole*), to be the real heroes. True, most of these novels are furnished with a sort of counter-hero, a Satanic antagonist of the other: Bubu, Raphaël in *Marie Donadieu*, and Croquignole; but they too are repetitive abstractions, rich where the other is poor, tenacious where the other is yielding, successful where the other is a failure. Dostoevsky's fertility permitted him an immensely wider range of characters, and consequently he was able to study suffering and the effects of suffering in a far wider variety of human types. His hero in *Poor Folk* is an ageing clerk; in *The Idiot* it is a prince. If poverty and the dream of a richer life urge Raskolnikov to crime and suffering, who shall say what tortuous mental torments bring Stavrogin to suicide?

Each writer overlaps the other, and it is clear that Philippe was no slavish imitator of Dostoevsky. His prose, that highly individual mingling of a poetical style which recalls Gérard de Nerval's, with pieces of a crudity in observation which rivals Zola in his most 'clinical' moments, is in no wise reminiscent of Dostoevsky. Philippe drew more on himself, on his personal experiences and his personal philosophy of life, than on Dostoevsky. Some elements of his work there are, however, which appear to have been derived from the Russian, or if not derived, at any rate strengthened and deepened by his frequenting of Dostoevsky's works and to a lesser extent Tolstoy's. The isolation and examination of these elements will bring us into the heart of the question of Dostoevsky's influence on Philippe.

Beneath the portrait of Dostoevsky which hung on the wall of his room Philippe had affixed a white scroll, renewed each time he moved, on which he had inscribed the saying of the master's: 'If it has been given to anyone to suffer more than another, this is because he is worthy of his greater suffering.'[1] Philippe found consolation in the thought, and would re-read it in moments of depression. 'At bottom', he confesses, 'it is quite untrue, but I assure you it is very consoling.'[2]

The motto resumes Dostoevsky's 'religion of suffering'. The gloominess of so many of his stories is relieved by the idea that suffering ennobles the sufferer, no matter how black his (or her) crimes or ignominy may be. It is those who suffer, not those who work good, who are at the summit of the moral universe: the martyrs, not the saints, have the highest seats in heaven. Besides, martyrdom confers saintliness; he who has suffered learns compassion, and thus is led to succour his fellows and do good, just as surely as the plant that is watered will bud and bear fruit. But the man who cannot suffer, the wealthy man whose fortune shuts him off from suffering, the voluptuary whose senses deter him from treading painful paths, the socialist or atheist (the terms are synonymous for Dostoevsky) whose intellect teaches him to strive

---

[1] 'Celui à qui il a été donné de souffrir davantage, c'est qu'il est digne de souffrir davantage.' Apparently an adaptation of certain lines in *The Idiot* (book IV, chapter 5). In the current French translation these ran: 'Qui a pu souffrir plus que les autres est, par conséquent, digne de cette souffrance.' (Derély's translation, vol. ii, p. 270.)

[2] Letter to Vandeputte, 27 Nov. 1899.

for a world in which suffering is abolished—all these are lost souls:
they are the Fyodor Pavlovitches, the Prince Valkovskys, the
Svidrigailovs, the Kirillovs, and the Ivan Fyodorovitches.

Did Philippe accept this doctrine? Not without reservations.
There were moments when, in fact, he felt it was 'at bottom quite
untrue'. He aspired to a state of society in which suffering should
be, if not abolished, at any rate minimized; and he was fully aware
of the human debasement that poverty causes, a debasement of
which Dostoevsky was apparently oblivious. In reply to certain
objections to *Le Père Perdrix*, he told his correspondent: 'Everything you reproach me for I put in deliberately. I wanted to show
in Perdrix a blameworthy resignation. Do you know Knut Ham-
sun's book called *Hunger*? You see there how hunger flattened out
its victim. It is the very subject of the book just as poverty is the
subject of mine.'[1] It is in this light accordingly that one should
interpret Perdrix's remark to Jean Bousset, after the latter has lost
his job for a movement of revolt against authority, inspired by pity
for the oppressed: 'Oh! mon ami, tu es un petit bêta. Moi, je suis
un vieux malheureux. Pourquoi t'en mêler? Il faut laisser les malheureux pour ce qu'ils sont.' Philippe was under no mystical
illusions about the effects of suffering; it may fortify a man, just as
it may abase him; but it fortifies him by robbing him of humility,
by awakening in him a desire for vengeance, by perverting his
development. In *La Mère et l'enfant* he describes how harsh and
unjust treatment at the hands of the school usher made him dream
of becoming an officer so as to be able one day to lord it over other
men in his turn. He works harder at his books, sustained by this
sour ambition.

But Philippe was capable, too, of celebrating suffering just as
Dostoevsky did, and in passages highly reminiscent of the Russian
novelist.

I know that unhappiness is sacred, I know too that those who have
failed and those who are backward are the survivals of innocent men.
I should like to kiss a convict and tell him: 'You are sanctified, I love
you as I should have loved you when you were a child. I love you because
all of human sorrow has descended on your countenance and dis-
figured it.'

These words occur in *La Mère et l'enfant*, but Philippe's reasons

[1] Letter to André Ruyters, Dec. 1902.

for loving the convict are essentially the same as those Raskolnikov had for loving Sonya.

'It was not before you that I bowed myself to the ground, but before all human suffering,' he said with a strange air, and went and leant against the window. 'Listen', he went on, coming back to her a moment later. 'A little while back I told an insolent person that he was not worth your little finger even, and that I had done my sister an honour in inviting her to sit beside you. . . . In speaking thus I was thinking not of your dishonour or your faults, but of your great suffering.'

Thus the hero and heroine in *Crime and Punishment*.

Those who suffer most sometimes give proof of surprising virtues —suffering in particular creates bonds of sympathy between the sufferers, as Dostoevsky had discovered in Siberia, and as he insists so frequently in *The House of the Dead*. In *La Mère et l'enfant* once more, Philippe notes:

In humanity at its lowest, among convicts in prison, soldiers in barrack-rooms, beggars on the high-road and children at school, you will find goodness. I remember, one autumn evening, in my childhood, seeing two tramps sitting on the edge of a ditch. Each had an arm about the other's neck, they were sitting close up to each other, they were squeezing hands and kissing each other. Life was hard on them, like the usher at school, but they united their hearts.

Dmitri Karamazov, bound for the mines of Siberia, feels convinced he will find love and strength flowering among the dregs of humanity: 'You can quicken to new life the hardened heart of a convict, heal it, and in that den save a great soul purified by the knowledge of suffering, making a hero of him.'

There exists then a curious dichotomy in Philippe's conception of suffering. His native wit, his immediate judgement, told him that suffering results from evil, results in evil, and ought to be done away with. But his admiration for Dostoevsky led him to adopt occasionally the Russian's attitude, which was in direct contradiction with his own intimate conviction, and so he writes an occasional page which seems to exalt some ill-defined but sovereign virtue which suffering possesses. The influence of Dostoevsky seems to have been strong enough here to have reversed momentarily the natural trend of Philippe's thought.

Suffering, however, may take more than one form; and if Philippe was fundamentally in conflict with Dostoevsky over the value of material suffering, he found perhaps more room for agreement when he came to treat of moral suffering. The martyrs in Dostoevsky's books, the humiliated and oppressed, the wretched and tormented, are not always sunk in penury. In *The Idiot*, for instance, there is scarcely a single scene set amidst conditions of material poverty; but how many characters are there deserving of pity—Nastasya Filippovna, Ippolit, Ganya, Rogozhin, even Myshkin. Physical infirmity (in the case of Ippolit and Myshkin), defects of character which are so many fissures in the cup of happiness (in the case of Ganya and Rogozhin), the obsession of past shame (in the case of Nastasya)—all these things, and many more, are the ills on which suffering may batten.

And in Philippe's books too, suffering is not merely the suffering of the empty stomach or the disease-ridden body. Moral suffering has its place, a place constantly enlarged as the author progressed in mastery of his art. His first book contains one story (*Le Journal de Roger Jan*) which is an attempt at describing a cankered soul, in revolt against life and the body, who ends in suicide. It is the least satisfactory of the *Quatre histoires*. Thereafter Philippe was careful to anchor his suffering heroes to the sea-bed of material poverty. All of them, 'la pauvre Marie', the child in *La Mère et l'enfant*, Jean Bousset, Perdrix, Pierre Hardy, are poor in this world's goods; but they are also, and chiefly, the 'poor in spirit' of the Gospels. They are not revolted proletarians: like Dostoevsky himself, Philippe was incapable of painting the social rebel.[1] *La Pauvre Marie* is a study of a crippled working girl, who is taught in a series of discouraging lessons that life has thorns but no roses for her. 'She understood that those who can walk and who are strong must go their way, but those who are infirm must stay at home. There is a life for each one of us: beautiful for those who are beautiful and ugly for those who are ugly. Marie resigned herself to hers, but not before she had made many bitter reflections.' Makar Devushkin, in *Poor Folk*, sees himself deprived of the one joy of his life for no other reason than that he is of the race of those who are not destined to happiness: his poverty, his age, his ugliness, his lack of spirit are all at fault, but nothing of this is his fault—hence the piteousness of his case. The idea, which is stated in *La Pauvre Marie*, that 'God is pleased only by the incense that rises from beautiful shrines, satisfies the love only of lovely women and the desires only of strong

[1] The 'social rebels' in *The Possessed* are caricatures, not portrayals.

men', is implicit throughout Philippe's work, as it is in Dostoevsky's too. What measure of personal philosophy is here, and what measure of the influence of Dostoevsky's thought, it would have been diffi-cult, no doubt, for Philippe himself to determine. Dostoevsky may have done no more than confirm Philippe in his outlook: for the letters we have, written in his early twenties, are full of complaints and steeped in melancholy. Philippe gives the impression of being as constitutionally unable to grasp the flower of happiness as are his characters.

Philippe divided men into two classes: the rich and the poor: and these two classes only. He never showed any sign of realizing that the rich, too, may have their sorrows. The rich are, in fact, beyond his ken, or when they occur, they are regarded only through the eyes of the poor. They are the source of evil, the exploiters, the enemies: sinister in their activity, repellent in themselves. They are the squire, Monsieur Gaultier, who will not lift a finger to help a poor but clever lad to a career; they are the fat doctor, Monsieur Edmond, who tyrannizes over Perdrix; they are the class of selfish sensualists who pay honest girls starvation wages and drive them on to the streets where they minister to their pleasures.[1] This aspect of Philippe's analysis of society is alien to Dostoevsky and more akin to Tolstoy—Tolstoy, that is, after his eyes had been fully opened to social injustice when he started haunting the underworld of Moscow in 1881. *Resurrection* was translated when Philippe had already started writing *Bubu-de-Montparnasse*, and Tolstoy's graphic description of the lives of prostitutes in the Russian capital, but even more his firm pinning of responsibility on to the thought-less and selfish moneyed classes, aroused Philippe's joyful acclama-tion. 'Have you read Tolstoy's *Resurrection*?' he asks Vandeputte. 'It is one of the world's great books. Read it if you haven't done so already, otherwise your moral life will not be complete. There are things in it it is necessary to have read. You must tell me about it in your next letter. I repeat, you cannot afford not to read it.'[2]

Philippe's division of humanity into 'rich' and 'poor' does not, however, stop there. It is much more than an amateur economist's

[1] See the letters that Philippe wrote to Vandeputte when he was researching into the causes of prostitution and gathering material for *Bubu-de-Montparnasse*.

[2] Letter dated 14 Jan. 1900.

approximation, the partitioning of society into two classes, the haves and the have-nots, the propertied and the proletarian. It marks a split which runs far deeper, through the economic crust into moral substrata where Dostoevsky had sunk shafts. The concept of 'le Pauvre', as we penetrate deeper into Philippe's thought, gradually assumes ever broader dimensions, and the prototypes approximate more and more nearly to Dostoevskian figures.

When Pierre tells Berthe: 'We live in a world where the poor must suffer', he is not thinking so much of the three and a half francs he picks up for his day's work in a draughtsman's office, nor of the cruel compulsion on her to sell her body nightly to buy food. They are victimized, he and she, because they are defenceless. No reasoning, and no reorganization of society will change the nature of a sheep, but no reasoning either will alter the cruel injustice that the sheep should be the prey of the wolf. Pierre visualizes Maurice

astride on her shoulders, gripping her with his claws and thrusting them in her so that she should not escape. He forces her to walk. With all his weight he bends her to the ground, so that she shall be exhausted like an over-driven beast, so that she shall neither see nor hear. Pierre looked at Berthe. He said nothing. He took her hand and held it between his fingers so as to let his pity, quite simply, pass into her—like that—to do her a little good.

Pity, indeed, is the most one can offer Berthe: for even when she is for the time being delivered of Maurice, when he is in prison, she goes to her sister Blanche, another predatory creature, brazen, self-reliant, impure, who plunges her deeper into the mire.

Philippe, in creating Berthe, took her from the same mould as Sonya Marmeladov. Social injustice, certainly, drove both Berthe and Sonya on to the streets, but also—and this is more important —their very innocence, their altruism, one might almost say their spinelessness, led them both to adopt the miseries of prostitution: Sonya to save her family from starvation, Berthe to save Maurice from honest work.

The true prototype of 'le Pauvre', as Philippe conceived him, is represented by Jean Bousset in *Marie Donadieu*. 'He had neither charm nor good looks, but wore one of those hearts that crave to win everyone's approval and satisfy everyone's desires. Man lives by comparisons: people liked him because at every step he gave them the illusion of his defeat.' The Poor Man is marked out for defeat, will even welcome it and glory in his weakness. Jean Bousset is assailed by

a peculiar itch to sink still lower, to find his own people too high for him and to seek among the poor his true level and his faith. The business was not without its romantic side. . . . He reckoned himself among the weak, believed only in his private griefs, dilated on them and would have wished to weigh on the world's sorrow with all the weight of his youthful poverty.

He tells Marie: 'I should have been most wretched if I had been granted happiness . . . I had to, I had to be poor. I am an engineer, I could have been rich. I do not know how to be rich. That is why pity was invented.' These remarks are somewhat inconsequential, but Jean has a mystic's, not a rationalist's, logic. His drift seems to be that his poverty is not imposed from outside, it is an inner necessity of his nature, a germ such as that which makes this particular blade grow into a reed, never by any chance an oak-tree or a rose.

She seemed to delight in her sorrow, in the *egoism* of her sufferings, if I may be allowed so to express myself. This need to inflame one's sorrows, and the pleasure one can find in it, were things I can well understand: it is the pleasure of many humiliated and wounded hearts who feel themselves victims of fate and who are conscious of its injustice.

So writes the supposed author of *Insulted and Injured*, about one of the characters, Nellie. This desire for self-abasement, this hankering after the aggravation of ills already hard enough to bear, may be observed throughout Dostoevsky's work.

It is an odd thing [ponders Dolgorukov, the hero of *A Raw Youth*] I always had this trait, perhaps even from my earliest childhood: when people ill-treated me, thoroughly ill-treated me, outraged my deepest feelings, there always arose in me an unquenchable desire to submit myself passively to the outrage and even to anticipate the wishes of my persecutors—'See here, you have humiliated me, so I will humiliate myself still further—look at me, admire me!'

The same urge drives Raskolnikov to associate with Sonya, to confess his weakness and to disclaim his pretension to be considered an 'extraordinary man', and finally, to accept living with the dregs of humanity, the prisoners in Siberia; the same feeling inspires the hero of the *Letters from Underground* to call himself a rat, not a man, and compels the hero of *The Possessed*, high-born and gifted as he is, to marry the half-witted cripple girl, Marya Timofeevna. It is true that Dostoevsky, being a Christian, introduces the idea of redemption which justifies and gives point to these acts of abnegation.

Side by side with the enhanced vision of the Poor Man, there exists in Philippe's novels an aggrandized conception of the Rich Man. Philippe protested to André Ruyters[1] that it was wrong to suppose, just from reading *Le Père Perdrix*, that he was able to make only the poor live, and promised that in due course he would show himself capable of making 'the rich and the conqueror' live also. Philippe kept this promise. Maurice, in *Bubu-de-Montparnasse*, is indisputably a living figure, and it is clear that he is intended as a conqueror from the way the book ends. Raphaël in *Marie Donadieu* and Croquignole are further types of the same kind. Is poor he who yields: is rich he who takes. The poor are in fact the weak, the masochistic, who are also the lovable, the human, the poets even; the rich are the strong, the redoubtable, men of action, beasts of prey: although, in their way, they are as innocent as Blake's Tiger. Jean thus describes his rival Raphaël, one of the 'rich': 'You came on the scene with your life, with a way of gathering up in your hands the human material and setting it down in front of you. I don't know if you see through it quite, I don't know if you understand it, but I do know you possess it.'

Dostoevsky had called such men 'normal men', and Philippe may have read, in Halpérine-Kaminsky's adaptation of *Letters from Underground*, certain passages which foreshadow his own creations. The Underground Man (who is, after all, simply one of Philippe's 'poor men' having lost his youth and grown embittered by forty years of 'poverty') speaks of them as

the people who can avenge themselves and in general look after themselves. . . . The man who acts without thinking is in my view the real, the normal man, such as his tender mother Nature desired him to be. I am to the last degree jealous of this man. He is stupid, I agree, but who knows? it is perhaps laid down that the normal man must be stupid. Perhaps even this stupidity is a form of beauty.

They are stupid but they are well equipped for life, with teeth and claws; their opposites, the poor, the underground folk, are intelli-

[1] Letter quoted above.

gent but ill-equipped, and lack the strength of their desires. The rich say little: the poor talk endlessly ('I am a chatterbox', says Jean Bousset, but he understates his case), but they never act. 'But after all' asks Dostoevsky's Underground Man, 'this chattering, isn't it the sole destiny of every intelligent man?—this chattering, which is simply the action of pouring nothingness into the void.'

There is a fixed pattern to at least three of Philippe's novels: *Bubu-de-Montparnasse*, *Marie Donadieu*, and *Croquignole*. In each there are two protagonists: the rich man and the poor man, and between them is the woman. Berthe stands between Pierre and Maurice; Marie between Jean and Raphaël; Angèle between Claude and Croquignole.

The pattern is recurrent in Dostoevsky too. In *Poor Folk*, Varvara Alekseevna stands between Makar and the unnamed suitor who eventually bears her away. In *Insulted and Injured* Vanya represents the 'poor man' who loves Natasha but will never make the struggle to win her; Alyosha, for all his weakness, plays the part of the 'rich man', because he is the real winner by his charm and fascination. Natasha stands between the two. But in this novel Dostoevsky has complicated the issue by overlaying this primary pattern with a secondary one, in which the two women (Natasha, the weaker, Katya, the stronger) struggle to possess Alyosha, the passive central figure. The distribution of the sexes is oddly reversed.

The same pattern is evident—though subsidiary—in *The Possessed*, where a triangle is composed of Stavrogin, Shatov, and Shatov's wife. It is more obvious—though still providing only a sub-plot—in *The Brothers Karamazov*, where Ivan and Dmitri are both suitors for the hand of Katerina Ivanovna. It is at the very basis of that short story of Dostoevsky's, *The White Nights*, the flavour of which is most nearly identical with the atmosphere of Philippe's books. Here we have the girl Nastenka, loved by the shy dreamer who is the narrator, but leaving him for the 'lodger' to whom she had first pledged herself. But, most brilliantly of all, the pattern is exemplified in *The Idiot*. Myshkin represents the 'poor man', notwithstanding his respectable income: Philippe would have regarded him as such because he converses on a footing of equality with lackeys and children, because he is harmless, because of his timidity with women, and because compassion is his strongest emotion. Rogozhin is his antithesis—excessively wealthy, endowed with immense animal strength, using his riches, physical and material, quite ruthlessly, to buy his pleasure where he can. Nastasya Filippovna is the woman set between these two.

A mere conflict between two rivals for the hand of a woman would, of course, have been the most banal of themes: and that amounts to no more than the scaffolding of the edifice. The pattern of this dualism between rich and poor has certain constants, in Dostoevsky as well as in Philippe, which give striking evidence of the strength and nature of the influence of the Russian author on the French one, and which show how far the idea transcended its origins.

To begin with, the poor man is both intellectually and morally the superior of the rich man. Ivan Karamazov is Dmitri's clever brother, but he knows that he will have to yield precedence to Dmitri, stupid but strong, in the estimation of Katerina Ivanovna. Myshkin is almost a saint on earth, with all the wisdom of the innocent. 'You have a gentleness and innocence which the Golden Age itself never knew', Keller tells him; 'and at the same time you read in the hearts of people like the most keen-witted of psychologists.' Makar Devushkin is full of high sentiments, and continually accomplishing acts of self-devotion: while of the man who eventually marries Varvara Alekseevna we hear little, but the little we hear is not reassuring. And among the counterparts of these figures in Philippe's writings, the same qualities are apparent. Pierre Hardy is a poet and a philosopher, and he sets himself the task, from motives of philanthropy, of rescuing Berthe Méténier from vice. Jean Bousset is generous, altruistic—we see him in this light chiefly in *Le Père Perdrix*. In *Marie Donadieu* he is the incarnation of goodness; he says of himself: 'I have always liked knowing men. I get to know them with deference and in all my feelings there mingles a strain of timidity.' Claude is full of gentle attentions for Angèle (in *Croquignole*), persuades her delicately to spend less time at work, to go for walks with him; he is childlike in his dealings with her, just as Myshkin is in his talk with Nastasya Filippovna. Claude's antithesis, Croquignole, is a sensual, refining on his sensuality. A further revealing detail—he inherits a small legacy, and leaves the ranks of the poor, for the Devil claims his own.

It is a further characteristic of this pattern, that the 'rich man' always gains his object. The woman is passive in his hands: he wields a fascination over her that is more powerful than all the gentleness and understanding of the 'poor man'. Thus Rogozhin, mingling among the crowd which gathers to watch Nastasya in her bridal dress drive to the church, where Myshkin is awaiting her, catches her eye with his magnetic gaze: immediately she leaps out of her carriage and goes to him—and to her death at his hands which she had foreseen. Mavrikiy Nikolaevitch, one of the characters in *The Possessed*, suspects Stavrogin (whom we can classify with no hesitation as a 'rich man') of being his rival for the affections of Lizaveta Nikolaevna. He takes the extraordinary course of asking Stavrogin to marry her, because, as he says, 'if she were standing in the church at her wedding and you were to call her, she'd leave me and everyone else and go to you'. The dénouement of *The White Nights*, when Nastenka rushes away from 'the dreamer' as soon as she hears the summons of her first lover, 'without saying a single word', is yet another instance of the almost magical powers of attraction the 'rich man' possesses.

Bubu-de-Montparnasse, *Marie Donadieu*, *Croquignole*, all contain episodes comparable with those we have quoted from Dostoevsky's novels. At the end of *Bubu*, Berthe follows Maurice without a murmur when he breaks into Pierre's room, and leaves Pierre without a word of explanation. Marie Donadieu confides to Jean that Raphaël has used her cruelly on occasion: but Raphaël has only to return and without even being bidden she follows him. All Claude's kindness to Angèle never results in her becoming his mistress: nothing perhaps was farther from his design; but Croquignole, chancing to enter her room with half an hour to fritter away, debauches her on the spot.

But the most remarkable thing about these triangles is the good understanding that frequently reigns between the two rivals. Dostoevsky built *The Brothers Karamazov* round two triangles: Dmitri—Grushenka—Fyodor, and Ivan—Katerina Ivanovna—Dmitri. The first of these triangles is of the more commonplace type: the two men are snarling at each other, and the woman coquets with both. The second has a different nature. Ivan has no jealousy for Dmitri: he does not hate him for being an obstacle in the path of his love. Similarly Vanya and Alyosha, in *Insulted and Injured*, are on the best of terms one with the other, and Alyosha confides to Vanya all his feelings about Natasha, although he knows the other loves her too. Myshkin, fully cognizant of Rogozhin's love for Nastasya, goes and visits him, and together they discuss the different ways they love. They end by exchanging crosses in token of friendship.

When Raphaël has retaken Marie, Jean visits the pair of them in the evening and they converse together, calmly and without a trace of rancour. Raphaël tells Jean: 'For my part it would have been very difficult for me not to love you. You are so limpid and your voice speaks from the depths.' And Croquignole himself confides to Claude that he has seduced Angèle. The confession is not meant as an act of refined cruelty, for the two are good friends; Croquignole's intention is simply to unburden himself in all good faith. And Claude listens dumbly, without a word or gesture of revolt or reproach. 'Motionless, clasping his head between his hands, he received his grief as one receives it usually, silently, already preparing its dwelling-place.'

Although the theme of love has no part in *La Mère et l'enfant* or *Le Père Perdrix*, in the other books of Philippe it is a mainspring of action. But the division of the world of men into rich and poor holds here too; and love has two faces, according to whether it is the rich man who loves or the poor man. And here, too, Philippe is paralleled by Dostoevsky.

The Raphaëls and the Croquignoles, being men of action and not men of thought, men of the physical, not the spiritual world, are great sensualists, Don Juans after their fashion; but the Jean Boussets, the Claude Buys, with whom they clash, love romantically, platonically, chastely, through a distrust of their power to win their women and a fear for shattered ideals as soon as their love enters the physical plane.

Exactly the same opposition is observable in Dostoevsky, between the sensualist Dmitri and the intellectual Ivan; or between Myshkin and Rogozhin. Myshkin explains to Rogozhin: 'I do not love *her* with love, but with compassion.' This is beyond Rogozhin. 'Do you think I am deceiving you?' asks the prince. 'No,' replies the merchant, 'I believe you, only I don't understand the first word about it.' The sensualist lives in so different a world from the chaste man that he cannot understand him. Croquignole is astounded when he learns that Angèle had never been Claude's mistress, and is inclined to put the blame on him for the whole catastrophe.

Si tu avais pris la précaution de coucher avec elle le jour où tu l'avais connue, elle aurait tenu à toi, elle aurait résisté, je n'aurais pu rien faire. Je suis un salaud, ça c'est comme tu voudras, mais enfin, voyons, pourquoi n'as-tu pas couché avec elle? Elle ne te plaisait donc pas? Alors, pourquoi te fais-tu de la peine? Bois donc, va, ça passera.

Vogüé noted, with a good deal of acumen, that Dostoevsky in his novels represented love only in two forms: as a kind of mystical devotion, devoid of desire; or as a brutal and headstrong passion. 'Hence one of the most inexplicable qualities of his art; this realist, who abounds in risky situations and in the crudest of stories, never evokes a suggestive picture, but solely desolating thoughts; I defy anyone to quote in all his books a single line meant to quicken the senses or in which woman appears as a temptress.'[1] The generalization lays itself open to certain objections; but it can be maintained as a broad statement of tendency. As examples of the first type of love, the 'mystical devotion devoid of desire' which is rooted in altruistic compassion, not in egoistic sensual attraction, there are the Sonya–Raskolnikov pair in *Crime and Punishment* (specifically cited by Vogüé), Shatov and his wife in *The Possessed*, Makar and Varvara in *Poor Folk*, but above all, Myshkin and Nastasya Filippovna in *The Idiot*. As examples of the second type, the 'brutal and headstrong passion', we have Svidrigailov's pursuit of Dunya, Fyodor Pavlovitch's lusting after Grushenka, and Rogozhin's love for Nastasya Filippovna.

Shatov had lived with his wife for less than three weeks when she left him for Stavrogin. After three years' absence she returns, in the final stages of pregnancy. And Shatov is radiant:

There was a thrill of extraordinary and unexpected feeling in his soul. Three years of separation, three years of the broken marriage had effaced nothing from his heart. And perhaps every day during these three years he had dreamed of her, of that beloved being who had once said to him 'I love you'. He was fiercely modest and chaste, looking on himself as an absolute monster, detesting his own face as well as his character, comparing himself to some freak fit only to be exhibited at fairs. . . . But here was the one being who had loved him for a fortnight (that he had never doubted, never!); a being he had always considered immeasurably

---

[1] Vogüé, *Le Roman russe*, p. 151.

superior to him in spite of his perfectly sober understanding of her failings; a being he could forgive for everything, *everything* (there could be no question of that—indeed it was quite the other way about, he was convinced he was entirely to blame)—this woman, Marya Shatov, was in his house, was with him again . . . it was almost unbelievable!

When, from exhaustion, she falls asleep, he watches over her, and ponders:

Poor thing, how worn out she is, what she must have been through! Her pride prevents her from complaining. But she is quick-tempered, very quick-tempered—that's because she's ill; an angel's temper gets frayed in illness. How dry her forehead is, it must be hot—what dark rims she has under her eyes, and . . . and yet how beautiful the oval of her face is and her rich hair, how . . .—And he made haste to turn away his eyes, to walk away as if he were frightened at the mere idea of seeing in her anything but an unhappy, worn-out human being who needed *help*—'how could he think of his *hopes*, oh, how mean and base man is!' And he slunk back to his corner, sat down, buried his face in his hands and once more plunged into dreams and memories . . . and once more hopes revisited him.

Or take Myshkin's proposal of marriage.

I know nothing, Nastasya Filippovna, I have seen nothing, you are right, but I . . . I would consider myself honoured by your choice, far from thinking I should do you an honour in marrying you. I am a nobody; you have experienced suffering and come out pure from such a hell; it's a great deal . . . I . . . Nastasya Filippovna, I . . . love you, I would die for you, Nastasya Filippovna, I allow no one to say anything against you, Nastasya Filippovna. . . .

Later, Myshkin tells Rogozhin: 'I do not love her out of love, but out of compassion', and Rogozhin's reply is significant: 'As far as I can judge, your compassion is stronger than my love.' Meditating this saying on his own, Myshkin begins to feel that Rogozhin's love will perhaps alter and purify itself as sympathy replaces lust.

Rogozhin does himself an injustice: he has a great heart, capable of suffering and sympathizing. When he learns the whole truth, when he realizes how much this poor, distracted, half-witted creature is to be pitied—will he not forgive her all the past, all she has made him suffer? Will he not become her servant, her brother, her friend, her providence? Compassion will be for Rogozhin himself a school in which he will mature. Compassion is perhaps the chief and only law of human existence.

The hero of *The White Nights* declares his love only when he has seen Nastenka in tears, having been cast off, as she thinks, by her first lover.

You would never have known that I love you, I should have kept my secret; but the fault is yours; you forced me to speak; I saw you weeping, I could not stand it, I told you everything, and . . . you have not the right any more to send me away. . . . A moment ago, when you were crying, I couldn't keep still; when you were crying, you know, because another man had rejected your love. I felt in my heart so much love for you, Nastenka, so much love! And I could not keep quiet. . . .

Compassion plays an overwhelming part in the affection which Philippe's 'poor man', in his various incarnations, feels for the woman he chooses. In Pierre's relations with Berthe Méténier, the prostitute he sets out to 'redeem' (as Myshkin may have wished to redeem Nastasya), 'there was never any love . . . but there was something which surpassed it: there was trustfulness and kindness.' Pierre encourages her in her day-dreams of returning to a normal life, getting employment in a florist's shop, becoming a dancer at the Moulin Rouge, or an assistant in a tobacco stall, and tells her: 'The days you feel depressed, you must come and see me. . . . You should know how much joy there is for a man and a woman to suffer together. . . . So come, come. Really it is good to help unfortunate girls. They call that—relieving suffering humanity.' One night, in despair, she visits him. Her sister, with whom she has been living, has been sent to hospital and she is at her wit's end to know how to scrape together the money to pay the rent for their room. She asks to stay with him, and he, knowing that a night 'lost' in this way means a morrow without a meal, is moved to the core.

He pressed her to his heart and held her there warm for a long while, with burning tenderness and uttering a little moan of pity which flickered like a flame. He said nothing, he was not conscious of her as a woman, he wrapped himself up in this sorrow and he would have liked to cry out 'Poor little saint, poor little saint!'

All these scenes in *Bubu-de-Montparnasse* border on the maudlin. In subsequent novels Philippe avoids such excessive sentimentality, but the 'poor men' among his characters retain an approach to women in which puritanism is mingled with mysticism. Jean Bousset, while Raphaël is away from Paris, tells Marie Donadieu—whose virtue is of the easiest: 'Woman is a science, not a pleasure.

Of all the creatures in the world, she is the one who can teach us the most.' He talks to her endlessly, and Marie resorts secretly to a stranger in the neighbouring flat whose ardours are not purely cerebral. Finally she pretends to fall in with his ideas: he can conceive of love only by the mediumship of pity. ('As for me,' he says, 'I should have liked to bring you my body crucified. I have not suffered enough for you to love me. . . . Isn't it true that you would have been happy to tend the wounds on my hands?') So she invents a story that Raphaël once kicked her in the stomach in an unjustified fit of jealousy: she arouses his pity, and they become lovers.

Jean remains an inexhaustible embroiderer on the same theme.

I used to tell myself: There are no women, or rather, if there are any, they will not be worthy of me. For a long while I thought of crippled girls. Don't you agree, cripples are sad, so they are intelligent as one is if one is sad and then they have need of consolation. I needed to be afflicted in my life, life had to be afflicted too and I needed to console all those it had touched.

It is quite likely that Philippe was thinking of Marya Timofeevna, the crippled girl whom Stavrogin married, or else of Raskolnikov's first love, the daughter of his landlady who had died before the novel opens. 'She was ugly rather than pretty. Really I can't think why I was so attached to her then,' comments the hero of *Crime and Punishment*, 'perhaps I loved her because she was always ill. . . . If she had been in addition crippled or hunchbacked, I believe I should have loved her the more.'

The second form that love takes in Dostoevsky, the mad passion of the animal in rut, has a certain place too in Philippe's books. One of the *Quatre histoires de pauvre amour* describes how three starved tramps, having inflamed their imaginations by gloating over erotic memories, see a woman pass in the twilight, rush in pursuit of her and rape her. In a certain scene in *Crime and Punishment*, Svidrigailov has decoyed Dunya, Raskolnikov's sister, to his room and all but assaults her there, while in *The Brothers Karamazov* Fyodor Pavlovitch is supposed to have violated a helpless idiot girl; the secret shame gnawing at Nastasya Filippovna's heart probably goes back to a similar indignity put on her by Totzky while she was a young girl. But more commonly, in Philippe, the attachment of his heroines to the 'rich' men is based on a normal give-and-take of carnal pleasures: thus Marie Donadieu and Raphaël Crouzat, Madame Ferrand and Croquignole; these relationships are just as straightforward as those contracted by the 'poor man' are complex and tortuous.

Undoubtedly Philippe's own attitude to women is reflected quite as much in his books as anything he may have adopted out of Dostoevsky: here, as elsewhere, the task seems almost hopeless of disentangling Philippe's personal contribution from the elements he may have borrowed from the Russian, simply because his own spirit and outlook had so much in common with the spirit and outlook of Dostoevsky. Philippe seems to have lacked both the manner and personal charm which might have captivated women, and probably as a consequence he was timid in his dealings with them. His letters exhale frequent complaints about his melancholy and longing for companionship.

Sometimes I try to think my solitude is a fine thing, and persuade myself that woman is evil, that love is an inferior passion, but I cannot convince myself. I feel too deeply the reverse. It seems to me now that women are wonderful jewels that only very rich people can afford. I regard them without envy, as I should regard a king's crown. I never even dare to think that one of them could love me. And yet, at the bottom of my heart, I am torn by intense suffering.[1]

And the whole history of Pierre's 'compassionate' love for Berthe was a transposition of Philippe's own relations with the street-girl Maria: we can follow in advance many of the vicissitudes of the novel in reading his correspondence. And not only in *Bubu-de-Montparnasse*, but in each one of his novels his own experiences at Cérilly and at Paris were always a reservoir which provided themes and incidents. His reading of Dostoevsky was, relatively, a subsidiary channel of inspiration. And yet, before Gide, no writer in France, probably, was more deeply influenced by Dostoevsky. The ideas of the Russian converged with his personal beliefs, strengthened and enlarged them.

The influence of Dostoevsky on Philippe is certainly of greater importance than that of any other writer. The 'sentimental realism'

[1] Letter to Vandeputte, 15 May 1898.

of Dickens has been suggested as a contributory factor; and it is true that Philippe, as we have seen, felt warmly about this English novelist. But the victims of society on whom Dickens empties his sympathy—the Little Nells, the Oliver Twists—are all of them innocent, unstained creatures: a woman dishonoured, even though society bears the blame, inspired him with a kind of shrinking dread. Dickens's 'social pity' did not venture outside the foundlings hospital or the Marshalsea prison. Analogies with Tolstoy have also been drawn; but no close parallel exists. Tolstoy's multitudinous characters, his puritanism and his strong sense of family bonds, above all his apparent remoteness from the scenes he paints, inevitable in an artist who brushed such broad canvases, all these qualities are antithetical to Philippe's. Also, it was not until he wrote *Resurrection* that Tolstoy attempted to put into the novel the underworld of city life, and, as we have noted, Philippe had conceived, planned, and partly written *Bubu-de-Montparnasse*, his own variation on the theme, before Wyzewa completed his translation of Tolstoy's masterpiece. Finally, by his socialism, which looked to a better world where individual happiness should be achieved by the abolition of class differences, Philippe was at variance with Tolstoy who condemned revolutionary socialism and pinned his hopes on spiritual reforms.

Thomas Hardy may have influenced Philippe. The hero of *Jude the Obscure*, for instance, is a true 'Poor Man' as Philippe understood the conception, coming from peasant stock, battling against a hostile society: but Hardy's atmosphere, like Tolstoy's, is unconfined, wind-swept, like the Egdon Moor he describes with such intensity of feeling at the beginning of *The Return of the Native*: Fate and the structure of society pit themselves against the puny frames of his heroes. In Philippe's books the air is stiller and closer, whispers and undertones are audible, the enemy is near at hand and tangible.

The only writer who may possibly—at one stage at least—have meant more to Philippe than Dostoevsky was Nietzsche. 'I am nearer perhaps to Nietzsche than I am to Dostoevsky. Don't imagine I'm showing off, as things are at present I have never said anything more true.'[1] Philippe, when he wrote these words, was commenting on an article Vandeputte had written about *Bubu-de-*

[1] Letter to Vandeputte, 30 May 1901.

Montparnasse in *L'Idée libre*, but the sally needs to be taken with some caution. It is fairly clear from his correspondence that Philippe did not 'discover' Nietzsche until after *Bubu-de-Montparnasse* was written. It is in a letter dated 31 December 1900 that he first mentions the German philosopher, and the tone in which he writes could have been used only by an excited neophyte.

It is legitimate, however, to consider that *Marie Donadieu* was affected by his reading of Nietzsche.[1] Philippe makes Jean, at the end of the book, refuse Marie who returns to him: Jean sees himself now as a 'superman' in a sense, and mutters heroic maxims to sustain his resolution. 'A man must not sell his soul to gain a woman. . . . Do not let yourself be held up by little things before you have reached the big things.' Jean has grown out of Marie, so he tells her, grown out of love, and is pressing on to new horizons. 'I know other feelings than tenderness, I know emotional play of a higher order than love.' But Dostoevsky continues to haunt Jean Bousset-Philippe:

> To be sure, I once knew a woman, and, thanks to her, one day when my blood was streaming from my heart like a new nation—on that day everything, everything—Paris, love, money, all that seemed to me scarcely a child's game, a tiny village in which one stops one day to greet a memory. I remember that Dostoevsky, in one of his books, speaks of 'the living life' and says that it must be perfectly simple, that the day someone discovers it, people will be quite astonished by it. Well, that evening, I discovered 'the living life'.

The truth is that Nietzsche, in many respects, is complementary to Dostoevsky, and Philippe was led on to him quite naturally. Nietzsche himself called Dostoevsky 'the only man who taught me something in matters of psychology', and Philippe is reputed to have declared that 'in *The Possessed* the whole of Nietzsche is already apparent'.[2] The same essential question was asked by the Russian and the German—the question, 'What is a man fit for, what can a man do, what are the bounds of the permitted?' Raskolnikov's arguments, which motivate and justify to himself his crime, the meditations of the Underground Man, the discussions the

[1] However, the author of the standard work on Nietzsche's influence on French writers and thinkers (Geneviève Bianquis: *Nietzsche en France*, 1929), does not even mention Philippe in her pages—a hint that the influence was subsidiary.

[2] See Henri Bachelin, *Charles-Louis Philippe, sa vie, son œuvre* (1929), p. 29.

Devil has with Ivan Karamazov in a fever-dream, all these are premonitions of Nietzsche. It is not only in *The Possessed*, but in the greater part of Dostoevsky's outstanding works, that 'the whole of Nietzsche is already apparent'. The essential difference between the two thinkers is that Nietzsche preached that 'everything was permitted', whereas Dostoevsky put this doctrine into the mouth of the Devil and his advocates the atheists. Raskolnikov renounces the theory of the superman and replaces it by the Christian practice of renunciation and repentance which lead to redemption.

It is clear that there is no far call from Philippe's 'strong' or 'rich' man to Nietzsche's superman. Is one to understand that Philippe, in his new-won enthusiasm for the author of *Menschliches Allzumenschliches*, began to transfer his sympathy from the passively suffering, 'poor' hero of the earlier books to the creatures of remorseless will-power to whom he had opposed them? Or was the enthusiasm for Nietzsche purely transitory? Without attempting to give a positive answer, we may observe at least that in his last completed novel, *Croquignole*, the 'superman' hero, having pursued his course reckless of the feelings of others, ends, just like Stavrogin, Smerdyakov, Svidrigailov, or any of Dostoevsky's satanic heroes, in committing suicide. One might venture to conclude, then, that after a brief phase during which the balance tipped the other way, the influence of Dostoevsky prevailed and, taking it all in all, proved to be of more permanent validity for Philippe than that of Nietzsche.

XI

TOLSTOYISM

NOVEL-WRITING was not the only, nor even perhaps the
most important, field of activity in which the influence of
Tolstoy made itself felt. The world-wide interest he aroused
from the mid-eighties until his death in 1910 can only be partly
explained by his prestige as a novelist. It was 'le tolstoïsme' on
which attention centred; Tolstoy's artistic achievement was subsidiary.

The Cossacks, War and Peace, Anna Karenina and the rest of his
earlier, fictional work had found a great and appreciative public;
the pamphlets, manifestoes, the polemical and didactic utterances
which followed on his 'conversion' in the early eighties—a vast
output now all but forgotten—were devoured by the French with
a different sort of enthusiasm. Relating as they did to the most
intimate workings of human behaviour as well as to the broadest
aspects of social institutions, they added up to a challenge to the
accepted ideas of nearly every individual: Tolstoy's iconoclasm
bore almost as fiercely on the use of tobacco as on the practice of
raising armies for war. He dwelt on a vast number of extremely
burning topics; and the solutions he offered were nearly always
extremist.

From 1890 or before, until his death, the 'prophet of Yasnaya
Polyana' was a major force to be reckoned with in the world of
ideas. As early as 1893 Wyzewa wrote: 'The moral papers of Count
Tolstoy have not so far fully converted anyone; but there is no one
now who does not take them seriously, and their influence on every
truth-loving spirit becomes stronger each day. I cannot think of
any philosopher since Rousseau whose words have commanded
more attention.'[1] Efforts were made to formularize and summarize
the attitude of Tolstoy towards modern civilization, to answer the
challenge implied in his destructive criticisms of contemporary
society and religion, or to reinforce them. Tolstoy was a living and
dynamic force, issuing an uninterrupted stream of manifestoes on
current problems, delivering himself personally of his opinions to
visitors, inviting discipleship or renegation: nothing of the kind,

---

[1] Wyzewa, 'Revues russes', *Revue des Deux Mondes*, 15 Oct. 1893, pp. 940–1.

perhaps, had been seen since Voltaire established himself at Ferney.

The influence of Tolstoy's didactic writings was, of course, not confined merely to France, or even to Europe. Before long it had spread over the whole world, from America, where a prominent New York figure in the nineties, Ernest H. Crosby, declared public allegiance to the principles of Tolstoy, to Japan, where a colony of disciples was formed to put into practice his precepts, and to India, where Mahatma Gandhi (perhaps the last of the 'tolstoïsants') found a buttress for his ideas in Tolstoy's doctrine of non-violence, and used it as a most effective political weapon.

Literature, being a human and social activity like any other, was in its turn weighed on the scales of Tolstoyism, and found wanting. Although art was not subjected to the scourge of Tolstoy's denunciation until relatively late in the development of his philosophy,[1] his denial of old gods was implicit in the abrupt cessation of literary production after the completion of *Anna Karenina* in 1877; and thus, before even Tolstoy had won his reputation in France as a novelist, the news was circulated that he had declared his intention never again to write a novel. The philosopher-moralist he had now become was seemingly no longer content merely with striking an occasional didactic note, such as had not infrequently sounded, in *War and Peace* and *Anna Karenina*, above the crash of buildings in burning Moscow and the merry waltz music of St. Petersburg ball-rooms. In future he would write, if write he must, only to teach mankind, never to amuse.

His earliest French commentators, de Cyon, Dupuy, were not over-distressed by the new phase in Tolstoy's development: it was not then realized that the philosophical preoccupations were to banish literary activity, at least for a long time to come. Vogüé was the first to take alarm. Catholic and conservative that he was, the French critic found nothing in it but

the first stammerings of rationalism on the religious side, and of communism on the social side; the old millennial pipe-dream, the tradition passed down, from its origins in the Middle Ages, by the Waldenses, the Lollards, the anabaptists. Happy Russia, where these sweet fancies (ces

---

[1] *What is Art?* was published in 1897; but an earlier book, *What then should we do?* (1886) contained some scathing comments on those who make a livelihood out of writing books, painting pictures, or composing music.

belles chimères) are still new! In the West, the only surprise we shall have is to come across these doctrines from the pen of a great writer, unsurpassed in his observation of the human heart.[1]

There was the rub: for those who had entertained so strong an admiration for Tolstoy's literary achievements, his renunciation of the pen was felt to be an almost criminal apostasy. 'My grudge against his doctrine is all the greater', Vogüé adds, 'because it robs me of masterpieces condemned to be stifled in their cradle.'[2] Hennequin is equally baffled by the metamorphosis. 'The most gifted psychologist of our time . . . has fallen in the last few years to compiling a petty manual of practical morality containing only a few rules, which are, however, such that the most religiously minded of men would be looked on as mad if he were to try to put them into operation.'[3] Rod testifies that 'the majority of those who admired *War and Peace* and *Anna Karenina* shrug their shoulders, declaring that the old master—the stamp of whose genius it is, however, hard not to recognize in each of his new books—is no more than an eccentric or a sick man seized by mystical delirium'. True, in Rod's view, this is a summary judgement which he considers it his duty to rectify.[4]

As time went on it became more and more evident that Tolstoy was in full earnest, and that there was slight hope that he would go back on his decision never again to turn his hand to non-didactic literature. 'We are to-day,' writes Léon Daudet in 1894, 'the amazed witnesses of this spectacle of a spirit rich in all manner of talents who is tearing off his badges one by one.' The one circumstance that still compels admiration is the strength of purpose with which Tolstoy has so ruthlessly put behind him his past in order to devote himself whole-heartedly to his mission.[5]

At intervals there were, as it seemed, flashes of the older Tolstoy: certain of his publications in the eighties and nineties, *The Death of Ivan Ilyitch, The Kreutzer Sonata, Master and Servant, Resurrection*, while they were all more or less tendentious, betrayed the supreme artist that Tolstoy remained almost in spite of himself. Some critics, among them so eminent a one as Théodore de Wyzewa, held that Tolstoy's conversion had, in fact, a saving

[1] Vogüé, *Le Roman russe*, p. 338.   [2] Ibid., p. 339.
[3] Hennequin, *Écrivains francisés*, pp. 236–7.
[4] Rod: *Idées morales du temps présent*, p. 239.
[5] L. Daudet: 'Les Grands Évolutifs', *Nouvelle Revue*, 1 Jan. 1894, p. 187.

influence on his talent. His later tales and novels are infused with
a certain element lacking in *War and Peace*, 'and which makes of
them more touching, if not more accomplished works of art'. The
technique is the same, the artistic mastery unimpaired, but these
gifts are now used to a practical end. 'By the single fact of his conversion, Count Tolstoy has given his talent an impulse in a new
direction, which allows him to turn it to the best advantage.'[1] And
Leroy-Beaulieu later agreed with Wyzewa, declaring that it needed
a Russian to turn problem novels into superbly living works of art.[2]

For others in France who had learnt to love Tolstoy's first
manner, the infrequent literary masterpieces of his later period
were only the occasion for regrets that he should be dissipating
most of his energies on arid speculations. Waliszewski, discussing
Tolstoy's play, *The Power of Darkness*, which, forbidden in Russia,
had been given its first performance in Paris with outstanding success, summoned the author to produce yet more of such works,
'forsaking the scientific researches and philosophical speculations
which do not befit you. I am no Turgenev,[3] but I am quite certain
I am interpreting the wishes of thousands of your readers. . . .'[4]

Tolstoy's renunciation of 'pure' art was, however, final; and in
due course it turned to denunciation. *What is Art?* was translated
in 1898; and it became clear that Tolstoy's nihilism was not to
spare even those aesthetic ideals which formerly he had so magni-
ficently illustrated. The work finally cost him the sympathies of the
literary world, in France particularly, since it was French poets
and French novelists for whom Tolstoy, considering them to be
the vanguard of the contemporary movement in literature, reserved
his most savage vituperation.

Representative of the conservative attitude to *What is Art?* was
René Doumic.[5] The traditionalist found himself, in many respects,

---

[1] Wyzewa, 'Le Comte Tolstoï et la critique russe', *Revue des Deux Mondes*,
15 Mar. 1901, p. 459.

[2] Leroy-Beaulieu, 'Léon Tolstoï', *Revue des Deux Mondes*, 15 Dec. 1910, p. 825.

[3] Turgenev, on his death-bed, had written an appeal to Tolstoy destined to
become famous. Addressing his fellow-countryman as 'great writer of the Russian land', he called on him to return to his literary pursuits and to use the gifts
he had received from on high.

[4] Waliszewski, *Littérature russe*, p. 388.

[5] Doumic's ideas about Tolstoy's book were set forth in an article, 'Les
Idées de Tolstoï sur l'art', *Revue des Deux Mondes*, 15 May 1898, from which the
matter and quotations in these pages are taken.

in the fullest sympathy with the revolutionary. This somewhat
unlikely chance was, in part, due to a very real similarity between
the views of Tolstoy in matters of aesthetics and those held by
conservative criticism in France; but if the whole truth were known,
might not Doumic's favourable reception of the book be traced
also to the fact that Tolstoy had used his *Les Jeunes* as an important
source for documentation and had on one or two occasions in the
course of *What is Art?* quoted Doumic's words and complimented
him on his critical acuity?

Doumic does not, however, underwrite the whole of Tolstoy's
thesis. There were points in the pamphlet to which exception
might rightly be taken. Tolstoy is, for instance, too rigorous in the
application of his formulae. 'It is enough for us that a criterium of
art involves the rejection of Beethoven and the acceptance of Dumas
père: we conclude automatically that the criterium is erroneous.'[1]
Also, 'Tolstoy totally misunderstands the importance of form.'
Correctly applied, however, and used as a means, not an end, form
is a valuable aid to the propagation of a writer's ideas. From this
mistaken hostility to form Tolstoy's other errors derive: his disapproval of writers who live by their art; of literary schools and
coteries; of the activities of critics(!)

Tolstoy's idea that art should be the universal language could
without much difficulty, as Doumic was glad to point out, be
reconciled with the ideals of seventeenth- and eighteenth-century
French literature. And at many other points, by the value he puts
on simplicity of expression, by his reinstatement of a moral purpose in art, by his demand that an artist's life should be as irre-
proachable as his work, Tolstoy's doctrine is inseparable from
classicism. Tolstoy is to be complimented 'for having rejuvenated
the expression of ideas which are only old because they are true,
and for having returned to them by a new route'.

Doumic supports the Russian, too, in his denunciation of esoteri-
cism, 'the great danger which threatens modern art'; and, linking
up the ideas of *What is Art?* with his own and Brunetière's emphasis
on the part the writer must play in society, Doumic declares that
literature is at the cross-roads: 'Either it will go on being the idle
pastime designed to amuse a decadent society, in which case it will
rapidly perish from exhaustion. Or else it will gain understanding

---

[1] The references are to pp. 201–3 (for Beethoven) and p. 247 (for Dumas) in
Qu'est-ce que l'art? (Halpérine-Kaminsky's translation).

of the mission which it behoves it to fulfil, and which is to provide a unifying and uplifting power for the multitude of consciences adrift.'

The reasons why Tolstoy's book appealed to Doumic could, however, carry no weight with those (who after all were almost certainly in the majority in France) who were indifferent or antagonistic to the ideals of 'social art'; and Émile Faguet is probably in the right in saying[1] that *What is Art?* 'has, frankly, displeased nearly all of us'. He regards it as one more episode in the eternal struggle between the moralist and the artists: there is not the slightest doubt to which side Faguet inclines. His refutation of Tolstoy is acid. 'Quand on est un moraliste très convaincu, très passionné, et en même temps un esprit borné, on ne peut voir dans l'art, si l'on est combatif, qu'un ennemi; si l'on est timoré, qu'un danger; si l'on est indulgent, qu'une erreur; si l'on est dédaigneux, qu'une vanité. Et M. Léon Tolstoï est borné, combatif, timoré, indulgent et dédaigneux.'

Formulating his objections with greater precision, Faguet attacks Tolstoy's definition of art, which he thinks is far too narrow. Tolstoy had said that art was the means of conveying to all other men feelings one experiences oneself:[2] a child, having encountered a wolf, who tells the story in such a way as to communicate to others the feelings of terror and relief he experienced, may be said to have created art. Come, rejoins Faguet; this is not one half of art, no more than the fifth part. The question of beauty is ignored.[3] The child has created no beauty: but can there be any art without it?

Tolstoy's definition of art is falsified by overlimitation. By their fruits you shall judge them—and literary theories which only admit, as works of art, certain novels of Hugo, of George Eliot, which

[1] Faguet's remarks on Tolstoy's theory of art are contained in his *Propos littéraires*, 1ère série (1902), p. 311 et seq.

[2] What Tolstoy understood by art can be gathered from the following passage in *Qu'est-ce que l'art?* (p. 89): 'L'art n'est point, comme le déclarent les métaphysiciens, la manifestation de quelque idée mystérieuse de la Beauté, de Dieu; il n'est pas, comme l'affirment les physiologistes, un jeu dans lequel l'homme dépense son excédent d'énergie; il n'est point l'expression des émotions au moyen de signes extérieurs; il ne consiste pas dans la création d'objets qui plaisent; il n'est point surtout le plaisir. L'art constitue un moyen de communion entre les hommes s'unissant par les mêmes sentiments.'

[3] 'Apprécier une œuvre d'art suivant sa beauté, est en somme aussi étrange que de juger de la fertilité d'une terre d'après la beauté du site.' Ibid., p. 187.

appear to tend uniquely to the glorification of Beecher Stowe's *Uncle Tom's Cabin*[1] are, manifestly, abominably false. 'Into Tolstoy's definition of art, hardly anything can be fitted of what is called art, while certain things find their place which are perhaps not very artistic.'

Nothing, indeed, could be less likely to appeal to the French mind than this reversal of the normal order: utility (for the 'betterment of mankind' is after all utilitarianism writ large), was enthroned above beauty in the one sphere which is beauty's sanctified preserve.

Faguet analyses Tolstoy's method for arriving at a definition of art, as follows:

> To discover what art is, he has deliberately put on one side everything that men have deemed to be works of art; then he gives a definition of art according to his own whim; then, everything which failed to accord with this *a priori* and arbitrary definition, with what I shall call this 'spontaneous definition', he quite simply entered on the index.

And Faguet, sarcastically: 'Comme procédé de polémique, c'est assez bien trouvé; mais comme méthode philosophique, voilà du nouveau.' Faguet does not offer to provide his own definition of art. Perhaps the question was better left open, for the infinite cannot be defined by the finite, and art and beauty will cease to exist the hour that they can be resolved into words.

For French readers the most unfortunate part of Tolstoy's polemics was the crusade he undertook against certain notabilities or notorieties in French literature. Anyone who tries to assess the general drift of affairs among his contemporaries is liable to fall into serious blunders: and for one who, like Tolstoy, judges from afar, and devotes only a portion of his attention to the spectacle, the risks are even bigger. But the picture of Tolstoy as a benighted barbarian is most inaccurate, and when Faguet calls him 'a solitary dreamer, absolutely out of touch with the literary and artistic movement, receiving only distant and intermittent echoes of it', it is Faguet, not Tolstoy, who is the dreamer. The poets from whose writings Tolstoy quotes are those whom even to-day we should regard as most representative of that generation: Baudelaire, Verlaine, Mallarmé. The omission of Rimbaud should not surprise us,

[1] See ibid., pp. 264-5.

when we recall that virtually nothing of his poetry had been published until 1898, the very year of *What is Art?* The astonishing
thing about Tolstoy's literary judgements is not that he 'gave too
much importance to writers who had none', as was said by André
Beaunier,[1] but that he was so convinced of the soundness of the
criteria he had fashioned, that he could in all good faith dismiss the
huge reputation of the leading symbolists and pre-symbolists as
something wholly artificial, part of a sinister conspiracy of the idle
governing classes against the mass of mankind.

Decidedly, Tolstoy's *ars poetica* attracted little sympathy in the
country which had given so generous a welcome to his major works
in 1885: but then, Tolstoy had probably little expectation that
What is Art? would find champions or adherents among the literary
'professionals' he despised. The misfortune was that the book threw
a cloud over his reputation as a constructive thinker on other planes,
and shattered the confidence and admiration of many who had,
until then, followed with approving interest the development of
his philosophy.

This philosophy had not been enshrined by its author in a corpus
of a few major works like the systems of Kant, Schopenhauer,
Nietzsche, Bergson. Tolstoyism was a pragmatic rather than a
metaphysical system; his guiding principles once established, Tolstoy proceeded to apply them as a touchstone to every conceivable
sphere of human conduct, and his 'philosophical writings' consist
in a series of comments on all aspects of life, art, thought, religion.
It was left to others to attempt a synthesis of his thought. In France
this task was undertaken first by Georges Dumas (*Tolstoy et la
philosophie de l'amour*, 1893), who writes in guise of apologia that
Tolstoy's philosophy 'is very poorly known in France because it
has never been condensed; it seemed to me that it deserved to be
set forth systematically' (p. 190); and by Félix Schroeder (*Le
Tolstoïsme*, 1893), who states as his aim: 'in the writings which,
although scattered, are now nearly all accessible to French readers,
I have striven to follow . . . the formation of the doctrine to the
propagation of which the great novelist has henceforth devoted his
genius' (pp. 3–4). Among later ventures in the same field, the most
noteworthy are the works of Ossip-Lourier, who occupied a chair
at the University of Brussels (*Pensées de Tolstoï*, 1898; *La Philosophie de Léon Tolstoï*, 1899; *Nouvelles pensées de Tolstoï*, 1903;

[1] Beaunier, *Notes sur la Russie* (1901), p. 108.

Tolstoï . . . le Tolstoïsme, 1907). The religious aspect of Tolstoyism formed the basis of not a few university theses, submitted in the nineties by those aspiring to degrees in theology—both Catholics (É. Fremont, *Les Idées religieuses de Tolstoï*, 1892; L. Pellier, *La Morale sociale de Tolstoï*, 1893), and Protestants (P. Maffre, *Le Tolstoïsme et le Christianisme*, 1896; É. Majal, *La Pensée religieuse de Tolstoï*, 1899).

Such syntheses were faced with certain difficulties. Tolstoy was not always perfectly consistent in his pronouncements, which was perhaps inevitable since his thought was in continual evolution, and had as its basis a highly personal and arbitrary interpretation of the New Testament gospels. But on the whole, 'le tolstoïsme' emerged as a series of principles and an attitude of mind well-defined enough to permit of reasoned discussion.

To enter into an examination of Tolstoy's system here would be neither necessary nor useful: rather our interests lie in the reactions of the French to the extraordinary proposals Tolstoy made them. To some, especially the neo-Catholics and the body of opinion disappointed in the 'bankruptcy of science', there was much in the principles of Tolstoyism which appealed; pacifists also found a powerful reinforcement to their arguments; Protestants saw in Tolstoy's defiance of the Orthodox Church a second Luther in arms against a degenerate priesthood. But equally there was much, especially in detail, which repelled French habits of thought and personal behaviour—the exaltation of manual labour over intellectual pursuits, the sweeping condemnation of nearly all forms of artistic expression, Tolstoy's distorted attitude to sexual problems, &c.

Between outright dismissal of Tolstoyism as a utopian pipe-dream, and complete acceptance of it as the one path to salvation, there were obviously many middle roads; and along one or other of these most thinking Frenchmen travelled.

The social implications of Tolstoyism sprang directly from its moral and religious implications; from the New Testament commandment to render good for evil, Tolstoy deduced that resistance to an aggressive war, for instance, should not be permitted, that the prosecution of criminals in courts of law was indefensible, &c.

Right from the first Tolstoy's name became associated in France

with 'nihilism'.[1] Tolstoy had himself declared, in *Ma Religion*
(published in France in 1885): 'For thirty-five years of my life, I
have been a nihilist, in the exact meaning of the term, i.e. not a
revolutionary socialist, but a man who believes in nothing.' Tolstoy's interpretation of the Gospels led him to deny every claim of
society and civilization as it is constituted in the modern world;
but 'that does not trouble Tolstoy. He is scarcely more interested
in the State than the raskolnik (schismatic) who looks on the State
as the Kingdom of Hell.'[2]

Conservatives, as might be expected, regarded Tolstoy's social
theories, at the best, with humorous indulgence; when they were
less well-disposed, with anger and indignation.[3] Doumic relates
the story that Tolstoy told against himself, how he once went up
to a soldier whom he had seen ill-treating a beggar. Tolstoy asked
him reproachfully whether he had not read the Gospels. The
beggar had been asking for alms in a public place where this was
forbidden, and the unusually quick-witted grenadier retorted:
'Have *you* read *Military Regulations*?'—'Let us then', Doumic
draws the moral, 'read the New Testament, but let us not omit to
complete our studies by reading *Military Regulations* too. . . . Anyone, whoever he is, soldier or civilian, in the army or in life, who
refuses to mount guard, that man, for all the fine phrases you may
invent, is guilty of dereliction of duty.'[4]

These words of Doumic occur in a review he wrote of *Resurrection*. By publishing this novel (in 1899) Tolstoy went back on his
resolution never again to invent a story designed to be read by the
leisured classes; but the cause he had nearest at heart was better
served by this piece of fiction than by any number of pamphlets,
open letters, and broadsheets. The book was a vehicle for some
most vehement social criticism; and because it was a novel, and a
novel by Tolstoy, and the first full-length novel by Tolstoy for
twenty odd years, everyone read it, even members of that section
of the community which the author held responsible for the evils
he described.

Resurrection, according to another of its reviewers in France, was

[1] See Vogüé, op. cit., p. 280; Leroy-Beaulieu: *L'Empire des Tsars*, tome III,
pp. 541, 547.
[2] Leroy-Beaulieu, op. cit., p. 540.
[3] As, for instance, Paul Bourget. See above, p. 132.
[4] Doumic, 'Le Nouveau Roman de Tolstoï', *Revue des Deux Mondes*, 15 Feb.
1900, p. 934.

'above all an indictment of the bourgeois way of life',[1] and it
reaped praise or blame largely according to whether the reader was
dissatisfied or content with the social order. A revolutionary like
Charles-Louis Philippe praised Tolstoy's new novel to the skies;[2]
conservatives regarded it with distaste, spoke of the 'defects in
[Tolstoy's] analysis of society', and insinuated that Tolstoy's
philanthropic emotionalism was turning his head.[3]

Édouard Rod, in a novel (*L'Inutile Effort*, published in 1903),
reported (a little satirically perhaps) a typical discussion of the book
at a Parisian dinner-table, by a gathering fairly representative of
cultivated French circles at that time. More vividly than in the
book-review columns of the periodicals, we can catch here the
vibration of the shock which *Resurrection* produced in 'polite
society' at the opening of the twentieth century.

The discussion is started by Gastellier, an architect.

A man who went in for every bold novelty, every piece of exoticism,
always eager to adopt new fashions and shore up dubious reputations,
the architect was one of the anonymous factors in the cults which swept
Paris; he supported with the eloquence of the beer-parlour advanced
opinions that he did not always understand, and which were justified or
upset, depending on whether his admiration happened to go to men of
genius or charlatans, between whom he made no distinctions. For two
or three minutes he talked, loudly uttering a flood of exclamations, in
which figured such words as 'enormous—sublime—truth'.

Gastellier is interrupted peremptorily by Mme Du Rosoy, a
woman of the world 'whose enormous bosom swelled behind a pink
bodice'. Her verdict, delivered 'with an energy which made her
shoulders quiver' is: 'Tolstoy has a great deal of talent, no one can
deny it. An immense talent! But his book is a bad one.'

Her husband chimes in to the effect that 'the subject is un-
pleasant' and other guests add that it is not even new. But Gastellier
is not so soon suppressed. 'The subject is not new, because there
are no new subjects. But it is eternal, wonderful! And with what
power this old moujik handles it! It becomes a terrible indictment
of the rottenness of our society, a speech in defence. . . .'—'Of

[1] M. A. Leblond, 'La Justice russe, d'après les œuvres de Gogol, Dostoïevsky,
Tourguéniev et Tolstoï', *Revue Bleue*, 11 Nov. 1899, p. 626.

[2] See above, p. 161.

[3] H. Bordeaux, 'La *Résurrection* de Tolstoï', *Revue Hebdomadaire*, 6 Jan. 1900,
p. 133.

unmarried mothers, my dear Sir, of unmarried mothers!' bursts in
Mme Du Rosoy. 'A class well worth defending, I must say! The
idea of Nekhludov marrying this Maslova, no, but really, can you
imagine it? He, a prince, a real prince! . . . It's raving madness,
I declare.'

M. Arondel—a lawyer, counsellor in the Court of Appeals—
speaks with the voice of calm good sense:

You should say, it is the morbid manifestation of a stricken conscience,
and from this point of view I believe the book has a high moral value.
These extravagant ideas do occasionally ripen in disordered minds under
the pressure of fear or remorse. But Tolstoy imagines perhaps he has
proved heaven knows what truth of general import, and that is where
he begins to go off the rails. His novel is not a speech for the defence or
for the prosecution; it is only a story . . . rather a long one, and which
would have a bad effect if it were taken too seriously.

And Arondel develops the idea: Nekhludov was certainly at fault
in seducing Maslova, but with the passage of time the misdeed
became irreparable, and all Nekhludov's efforts to right the wrong
only worsen the situation: 'His idea of saving her is that of a school-
boy. And, as he cannot raise her to his level, he would be preposterous and blameworthy in marrying her, that is, in introducing
her into regular society, where she would create a scandal.' Nekhludov should have contented himself with behaving more thought-
fully in future. Arondel's advice to him would be: Choose a wife
of your own class, raise up an honest family, and warn your
children against the siren-calls of passion(!) 'That is how he could
resurrect in the true sense of the word and become a useful member
of society!' As for his victim, it is true that the good advice
Nekhludov can give to his children does not help Maslova, but
'society will profit more than if she became a princess, and perhaps
the mother of his children. In any case a person of her kind could
not really be interesting. . . .' The mask is dropped: M. Arondel's
words are spoken by the very voice of upper middle-class society,
secretly outraged by Tolstoy's aspersions and endeavouring to
refute them by specious arguments about the good of society in
general: in truth Arondel is concerned with the good of his class
alone, the ruling class in the Third Republic as Nekhludov's was
the ruling class in Tsarist Russia.

Much as *Resurrection* may have displeased those who controlled
the destinies of France at the turn of the century, it can scarcely be

said that Tolstoy gratified any more those men who sought to overthrow the bastions of political and economic power. Tolstoyism was almost as suspect to the political Left as to the political Right. Tolstoy had in common with other social revolutionaries, or merely Fabian socialists, only his desire to overthrow or refashion the State. The methods by which he proposed to achieve this end were diametrically opposed to theirs. Violent means were condemned as an infringement of the law of charity, constitutional means were ineffective, since they could only alter the framework of society, whereas the evil lay in the heart of man. Consequently, Tolstoy evoked little sympathy either among the 'terrorist' radicals or among democratic socialists. Georges Dumas wrote: 'His socialism in every aspect . . . is too elastic, and can lie down with every kind of tyranny. Tolstoy protests, it is true, against social wrongs, against man's oppression of man, but his protests run a great risk of being unavailing, if to the oppressors he can speak only of love, and to the victims, only of resignation.'[1] Jean Jaurès was afraid that Tolstoy loved the people for those very virtues—piety and resignation—which perpetuated their misery, 'and then it seems that we are faced with this terrible paradox that Tolstoy, while loving, pitying, and admiring the people, would cease to be on their side if the people ceased to be resigned to their fate, or if they did not adopt the pacific means that Tolstoy wishes to force on them'.[2] Jaurès had little faith in passive resistance as a weapon of combat.

The outstanding features of the religious side of Tolstoyism are firstly, the founder's arbitrary and personal interpretation of the Scriptures, and secondly, his rejection of and contempt for all Church teaching, dogma, ritual, &c.

Tolstoy's method of reading the Bible he has described quite candidly: of the words of Christ as recorded, he underlined with a red pencil those which appeared to him to be genuine: the anthology of sayings that emerged constituted the true Testament.

Such a basis for religious faith could not but appear ingenuous in France, especially among Catholics who in any case had scant patience with private interpretations of the Word of God. Their shocked bewilderment was voiced by Jean Lionnet in his *Évolution des idées chez quelques-uns de nos contemporains* (1903); and an even

---

[1] G. Dumas, *Tolstoy et la philosophie de l'amour*, p. 201.
[2] Jaurès, 'Léon Tolstoï', *Revue Socialiste*, 1911, p. 206.

more forceful attack on the religion of Tolstoyism was launched, after its founder's death, by Paul Bourget. He argued, conventionally enough, that religion, a phenomenon of an essentially gregarious order, has never existed and never will exist outside a church of some kind, and that a man proposing the organization of 'individual religion' has about as much hope of success as one proposing to square the circle. 'The last thirty years of Tolstoy's existence were spent twisting and turning, in feverish revolt, in enthusiasm and impotence, about this insoluble problem.'[1]

Protestants had not quite the same reasons for disliking Tolstoyism as Catholics had. A fair sample of Protestant thought on the subject is provided by Édouard Rod's essay on Tolstoy in his *Idées morales du temps présent*. The chief point the author is concerned to establish is that there is nothing transcendental in this new philosophy. Tolstoy is a man of action, not a contemplative. His belief in God is founded on none of the customary props that men use for faith—such as the desire to rise above terrestrial occupations and to seek the traces of divine influence in human affairs, or the hope of being rewarded in Heaven for good deeds done on earth, or the inability to tolerate the idea that death will bring dissolution of the personality. Tolstoy draws a strict dividing-line between the knowable and the Unknowable, and does not attempt to overleap it. He is not a mystic, but a moralist pure and simple.[2]

Founded as it was on reason, abjuring all theological apparatus and mystic appeal, this arid doctrine could have had little following in France. Rather it was the secular face of Tolstoyism, the appeal for a renewal of the practice of the Christian virtues, which aroused the enthusiasm of such disciples as he found in France. Tolstoyism was 'not so much a religion as a philosophy, and less a philosophy than a code of morals, or better still, a conception of life'.[3] Georges Dumas took Tolstoy's philosophy to be the source of the neo-Christian movement, itself a reaction against Bentham and Stuart Mill who had regarded virtue as just 'enlightened self-interest'. Tolstoy aimed at establishing the doctrine of love without making it depend on divine revelation or command. 'In a word, the object is to make a natural and rational philosophy out of this religion which for so long we have been led to believe flies in the face of

---

[1] Bourget, *Pages de critique et de doctrine* (1912), p. 169.
[2] Rod, op. cit., pp. 243–4.
[3] Beaunier, op. cit., p. 213.

nature and reason'—a kind of union of the spirit of science and the spirit of Christianity.[1]

This would have spelt the end of religion, in the forms it had taken hitherto: this is why he found no apologists, let alone adherents, among believing Protestants or Catholics. But the odour of sanctity which still clung to Tolstoyism made it no less repellent to the average free-thinker. Generally speaking, Tolstoyism as a religious doctrine made no headway in France, for no one was prepared to take it seriously.

Although there is little reason to suppose that Tolstoyism gained the slightest foothold in France, although, in fact, far from being accepted as a practical guide to living, the consensus of opinion was that its implementation was not feasible—nevertheless, Tolstoyism had, undeniably, a strong appeal, and for a period, no doubt, provoked many a heated argument.

The renown Tolstoy had won himself previously in the realm of literature admittedly increased the sensationalism of his spectacular abandonment of art and his assumption of the mantle of the prophet-preacher. But the great emotions aroused by his thought cannot be accounted for by any extrinsic interest attached to the man himself, nor by the revolutionary and uncompromising nature of his teaching. Tolstoy's 'crisis' and 'conversion' illustrated a form of spiritual anguish widespread in Europe in the late nineteenth century. Tolstoyism was a myth and a symbol.

Never has a moral crisis been greater or more painful than that of the age in which we live—and in every country. Every mind awaits some great event. Those of higher intellect strive, after their cast of mind, to peer behind the mysterious veil of the future. Every sincere and conscientious pronouncement awakes sympathetic echoes in human hearts. And that is why no voice, for many centuries, has resounded over the world so sonorously as Tolstoy's. In a time when it was so needful to adduce new proofs of truths so often demonstrated, he has succeeded in compelling the most hardened to hearken his word. The religion he preaches, the religion of Work and Love, is too pure not to wake suffering souls, especially in the present hour of moral and social faint-heartedness. The example of his own life is too fine not to arouse echoes in every corner of the world.[2]

[1] G. Dumas, op. cit., p. ix.
[2] Ossip-Lourier, *La Philosophie de Léon Tolstoï* (1899), p. 186.

Tolstoy offered an escape from a dilemma familiar to his age:
the perennial dogmas of Christianity having been shattered or
corroded by the discoveries of material science, man was left without a spiritual objective in living. Tolstoy himself has described
how the urge to suicide was, before his conversion, so strong in
him that he carefully hid his firearms in order not to be tempted to
use them against himself.

Tolstoyism was a substitute for the older ethical systems of the
great religions (Christianity in particular) which explained the
injustices and imperfections of this world as a test of spiritual
quality, and promised bliss after the grave for those who had
suffered on earth and retained their faith. Tolstoy held out no such
hope for his disciples; but he maintained, vigorously and un-
tiringly, that personal happiness in this life, if only the genial
contentment of the sagacious moujik, was attainable through the
universal observance of certain precepts.

The appeal of Tolstoyism was to those earnest minds who felt
they needed a moral authority on which to regulate their lives, but
whose reliance on the consecrated religious-ethical system had
been broken against the rationalist scepticism of the eighteenth
century and the scientific materialism of the nineteenth.

The active, practising and proselytizing 'tolstoïsants' in France
were probably very few: quite apart from the claims of other
solutions to the problem of the meaning of life, the code of
behaviour laid down by Tolstoy was difficult to put into operation.
But there were others—'le troupeau des snobs tolstoïsants' as
Péguy called them—those who professed to embrace the system
but who were merely following a whim of fashion and in actual
fact perverting and discrediting the master's word. These false
disciples were in all likelihood more numerous. Rolland pilloried
one of them in *La Révolte*, in the person of Mannheim. The details
of Rolland's pen-portrait are more revealing than any generalizations that could be hazarded about this type.

Mannheim

took up with every grotesque utopia—usually of the noblest sort. He
was too keen-witted and had too good a sense of humour to believe in
them entirely; he never allowed himself to be swept off his feet, even by
one of his crazes, and he never compromised himself in the application
of his theories. But he could not get along without a hobby-horse, and
he changed it frequently. For the moment his hobby-horse was

benevolence. It was not enough for him to be benevolent naturally; he wanted to appear so: he made a profession of benevolence, he paraded it. Out of a spirit of perverse antagonism against . . . German rigorism, militarism, Philistinism, he was Tolstoyan, evangelist, Buddhist—not too sure himself what he was—the apostle of a soft and spineless morality, unctuous, easily practised, full of effusive forgiveness of every sin, especially the sins of the flesh. . . . This Christianity of the gutter-snipe was only awaiting an opportunity to give way to some other hobby-horse—any one: that of brute force, for instance, the imperialism of the 'laughing lions'.

The vogue of Tolstoyism was quickly over. So long as Tolstoy remained alive and concerned himself actively and volubly with day-to-day occurrences, maintaining a voluminous correspondence with all manner of people all over the globe, remaining, in fact, in the public eye, then Tolstoyism was a force still to be reckoned with. But the manner of his death was such as to cause consterna-tion among the faithful: his undignified flight from his house and family a day or so before the end gave rise to speculation on the part of the indiscreet, and many of those who in his lifetime had ridiculed and opposed him the most thought, with the ultra-conservative Catholic Eugène Tavernier, that this final act was a gesture of despair, a confession of failure. 'In the end he saw him-self misunderstood by his admirers. . . . The goodwill and love which he preached by virtue of his individual authority alone, have sprung up in the shape of hatred and despair. He dies triumphant, hailed as a prophet, but convicted of having persisted in a muddle-headed and disastrous course.'[1]

The outbreak of the First World War seems to have marked the end of the age tormented by the essentially *personal* problems which Tolstoy spent the latter part of his life in resolving. In Russia the forces of militant socialism triumphed, and Tolstoy's gentle theorizing about the power of non-resistance to evil was ignored not only in his own country but abroad also. In post-war Europe the pressing questions did not centre around personal conduct, but around social and economic organization; and France, locked in a struggle for existence during these four years and emerging weakened, disrupted, and uncertain of her future, found little that seemed to concern her in the oracles of this pre-war ascetic.

In truth, Tolstoyism is essentially a philosophy for the satiated,

[1] Tavernier, 'Tolstoï', *Le Correspondant*, 25 Nov. 1910, p. 666.

designed to infuse moral vigour into the veins of a generation cloyed by too much security. In a post-war world in which it becomes increasingly evident that salvation—at least for the time being—lies in one form or another of social organization, types of primitive social anarchy such as Tolstoy proposes will obviously find slight sympathy. 1914, in fact, rang down the curtain on Tolstoyism as on innumerable other phenomena surviving from the nineteenth century.

XII

TOLSTOY AND THE YOUNGER GENERATION

IN 1886 Rolland and Suarès were both emerging from adolescence;[1] together, at the École Normale, they 'discovered' Tolstoy; and throughout the early manhood of both this figure continued to dominate the horizon and to influence the development of their thought. Unlike most of the other French writers in whom we have hitherto studied the impact of the Russian novelist, their outlook on life and their artistic ideals were not set firmly in certain moulds before they came to read the foreign masterpieces. In them one may look for a more flexible approach and a greater aptitude for enthusiasm: and one will not be disappointed. For Rolland, Tolstoy was 'the only real friend in all European art'; for Suarès he was the hero of the age: 'Tolstoy's heart and imagination are the widest space in the world to-day; and this old man is the only example vouchsafed to us of the Life Sublime.'

Suarès' first publication on the subject of Tolstoy dates from 1899; it was written on the occasion of Tolstoy's seventieth birthday the year before. In 1911, in the *Cahiers de la Quinzaine* (12th series, 7th cahier), he published *Tolstoï vivant*, in which the earlier study was completed by further reflections added between 1905 and 1910. Finally, in 1938, the entire essay or series of essays was reproduced in the volume *Trois grands vivants*,[2] flanked by Suarès' studies of Cervantes and Baudelaire.[3]

To a certain extent, then, one is able to follow the evolution of the moral influence of Tolstoy on Suarès, and to observe the very pronounced shift undergone by Suarès' attitude to Tolstoy. The essay of 1899 shows Suarès still largely dominated by Tolstoy's

[1] Rolland was born in 1866, Suarès in 1868.

[2] Quotations from Suarès in this chapter are to be understood as having been taken from this publication, unless another reference is given in a footnote.

[3] In addition, he seems to have written a short article for Tolstoy's eightieth birthday, in 1908. I have been unable to discover whether this was published at the time it was written, and if so, where. It appears as chapter XLVI of *Sur la Vie*, a collection of essays by Suarès published in 1923, and is there headed 'Tolstoï parle'.

thought, and even more by the grandeur of Tolstoy's figure. In the later essays one can perceive a distinct loosening of these bonds of sympathy.

If, from our special point of view, Rolland's book on Tolstoy is almost too judicious an account, Suarès' study seems at times to escape completely from the subject. In seeking evidence of the influence of Tolstoy on the two French minds, we are hampered by the objectivity of the first quite as much as by the excessive concern of the second to set up his own views in opposition to those of Tolstoy. Suarès does not so much give an interpretation of Tolstoy as use his conception of the Russian as a hook on which to drape his subtle generalizations. One can find examples of this digressiveness almost anywhere—the passage on humour, for instance (p. 139), on egoism (p. 143), &c. Suarès is not a critic, nor a biographer, not even an essayist, and least of all a philosopher; he is a poet: part of *Tolstoï vivant* (the *Prose de l'Évasion*, at the conclusion) is, in fact, a prose-poem. In such a man one looks not for logical argument, but suggestive phrasing; and there is no lack of this. To determine the general drift of his pages, occasionally brilliant and even witty, but not infrequently obscure, is not the simplest of undertakings.

'Je ne controverse point contre Tolstoï; je le montre' he declared (p. 110). But he held to this resolution only in his first essay; and although it is the longest, even here he shows by no means a universal picture—only certain facets of the man, of his life, his thought, his art—which Suarès found either particularly admirable or particularly pernicious.

In his first essay Suarès devotes surprisingly little attention to Tolstoy's artistic productions proper, save in so far as these shed light on his religious doctrine; in his later essays the literary work of Tolstoy finds scarcely any mention at all. In this Suarès is typical of the later interpreters of Tolstoy. An older man, Lucien Descaves, who had made his name in 1889 with a novel in the naturalist manner (*Sous-Offs*), might ask to be allowed to hold cheap all efforts to get to the bottom of 'Tolstoy's Doctrine', and limit his admiration to the works of art which were *War and Peace* and *Resurrection*.[1] But the more modern tendency was undoubtedly

---

[1] See the *Revue Internationale de Sociologie*, Mar. 1900. The remark was made in answer to an 'enquête littéraire' about Tolstoyism initiated by Marguerite Gerfault.

to take Tolstoy at his word and give more attention to the apostle than to the novelist.

In our chapter on Vogüé, we observed this critic wrestling with a dilemma: should Tolstoy be viewed as a 'realist', or as an 'idealist', the two being mutually exclusive? Suarès cuts the knot by rejecting the second alternative. Tolstoy is a realist, for Tolstoy 'is in perpetual quest of the truth, heeds only the truth, and neglects none of the elements of the truth' (p. 139). Suarès has nothing but contemptuous ridicule for Vogüé's view of Tolstoy as an apostle of social pity. Tolstoy is miles away from sentimentalism: he would have become an implacable satirist in the manner of Swift had it not been for his 'will to Good'. He is not at all indulgent. 'A burning love of truth is not compatible with indulgence: indulgence must be left to the spineless creatures, or to those who have grown tired of everything, even of truth' (p. 154). Tolstoy's analytical genius, not sparing even those he loves the most, his 'brutal sincerity', drove him eventually to solitude. The charity to which he aspired forbade him the exercise of the perspicacity which is part of his nature: in order not to judge men he fled them. This explains why he stopped writing novels. Suarès may well have hit on at least part of the truth here.

Like Rolland, Suarès was perplexed and disturbed by Tolstoy's strictures on art itself—the search for and the cultivation of beauty. In this first essay he presents a fairly objective account of Tolstoy's aesthetic ideals. He shows that in appreciating art merely in terms of its social usefulness, Tolstoy is reasoning soundly in accordance with his premisses. Suarès, however, denies the premisses.

To Tolstoy's classical (or Platonic) outlook Suarès opposes that of a belated Romantic, convinced of the relativity of beauty. Tolstoy's stipulation that art should be universally intelligible is 'justified as a principle, but the searching test of time has rendered it doubtful'; his further stipulation that art should unite men by treating what is of common interest to them all is also allowed by Suarès, with the important reservation that those for whom the artist is asked to work should not be too far removed from him intellectually: Tolstoy's 'paysan chaste, égaré dans un musée' is tacitly eliminated by this condition (pp. 104–5).

Suarès will return to the discussion of Tolstoy's aesthetic ideas in his later writings: he will be much more violent, then, in his repudiation of them.

In this early essay, Suarès gives more space to Tolstoy's religious philosophy than to any other aspect of the man and his work.

Firstly, he considers how far this preaching can be put into practice. Tolstoy's fundamental idea is that of the Gospels, that men should become as little children, to enter into the Kingdom of Heaven, to enter on to the Happy Life. Tolstoy's God is 'the God of a nation of passionate children, ablaze with longing for this happy life' (p. 91). But the Christ-like idea cannot be put into effect in a hostile world: the community of children will be massacred by a horde of Turks, and 'the race of evil-doers will profit by the righteousness of the righteous, in order to perpetuate their own evil-doing. In Tolstoy's mind, perfection is the exercise of defeat and martyrdom' (pp. 92–3).

Suarès does not pretend that an ideal is necessarily false because it is unattainable: in his view the principal objection to Tolstoy's theories is none of the rationalist ones which are commonly brought to bear. 'It is clear that his doctrine rests on an act of faith, like a religion' (p. 124). No, the principal objection is Tolstoy himself. Not his own deviations from his principles, not the contradictions which can be tracked down inside his doctrine, but his own character.

His arrogance first—this 'strange pride' which is 'the strength which reason puts in its arguments, and with which it pursues truth's enemy, either by sarcasm, or by contempt' (pp. 109–10). Then his egoism, the source of his strength. 'Proud, masterful and passionate, Tolstoy, who has rather unworthily been styled an egoist, is only an egoist in the sense that he has a strong soul, that he knows it, and that he does not conceal this strength' (p. 144). Then his passion: the most passionate of men pleads against the passions, and with effectiveness only because he is so passionate. 'If he was not born so full of strength, let alone of violence, he would not have been the heroic soldier of truth which he is seen to be. The saints who sow their saintliness abroad are those same violent men whom their saintliness condemns' (pp. 124–5). It is interesting to note that Suarès' whole argument here against Tolstoy is based on a double use of the word 'passionate'. Tolstoy's attack on the passions is according to Suarès invalidated because he conducts it himself with passion. But the passions Tolstoy combats are the passion for gain, the passion of lust: *his* passion is the passion of righteousness. Name it zeal or fervour and Suarès is confounded.

From this false start Suarès proceeds to examine Tolstoy's pacifism, and strays into some poisonous errors. Arguing along lines dangerously similar to those later to be followed by Benito Mussolini,[1] he states that wars are inevitable—they are either waged by strong nations or incurred by weak ones. Tolstoy gives the palm to the latter; but 'he forgets to weigh the ransom of this short-lived good, to calculate the price it costs. Rome the conqueror is terrible; but Rome vanquished is rotten.' Even if peace at any price does not necessarily mean bowing the head, the love of tranquillity cannot be separated from weakness—'and, in my view, he who says weakness, says impurity. . . . Nothing is pure save that which resists, and does not fear to struggle' (p. 127). Socrates, then, in the hands of his jailers, Christ in the midst of his tormenters, are impure? Suarès' fatal propensity for blinding himself with the flash of words is nowhere more apparent: only a little reflection was needed to convince him that resistance by force of arms is only one possible way of defeating violence, and that according to many it does so only at the cost of engendering more violence. In abjuring this weapon Tolstoy had consecrated the possibly more effective one of passive resistance.

Suarès concludes that if war is violence, violence is strength. 'And moreover, nothing is worth anything, save by its strength. Tolstoy is the living proof of this. His incomparable life is that of a violent man. . . . And that is why there is no graver objection to Tolstoy's doctrine than Tolstoy himself' (p. 128). The absurdity of this confusion between material strength and moral strength, between the force of a bayonet charge and the force of a man possessed of a conviction of what is right and what is wrong, needs scarcely to be further underlined. Suarès' eyes seem never to have been opened to this contradiction, and the arguments he later developed to rebut Tolstoyism take their spring from this point.

Suarès' next essay, dated 1907, is entitled 'Pour et Contre Tolstoï'. In a preliminary section, he gives a few details about the changes in his attitude to Tolstoy—details which explain the change

[1] To whom Suarès devoted one of the essays in his volume *Présences* (1926).

of tone in his subsequent remarks. He started, he says, by a complete acceptance of the doctrine, in a 'passion for holiness'. But his
conversion was not a disinterested one: 'When I was most desirous
of lending myself to all men, then I chiefly wore the appearance of
wishing to master them and lay them in subjection.' He wrote to
Tolstoy, who did not understand him. 'At bottom, I wanted to be
a saint like him, in order like him to father immortal works of art.'
There is the note of sincerity here which seems to render faithfully
both the original enthusiasm of Suarès for Tolstoy, and the disillusion that followed when he realized that 'in art, it is not possible
that the passions should be silent'.

He has had to reject Tolstoyism—the scales have fallen from his
eyes. 'I see Tolstoy as he was, not as I once loved him. I know full
well he is not my man. He is no longer so righteous as I was inclined
to think in my credulity. . . . Tolstoy is not a saint: and he has no
love for artists.' His influence on Suarès has been partly good,
partly bad. He proposed conundrums, and gave the wrong solutions.
'He made me anxious, without delivering me of anxiety. Tula is
not the universe, and not everyone can turn moujik.' But the 'four
or five years' during which Suarès was directly under his influence
have not been entirely wasted, since they have led him to a deeper
knowledge of himself (pp. 177-9).

In the pages that follow there is little 'for', and much 'against',
Tolstoy. No opponent is so bitter as a disciple who has lost faith.
Also it must be remembered that in the interval Suarès had come
to love Dostoevsky: and it would appear that it is not possible for
a Frenchman completely to accept both the Russian novelists. For
Vogüé, Tolstoy eclipsed Dostoevsky; for Hennequin, Dostoevsky
obscured Tolstoy. Rolland, scarcely once in his published works,
refers to Dostoevsky, but on the other hand, when Gide mentions
Tolstoy, it is to disparage him mightily in the comparison.[1]

Suarès deals afresh with many of the points he had touched on
in his earlier essay: but his attitude is immeasurably more hostile.
Now, he is inclined to regard Tolstoy's arrogance as an inexcusable
lust for domination. The apostle is only the despot in disguise. 'To
convert others is to become their master. Be it in the name of truth,

---

[1] Notably at the beginning of *Dostoïevsky*, but also, and most outspokenly, in
one of his most recently published works, the *Journal, 1939–42* (see the entry
for 10 Sept. 1941).

or of right, or of the law of the fist, it is always force. . . . When Tolstoy preaches, he tries to be the strongest, as in the days when he pilloried Napoleon with such wrathful zest' (p. 206).

His 'ferocious ego' drives him to demolish his rivals in the world of art—Shakespeare, Ibsen, Beethoven, Wagner (Tolstoy's essay on Shakespeare had appeared only that year, 1907, and was probably the occasion for Suarès' outcry). Tolstoy sweeps away the summits and is left with a desert in which he alone stands erect, the new prophet of a Christ doubtfully invoked. 'Gospel in hand, Tolstoy detests superiority. Every rival has to give way before him.' His idea of popular art is a mere pretext—'il a toujours un moujik dans sa poche pour lui donner saintement raison', and Suarès derides this idea fiercely. 'The moujik! What a fine judge of art and thought! Schopenhauer shall be no philosopher, because the moujik does not understand the first word about the Will to live; and because also he cannot understand the Quartet in C sharp minor, because a sketch of Rembrandt's means nothing to him, we are asked to condemn painting and music' (pp. 224–5). We are no longer sailing along an argument, but twisting in the midst of a hurricane of invective.

Between Suarès' aristocratic ideal of art, and the democratic, not to say proletarian ideal of Tolstoy, a great gulf is fixed. Suarès points out to Tolstoy that 'the mind of the common man and the minds of great artists may not differ in their nature, but they differ in the ways they have been exercised'. Culture is not to be left out of account: but questions of morality are.

Art is not made for good or evil. It is made to transport man at one bound into a higher sphere. . . . Hence, it is always a power for good. What matter if it causes the weaklings to perish. I should like to know what is to save them! Red meat kills the babe at the breast; it is not meant for sucklings, but for the athlete. The history of the world is darkened by moralists inviting men to become sucklings [pp. 188–9].

Tolstoy's utopia is the tomb, for Suarès. 'To make a pact with death, and have done with death, that is what Tolstoy understands by living. God and righteousness are only inferior substitutes for the Void.'[1] His social ideals—the equal division of the land, goods held in common, a world of contented villagers—what food is this for the spiritual hunger of real men?

[1] Suarès, *Sur la Vie*, p. 352.

How he underrates the world, after all! The most horrible thing in Tolstoy and in religions like his, is that however useful they are for the village, they will always be unusable by those two, three, ten or a hundred men who have infinitely more of the man about them than all the villagers. I am a man; I don't go around begging for crumbs [pp. 208–9].

This is nothing more than Raskolnikov's argument in justification of his murder of the usurer, at any rate in its early stages, as he puts it to Porfiry: one perceives how the fascination of Dostoevsky has taken toll of Suarès' loyalty to Tolstoy.

Suarès' faith is in fullness of being. Tolstoy's, as he sees it, in restriction of being. 'Goodness is everything which contributes to life. Everything that enriches the living creature is good. Everything that contributes to death and bears us towards it, is evil. That is my charity, which Tolstoy detests: it is not social' (p. 217). His guiding principles are individualism, aristocracy, the strong prevailing over the weak; Nietzsche, in fact, even more than Dostoevsky, has replaced Tolstoy in Suarès' affections.

In the end, Suarès, 'poète tout brûlant de l'amour de la renaissance italienne', as Rolland described him, found Tolstoy altogether too uncomfortable a bedfellow. He admired him for his strength, but detested him for the use to which he put that strength. The individualist in Suarès abominated Tolstoy the anti-individualist; and the lover of life, too, was revolted by the immolation of the passions urged by Tolstoy, his yearning after death. 'He condemns everything I strive to preserve and absolve' (p. 191). Suarès had become as thoroughgoing an 'anti-tolstoïen' as it is possible to imagine.

Tolstoy's last act before his death, his flight from his ancestral domain, in some measure rehabilitated him in Suarès' eyes: and in 1910 he wrote the 'Prose de l'Évasion', a kind of hymn to the 'cher vieillard', who had at last chosen holiness as the better part of patience, and who had gone out into the desert like the hermits of old. Tolstoy's inability to shake himself free from the atmosphere of prosperity at Yasnaya Polyana had troubled Suarès as it had many other Frenchmen.[1] Tolstoy, he had written, 'sees a crime in

---

[1] 'Il dit aux autres: dépouillez-vous, suivez la parole du Christ, mais il n'a ni assez de vertu ni assez de volonté pour se soumettre à son propre enseignement. . . . Ah! s'il s'était dépouillé de tout, s'il s'était résigné à gagner son pain à la

the ownership of land; but all his family commits it with him, and along with them he profits by it' (p. 205). This final act was a gesture of liberation: the poet in Suarès saw the complete appropriateness of the further, and final, liberation which followed hard on—the liberation from the flesh, from life itself.

Romain Rolland never made a secret of the profound veneration he had for Tolstoy. Like Suarès he had a mind more attracted to personalities than to ideas: he had written lives of Michelangelo and Beethoven[1] before he wrote his biography of Tolstoy.

Rolland 'discovered' Tolstoy in early youth.[2] We have already quoted the passage at the beginning of the *Vie de Tolstoï*, where he describes the fervour with which Tolstoy was read and discussed by the students of the École Normale in 1886.[3] Elsewhere, he declares that in 1887, for two or three years, he had lived wrapped in the atmosphere of Tolstoy's thought: 'I was certainly more at home with his creations, with *War and Peace*, *Anna Karenina*, *The Death of Ivan Ilyitch*, than with any great French work.'[4]

Although he never met Tolstoy, Rolland was in correspondence with the Russian master. Six of his letters are, it appears, extant in the Lenin All-Union Library at Moscow. They have not been published, but summaries of them, and translations into Russian of certain passages, have been given in one of the series of the *Literaturnoe Nasledstvo*.[5] Only the first two of these letters are of any great interest for the light they shed on Rolland's attitude to Tolstoy in these early years. They are both concerned with Tolstoy's views on art—the one aspect of the Russian's philosophy which, as will be seen, aroused the misgivings of this most fervent of French 'tolstoïsants'.

sueur de son front, s'il avait mis à ses reins la besace du mendiant! L'acte eût peut-être été inutile, du moins fût-il apparu en harmonie avec ses théories!' This reproach, which occurs in a 'popular' biography written in 1909 (A. Séché and J. Bertaut, *Tolstoï*, p. 190), is one of those not infrequently voiced by Tolstoy's opponents during his lifetime.

[1] Both published 1907, *Vie de Tolstoï* published 1911.

[2] And not only Tolstoy among the Russians. 'J'ai dévoré tout autant Dostoïevsky, Gontcharov et les autres.' Quoted by A. Séché, *Dans la mêlée littéraire*, p. 127.

[3] See above, p. 56.

[4] Rolland, *Tolstoï, une lettre inédite* (1902), p. 7.

[5] *Russkaya Kul'tura i Frantsiya*, vol. ii, pp. 1007-1011 (Moscow, 1937). This volume contains also a facsimile reproduction of part of Rolland's first letter to Tolstoy.

The first letter is dated 10 April 1887, Rolland then being 21. He begins by saying how moved and troubled he has been by the recurrence of the theme of death in Tolstoy's writings, especially in *The Death of Ivan Ilyitch*.[1] He agrees with Tolstoy that the terror of death can be overcome by selfless living: but he suggests that devotion to art is one of the surest means of overcoming this fatal preoccupation with self. If this is true, he asks, why should Tolstoy condemn art in such outspoken terms?

Rolland probably wrote this letter as an immediate reaction to reading *What then should we do?* which was published in France in the spring of 1887. This book was primarily devoted to an examination of the problem of poverty and social injustice in an urban society, a problem with which Tolstoy had come into contact when he moved from the country to Moscow in 1881. The general argument of the book is that the rich and powerful classes of society are exploiting the poorer ones by luring them away from the land, where they are happy and at home, and forcing them to live an unnatural life in factories and in the streets, ministering to the pleasures and prodigal habits of the well-to-do.

Tolstoy considers the sciences and the arts, as commonly practised at present, to be quite useless to the ordinary man; and scientists and artists are *therefore* little better than parasites. The scientists are occupied with problems that cannot have the remotest bearing on ordinary life, and the artists are producing works that the common people cannot understand or appreciate. 'We [the artists] examine them [the ordinary folk] and depict them for our own pleasure and amusement, and we have quite left out of sight our real duty, which is not to examine and depict them, but to serve them.' Clearly Tolstoy was chiefly irritated by the pretentions of the naturalist school, as far as literature went, and his remarks seem to be largely aimed at Zola who at that time was quite as well known in Russia as in France.

Rolland must have found a great deal to discourage him in *What then should we do?* But the book contained also much to inspire him: for Tolstoy was almost certainly one of the sources from which Rolland drew his ideas on popular art, ideas which he

---

[1] The work had just appeared in France (late in 1886). There had been two translations, of which one (bearing the title *La Mort*) contained in addition Tolstoy's short story *Three Deaths*, and various death-scenes taken from *Sevastopol*, *War and Peace*, *Anna Karenina*, &c.

later strove to realize in the creation of a drama written for the
people and to be understood by the people. Tolstoy had written:
'Art, if it is art indeed, ought to be within the grasp of everyone,
especially of those for whose sake it was created' and again: 'Why
should not artists serve the people? In every cottage there are holy
images and paintings; the men and women of the labouring classes
can all sing, many can play on musical instruments; and all can
tell tales and recite poetry.' And from this book of Tolstoy's too,
Rolland may have drawn his ideal of the artist, an ideal magni-
ficently illustrated later on in the epic of *Jean-Christophe*:

> If men are really called on to serve others by intellectual work, they
> will need to suffer in the performance of this work, since it is only
> through suffering that spiritual fruit is borne. . . . A thinker and an
> artist will never sit on the heights of Olympus, as we are apt to imagine;
> he must suffer along with other men in order to find salvation or
> consolation.

Rolland's second letter to Tolstoy[1] was written in the September
of the same year (1887). The hero-worship is much more in
evidence. Rolland feels anxious to assure his correspondent how
close he is to him in his outlook on life. Like Tolstoy, he finds
the pursuit of knowledge a poor source of satisfaction, and no
remedy for the obsession of death (an unusual obsession, it must
be confessed, to trouble a man in his early twenties). He is struck
by the contentment of ordinary folk, who live and die possessed by
a simple faith, and feels such souls are more worthy of respect than
his intellectual contemporaries. He is persuaded that happiness lies
in self-sacrifice—but on what altar? He will admit that devotion to
art does not annihilate the ego, but is more liable to puff it up.
Does the solution lie in undertaking physical labour? He begs
Tolstoy to clear up his doubts, and asks him whether he found it
easy to suppress his own egoistic desires and impulses. Emphasizing his isolation in the midst of sceptics and dilettantes, he tells
Tolstoy he would like him to become his moral guide: 'Do you
suppose that if I succeeded in devoting myself with my whole
heart to the work you proclaim, that would free me completely
from despair and doubt, and I should no longer have any anxiety,
any repinings for my past life; that I could at one blow destroy
everything I had been since my childhood?'

[1] Reproduced in the periodical *Commune*, Jan. 1936.

Behind the exaltation of the tone of this letter one may discern the traces of a genuine spiritual struggle. The purity of Tolstoy's doctrine had an obvious appeal for Rolland, who at the same time felt it was more than he could do to renounce the promises that life held out for him. Like the young man 'possessed of great riches' in the Gospel story, he was unable to bring himself to renounce his possessions (the blossoming artistic gifts) and so turned away from this second Christ 'with a heavy heart'. If the letter betrays in the writer a certain adolescent propensity for identifying his personal problems with those of a great man, his complaints about feeling out of touch with his contemporaries in France are probably genuine. In *La Foire sur la place* he was later to satirize mercilessly the insincerity and corruption of intellectual and artistic circles in the Paris of his time.

Rolland had the satisfaction of receiving, in answer to these two letters, a reply subsequently published in the *Cahiers de la Quinzaine*, 22 February 1902. Tolstoy in this reply restated his opinion that most contemporary art was the luxury product of a society doomed to dissolution: he condemned not art itself but those modern profiteers who aim at making fortunes out of it, thus debasing it to the level of a lucrative trade. In a foreword to the published letter Rolland suggested that pseudo-artists and minor talents might be eliminated by the equal distribution of manual labour over the whole of the population. The real artists would continue to produce in spite of all obstacles, while the lesser ones would be discouraged and weeded out.

Rolland's third letter, dated January 1897, seems to have little object other than to remind Tolstoy of the conclusions reached to date in their correspondence. On 21 July 1901 Rolland writes to congratulate him on the recovery he has made from a serious illness, and tells him how necessary he is to Europe. A month later he wrote to ask for information about a dissident Russian sect, the Dukhobors. Finally, on 27 August 1906, Rolland sent a letter to accompany a copy of his recently published *Vie de Michel-Ange*. He tells Tolstoy he has been reading Birukov's biography[1] and has realized that Tolstoy's moral victories over himself have been won

---

[1] P. Birukov, *Tolstoï, vie et œuvres*, translated by J. W. Bienstock, in 3 volumes (1906–9). Rolland acknowledged it as his principal source of documentation in compiling the *Vie de Tolstoï* (in a footnote, p. 7).

only at the cost of severe struggles: such a man, too, was Michelangelo. Tolstoy thought little of this work of Rolland's, although
(in a letter to Dr. Makovitzky dated 22 August 1906) he says he
believes the preface to be 'masterly'.

To speak of a 'correspondence' between Rolland and Tolstoy is,
after all, to stretch the term. Tolstoy, as we have seen, addressed
only one reply to Rolland, and his silence no doubt pained his
French disciple. In later years, however, Rolland recognized that
Tolstoy could never have found time to answer all the appeals for
sympathy and counsel that reached him from every corner of the
globe. Tolstoy had to reserve his personal attention for those who
stood most in need of it: and Rolland, in the formative period
during which he wrote his first two letters, was in greater need of
spiritual comfort and guidance than in his maturity.[1]

It is probably no exaggeration to say that Tolstoy's passing in
1910 was looked on, even in France, as a more portentous event
than the death of any man of letters since Victor Hugo's in 1885.
All the longer established periodicals carried obituary articles,
some of which (e.g. that of Anatole Leroy-Beaulieu in the *Revue
des Deux Mondes*) almost reached the dimensions and importance
of critical studies. The 'jeunes revues' tended to ignore the event,
a fact noted by Charles-Henri Hirsch as being not without significance: 'it is perhaps an indication that young writers to-day,
those not yet in their thirties, know about Tolstoy only by hearsay'.[2]

In addition to these obituaries, the death of Tolstoy was made
the subject of pastoral sermons and was taken as the text for political
speeches.[3] But Rolland's *Vie de Tolstoï* was the most imposing
monument raised to Tolstoy's memory in France in the year
following his end. Rolland himself was very ill, as the result of a
motoring accident, when the editor of the *Revue de Paris*, convinced that Rolland was 'the most "Tolstoyan" of all French
writers', pressed him to undertake the work.[4] It was published in
the *Revue de Paris* between 15 February and 1 April 1911, and
appeared in book form later in the same year.

[1] Ronald A. Wilson (*The Pre-War Biographies of Romain Rolland*, 1939, p. 76)
says that Rolland expressed himself personally to him in this sense.
[2] *Mercure de France*, 1 Jan. 1911, p. 175.
[3] Wilfred Monod preached a sermon on the subject of Tolstoy in Paris on
4 Dec. 1910; Jean Jaurès delivered an address in his honour on 10 Feb. 1911.
[4] Rolland, *Péguy* (1944), vol. i, pp. 348–9.

The *Vie de Tolstoï* is a piece of writing completely different from Suarès' series of monographs: it is a straightforward account, for the most part, of the life and writings of Tolstoy, presenting the known facts succinctly, while the views and glosses of the author are kept to a minimum. None the less it is indisputably a justificatory account: Tolstoy is whitewashed where this process is considered necessary, and Rolland defends him passionately against his detractors and belittlers. He alludes in the opening pages of his book to Lemaître's thesis, that Tolstoy owed the best of his thought to the French Romantics. Rolland does not deny this influence, but argues that

one must have a very mistaken view of Tolstoy's greatness and the strength of the fascination he wields over us, if one attributes these to his ideas. The circle of ideas in which art has its being is extremely bounded; art does not depend on them for its power, but on the expression it conveys to them, on the way the artist handles them, on the perfume of his life [p. 3].

All the same, Rolland devotes a large portion of his book to a restatement (and for the most part a sympathetic restatement) of Tolstoy's ideas on religion, the social order and social reform, and art. We have seen that it was this last subject, and Tolstoy's iconoclastic ideas about it, which interested and troubled Rolland most as a young man: his presentation of these ideas in maturity offers a peculiar interest. It is also in the chapters of the *Vie de Tolstoï* which deal with Tolstoy's theory of art that Rolland comes nearest to condemning his hero.

There were portions of Tolstoy's critique of art which appealed strongly to Rolland, either because they corresponded with views he already held or because he had early in life been swung over to these views by Tolstoy's arguments. The objections of the Russian polemist to modern art may be summarized as a violent protest against its industrialization. Art pandered to the perverted taste of the spoilt darlings of civilization: artists who, by accident or design, tickled this taste, were rewarded beyond all reason for their services. In Tolstoy's case the grapes were by no means sour: he made a fortune with *War and Peace* and *Anna Karenina*, but his conscience troubled him so much about accepting royalties that when he came to publish *Resurrection* he stipulated that the proceeds should be set aside for assisting the Dukhobors.

In this revolt, not against art but against the artists who danced to the tune that the moneyed classes piped, Rolland joined whole-heartedly. The fifth volume of the *Jean-Christophe* cycle—*la Foire sur la Place*—is one long diatribe against the noisy Parisian clique of writers, musicians, journalists and politicians who had sold their ideals and consciences for money and position. In a later volume, *Les Amies* (still anterior to the *Vie de Tolstoï*), Christophe tells his friend Olivier that wealth kills art.

Does a rich man know what life is? Does he remain in close contact with harsh reality? Does he feel on his brow the brutal breath of poverty, can he smell the smell of the bread he has to earn, of the earth he has to till? Can he understand, can he even see, people and things? . . . Wealth cuts the links that bind man to the earth, so how could you hope to be an artist still? The artist is the voice of the earth. A rich man cannot be a great artist.

In the *Vie de Tolstoï*, Rolland delightedly draws attention to Tolstoy's indictment of the 'false artists who exploit and dishonour' art (p. 114), who

without wishing or being able to do anything useful for men, expect to be admired and served blindly, setting forth as dogmas an impudent religion of science for the sake of science and art for art's sake—a deceptive mask which they use as a personal justification and as the apologia of their monstrous egoism and nullity [p. 111].

But Rolland is scrupulous to show that this purging of the temple is accompanied, in Tolstoy, by the inauguration of a new and purer cult. The true art, according to the author of *What is Art?*, is a religion, in the earliest sense of the word—a binding together of mankind in a communion of love. 'Art must suppress violence, and Art alone can do this. Its mission is to found the sovereignty of the Kingdom of God, that is, of Love.' This saying of Tolstoy's finds unlimited support in Rolland, who interprets it as a clarion call to cosmopolitan art.

Yes, the sum-total of our art is no more than the expression of one caste, which itself splits up, from one nation to another, in little hostile clans. There is no single artistic soul in Europe which succeeds in unifying all parties and races. The most universal artist in our day was Tolstoy himself. In him we learned to love one another, men of all nations and all classes. And whoever has tasted, as we have, the heady joys of this vast love, can never again be satisfied with the rags and patches of the great human soul, which is offered us by the art of the European *cénacles* [p. 126].

In a previous chapter we have seen how a hostile attitude towards the Russian novelists became associated with a narrow parochialism in literary tastes and outlook. Rolland's firm rejection of such pettiness reaches back to when the dispute was at its most virulent, in the opening years of the twentieth century. Writing in reply to an 'enquête sur la littérature allemande' in the *Mercure de France* of January 1903, Rolland stated his conviction that a new period was dawning when national literatures would be all fused into one world art. The French race, he points out, is one of the most hybrid of all; that is the key to its greatness, its harmoniousness, and universality: 'The more European we are, the more true we shall be to ourselves.' Brunetière had proposed the ideal of cosmopolitan art: in Rolland Brunetière's hobby-horse becomes a magnificent aspiration.

The whole of the *Jean-Christophe* cycle might be interpreted as an allegory of the union of the French and Germanic spirits in a wider and deeper art; and in the eighth volume of the cycle, *Les Amies*, Rolland introduces Tolstoy's ideal of a 'religious' art as one of the later stages in the evolution of his hero's talent.

He was no longer content with a music which was a monologue, a speech delivered for oneself alone, still less with one which was a piece of virtuosity to be appreciated only by professional musicians. He wanted music to be a means of communion with other men. There can be no vital art save that which links itself up with other men. . . . Certainly, there are great artists who never express anything but themselves. But the greatest of all are those whose heart beats for all. He who would see the Living God face to face must seek him, not in the empty firmament of his thought, but in the love of men.[1]

To the central idea of *What is Art?* Rolland here supplies an inspiring affirmative.

Rolland, however, is constrained in his turn to note the many flaws in the negative criticism of *What is Art?* which had amused or irritated his forerunners too. But they are flaws of detail.

Rolland is more shocked by the comical irreverences into which Tolstoy is led by his fundamental postulates, than by the postulates

---

[1] Rolland, *Les Amies*, pp. 94-5.

themselves. He neglects to consider that in condemning, for instance, Shakespeare, Tolstoy is being quite consistent with his own principles. There is no 'moral' to be drawn from *King Lear* (the play on to which Tolstoy had concentrated his batteries),[1] other than the banal precept 'Do not put too much trust in fair words'. Shakespeare has no moral lesson to give his readers: therefore, says Tolstoy, his art must be bad. But Rolland, unwilling to admit that Tolstoy is arguing like a frowsty puritan, accounts for this onslaught on Shakespeare (whom he, Rolland, admired, it goes without saying)[2] by vague talk of a difference in temperaments: Tolstoy, 'le moins littéraire de tous les écrivains', was out of sympathy with the art of the English playwright 'qui fut le plus génial des hommes de lettres' (pp. 120–1). Rolland blames Tolstoy's enormities on to his vehemence which betrays him into rushing to conclusions, and on to the gaps in his artistic culture (p. 110).

Rolland might have added that Tolstoy was calamitously limited in his outlook on non-Russian culture in particular. In *What is Art?* it is mainly contemporary French art, not Russian art, that suffers at his hands. Tolstoy was not a 'good European'. One hardly ever, for instance, meets a 'sympathetic' foreigner in the whole of his fictional work, save only perhaps Karl Ivanovitch, the German tutor in *Childhood*, who was in any case modelled on an early memory. The German strategists in the Russian army in *War and Peace* are fools; in the same book the Gascon captain Ramball whom Pierre meets in Moscow is a figure of fun, a caricature of all Gascons. Tolstoy's short story, *Lucerne*, centres round the selfishness of rich foreign tourists in Switzerland, against which the generosity of a travelling Russian prince stands out in sharp relief. But this is an aspect of Tolstoy's nature over which Rolland, the supremely 'good European', naturally preferred to draw a veil.

Rolland has also to face the difficult task of reconciling Tolstoy's savage attack on Beethoven with his own veneration for this figure.[3]

---

[1] In *Shakespeare and the Drama* (1906).

[2] But if evidence is required, one may adduce Rolland's own statement in a letter: 'Malgré Tolstoï, Wagner, &c., Shakespeare est de tous les artistes celui que j'ai constamment préféré, depuis l'enfance.' (Quoted by Paul Seippel, *Romain Rolland* (1913), p. 35.) See also Rolland's own account of his discovery of Shakespeare in boyhood, in *Compagnons de route* (1936).

[3] Which also reached back to Rolland's infancy. His mother, who taught him the piano, first introduced him to Beethoven. See Rolland, *Souvenirs d'enfance* (1930).

Tolstoy had intended the *Kreutzer Sonata* to be a dual offensive—
on the seduction of music and on the institution of marriage.
Rolland puts forward an hypothesis which honours Beethoven while
it avoids making Tolstoy seem ridiculous. Tolstoy's only grievance
against Beethoven, says Rolland, is his power, the excellence of his
mastery of his art. Carried away by this music, Tolstoy indignantly
shakes off 'the domineering master who bows him to his will. . . .
The spirit is enslaved, and . . . the incalculable force of sounds can
do what it will with him' (pp. 144–5). True enough: but Tolstoy's
mistake, the writer continues, is to believe that music has this effect
on all audiences, and on every member of an audience. Most men
are too 'lacking in vitality' to feel music deeply: they consequently
incur no danger in listening to it.[1] And Rolland arrives at the
immensely soothing conclusion that 'despite his wounding unfairness to Beethoven, Tolstoy feels his music more deeply than the
majority of those who to-day praise him to the skies. . . . Beethoven
would have been perhaps better pleased with his hatred than with
the love of the Beethoven fans' (pp. 145–6).

In his final assessment of the value of Tolstoy's critical *obiter
dicta*, Rolland once more strives for a compromise which should
be creditable for Tolstoy while it allows no real validity to his ideas.
He explains that Tolstoy's criticism is 'worthless as a key to the
gates of new worlds, but invaluable if we ask of it the key to Tolstoy's own art. You should not require critical impartiality of a
man of genius. When Wagner or Tolstoy speak of Beethoven or
Shakespeare, it is not of Beethoven or Shakespeare that they speak,
but of themselves.' He also says: 'Tolstoy delivers his artistic
judgements from the vantage point of a religious faith' (p. 121).
And this faith, at any rate where Tolstoy himself is concerned,
'instead of stifling his artistic genius has quickened it' (p. 109).
This is a bold claim. The one work of Tolstoy's written almost
completely along the lines he himself had laid down as fundamental
to the best art is *The Four Russian Reading Books* (a collection of

---

[1] The same idea is at the back of a remark of Christophe's, speaking of
the audiences to whom his own musical compositions are played. 'Heureuse-
ment qu'ils sont aveugles et sourds. J'ai tant mis dans mes œuvres de mes
troubles et de mes faiblesses qu'il me semble parfois commettre une mauvaise
action, en lâchant dans le monde ces volées de démons. Je m'apaise, quand
je vois le calme du public: il porte une triple cuirasse.' (*La Nouvelle Journée*,
p. 95.)

tales and fables, intended to be read by Russian peasants). Undoubtedly they contain many specimens of an admirable narrative art. Rolland himself speaks highly of this collection, but he does not find the eloquent phrases to describe it that flow from his pen when he is presenting *War and Peace* or *Anna Karenina*. And in *Resurrection*, the one long work of Tolstoy's written after he had published *What is Art?*, Rolland is compelled to admit that the desire to give the entertainment a moral bias threatens to ruin the book as a work of art (p. 154).

Between the letter Rolland wrote to Tolstoy in 1887 and the pages he writes in 1911 there is little fundamental difference. Already in 1902 Rolland's opinion of Tolstoy's artistic criticism, its defects and its merits, was fixed: 'If I am sorry that Tolstoy often made mistakes in appreciating this or that great man . . . if I am sorry too that he judged French art by a handful of ridiculous decadents . . . on the other hand I find his general judgement on art is absolutely sound.'[1] Rolland was and remained a 'tolstoïsant' with the one reservation that he would give art a higher place in the hierarchy of human activities than Tolstoy would. He does his best to present Tolstoy's point of view in a way more nearly in conformity with his own: but the discrepancy is visible.

Allowance, however, must be made for the undercurrent of reverence, not to say idolization, which is noticeable throughout the *Vie de Tolstoï*. This was due no doubt in some measure to the circumstance that it was written so soon after Tolstoy's death: and one suspects that for this reason Rolland was occasionally shy of expressing his opinions with complete frankness. Elsewhere in his writings he displays a more overt irritation with Tolstoy's critical obtuseness. At one point, Christophe falls under the spell of Tolstoy.

He had become an enthusiastic admirer of his, he shed tears while reading his books, he wanted to set one of his folk-tales to music, he had asked the author's permission, he had sent him his *lieder*. Tolstoy had not said a word in reply. . . . He had had Christophe's music played to him, and it had irritated him; he could not understand it. He called Beethoven a decadent, and Shakespeare a charlatan. On the other hand, he had a craze for the simple little masters, for the harpsichord music

[1] Rolland, *Tolstoï; une lettre inédite*, pp. 8–9.

which delighted Louis XV; and he considered *la Confession d'une femme de chambre*[1] to be a Christian work.[2]

Rolland takes no exception to Tolstoy's ideas on social reform: they touched him less. It is evident—and this is the crux of the matter—that Rolland was a 'tolstoïsant' not on rational, but on emotional grounds. It was not by Tolstoy's logic that he was convinced—a logic perfectly consistent, perfectly ruthless, but as headlong and heedless as a machine careering with brakes locked on a slippery and precipitous road. It was by the appeal of this magnificent and solitary figure, a giant of power clothed in loving-kindness, that Rolland was mesmerized. His cult of the great found satisfaction, as did his deep humanity: and these are the two strands that run through Rolland's most lasting literary achievement, *Jean-Christophe*.

It would be surprising if careful sifting of this novel-cycle did not reveal at any rate some grains of borrowed metal. So loving an acquaintance with Tolstoy's mind and work could scarcely have failed to influence Rolland when in his turn he sat down to write. It may be assumed that the ten novels that make up the *Jean-Christophe* cycle will be more likely than Rolland's later works to betray the influence of the Russian, since they were written, with one exception only, during Tolstoy's lifetime,[3] hence over a period when his presence was felt most strongly.

Yet some analogies that have been made between Tolstoy's art and Rolland's have been over-hastily arrived at.

It was to describe *Jean-Christophe* that the term 'roman-fleuve' was invented.[4] But this is not to say that by his use of the cyclical novel Rolland gives evidence of having fallen under Tolstoy's influence, and that there is necessarily a connexion between the multi-volumed novel of the Russian and the *Jean-Christophe* sequence.[5]

---

[1] Rolland probably intended an allusion to *Le Journal d'une femme de chambre*, one of Octave Mirbeau's better-known novels. This writer had a great vogue in Russia at the beginning of the twentieth century (see É. Haumant, *La Culture française en Russie*, 1913).   [2] Rolland, *Les Amies*, p. 175.

[3] Order and dates of publication of these novels are as follows: *L'Aube*, 1904; *Le Matin*, 1904; *L'Adolescent*, 1905; *La Révolte*, 1907; *La Foire sur la place*, 1908; *Antoinette*, 1908; *Dans la maison*, 1909; *Les Amies*, 1910; *Le Buisson ardent*, 1910; *La Nouvelle Journée*, 1912.

[4] By Rolland himself: '*Jean-Christophe* m'est apparu comme un fleuve' (Preface, *Dans la maison*).

[5] As, for instance, is suggested by Christian Sénéchal (*Grands courants de la*

Tolstoy achieves his voluminousness by the vast quantity of characters and the multiplicity of intrigues which are at all times present in his longer novels. Rolland follows the life-history of one single man;[1] the characters that enter into his books are only those who, at one time or another, enter into his hero's life, and as they cease to affect the hero, Rolland ceases, on the whole, to pursue their histories. Rolland had called *War and Peace* 'une Iliade moderne'; *Jean-Christophe*, one might say, is a lesser Odyssey. If Rolland is, like Tolstoy, sometimes long-winded, this is because of the detail in which he describes Christophe's unfolding soul, and partly too because he uses his novel (regrettably) to enounce his own opinions about German music, French politics, Parisian literary *cénacles*, &c. *Jean-Christophe* partakes more of the German *Bildungsroman*, of which Goethe's *Wilhelm Meister* is the type, than of Tolstoy's novel.

The theme of *Jean-Christophe* is personal to Rolland and one that Tolstoy would probably never have attempted. To narrate the life-history of an imaginary man of genius would never have occurred to a writer who denied the presence of genius in Napoleon, Shakespeare, Beethoven, and who probably in any case judged the word to be senseless. And Christophe himself has almost nothing in common with Tolstoy, as a personality, save one quality only, a burning passion for life. 'Always he hugs life to him, with the transports of a lover. He is "mad for life". He is "intoxicated with life". He cannot live without this intoxication. Drunk with happiness and unhappiness at once. Drunk with death and immortality.' That is Tolstoy, as Rolland saw him.[2] But Christophe feels life as an intoxication too, and bursts out in wild apostrophes to it: 'Dieu-abîme! Dieu-gouffre! Brasier de l'Être! Ouragan de la vie! Folie de vivre — sans but, sans frein, sans raison — pour la fureur de vivre.'[3] The feeling of intensified life enters into him at the crisis of adolescence with the force of a hurricane, and is accompanied by a thunderstorm: it is perhaps the tempest of inspiration. Christophe will feel it once more, when he is staying in the Alps and the storm-wind, the Föhn, raises him to a pitch of excitement and creative power.[4]

---

littérature française contemporaine (1941), p. 168) and by Serge Michelson (*Grands prosateurs russes* (1947), p. 88).

[1] With a long digression in *Antoinette*, where the reader almost entirely loses sight of Christophe.   [2] Rolland, *Vie de Tolstoï*, pp. 193-4.

[3] Id., *L'Adolescent*, p. 61.

[4] Id., *Le Buisson ardent*, pp. 321-3. Seippel (op. cit., pp. 160 et seq.) draws an

In a calmer state, lying in a wood one day, he is seized by a feeling of being at one with the entire living creation.

His hands beneath his head, his eyes shut, he listened to the invisible orchestra, the insects dancing frantically in circles, in a sunbeam, around the pungent pines, the trumpeting mosquitoes, the organ notes of the wasps, the swarms of wild bees. . . . All these voices, all this clamour, he heard them inside himself. From the smallest to the largest of these creatures there flowed the same stream of life: it bathed him too. Thus, he was one of them, he was of their blood, he heard the fraternal echo of their joys and sufferings; their strength mingled with his, like a river swollen by thousands of brooklets. He sank into them. . . . He swam along deliciously in the life that rolled along overflowing its banks.[1]

This pantheistic feeling is the echo of a mood felt by the hero of one of Tolstoy's earlier novels, *The Cossacks*. Olenin is there described lying in the Caucasian forests listening to the myriad-voiced swarms of the mosquitoes around him.

He felt cool, at his ease; he thought about nothing, had nothing to wish for. And suddenly he was overtaken by such a strange feeling of groundless joy and love for everything that, following an old habit of his childhood, he started to cross himself and give thanks to Someone. It suddenly occurred to him with particular vividness: here am I, Dmitri Olenin, a being so distinct from all others, lying here alone, God knows where. . . . Around me, dancing among the leaves which seem to them great islands, the mosquitoes hover and hum: one, two, three, four, a hundred, a thousand, a million mosquitoes, and they are humming round me for some reason, and each of them is a Dmitri Olenin as distinct from everything else as I am. . . . And it became clear to him that he was not a Russian gentleman at all, a member of Moscow society, friend or relative of such a one or such a one, but simply just such a mosquito, a pheasant or a swan as those that were living around him.

We have gone to the length of quoting these two passages side by side *in extenso*, in order to show the nature of the transformation Rolland wrought when he incorporated a scene or an idea invented by Tolstoy. The Russian gives us the raw material of the moment, communicates the impression of his hero's state of mind by showing us exactly what his thoughts and sensations are ('he felt cool

analogy between this episode and Tolstoy's brusque conversion, as recorded in the *Confessions*. In both instances, the scene is laid in a forest. Seippel quotes Rolland himself, however, as maintaining that there was no conscious imitation here.   [1] Rolland, *L'Adolescent*, pp. 64–5.

... he thought about nothing ... he was overtaken by a feeling ...
it suddenly occurred to him'). The French writer, as it were, digests
his hero's thoughts and sensations, and serves up a finished product. Tolstoy particularizes: Olenin feels that each mosquito is 'a
Dmitri Olenin as distinct from everything else as I am'. Rolland
generalizes: 'From the smallest to the largest of these creatures
there flowed the same stream of life: it bathed him too. ...' To
characterize the two artists in a simple formula, we may say that
Tolstoy was a psychologist, Rolland a poet.

It seems hard to avoid the conclusion, knowing as we do how
closely Rolland had read Tolstoy's books, that he was modelling
himself here on the Russian master. The settings of the two scenes
are identical, the essence of the two moods (the dissolution of the
sense of individuality in the face of impersonal nature, and the joy
this release brings) are likewise the same. The upshot of Olenin's
mood is resolution to keep this feeling of ecstatic happiness by
'doing good'—the perennial resolution of the average Tolstoyan
hero. Christophe's mood finds outlet in a burst of creative activity.

The antinomy Life–Death is a theme in the treatment of which
Rolland owes perhaps something to Tolstoy. We have seen how
Tolstoy's death-scenes stirred Rolland in 1887. Tolstoy's handling
of the subject is marked by a complete lack of squeamishness in
the details he supplies, coupled with the most faithful rendering
of the emotions (at times incongruous) of the bystanders. The early
volumes of *Jean-Christophe* are haunted by this theme, the theme
of 'the great Bugbear, which gnaws at all men, and which wisdom
strives vainly to forget or deny'.[1] Another boy dies of typhoid.
The incident gives Christophe nightmares. 'This dread of death
poisoned years of his childhood—and was only overcome by revul-
sion from life, by the gloominess of his life.'[2] The horrifying death
of his grandfather, which the little boy witnesses (and which Rolland describes in considerable nauseating detail), arouses a panic
terror. 'When he saw the old man's eyes turned inwards, the whites
showing bloodshot, horror froze him; and he dropped [the head
he was holding] with a shrill cry. He started up in terror, he
escaped and rushed outside. He was shrieking and weeping.'[3]
Later, when he sees his grandfather actually expire, he is seized with

[1] Id., *L'Aube*, p. 103.   [2] Ibid., p. 112.
[3] Id., *Le Matin*, p. 25.

a fit. Similarly the little Nikolenka in Tolstoy's *Childhood* shrieks
and rushes out of the room when he realizes that the odour that
clings to his mother's dead body is the odour of corruption. Jean-
Christophe is a maturer, more reflecting (and less natural) child than
Nikolenka, whose head is chiefly filled with his new-won importance as an orphan. Rolland's hero breaks forth into blasphemous
imprecations, hardly suited to his age. The lessons in realism which
Rolland took from Tolstoy were only half-learnt, in this case.

Christophe's father is drowned while drunk, and the young lad,
seated before the dead man, is assailed by thoughts closely re-
sembling those of Constantin Levin at his brother's death-bed.
'Seated by the bed, holding vigil over the last sleep of Melchior,
whose countenance now wore a grave and solemn expression, he
felt the dark peace of death enter into him. . . . How trifling did
everything appear next to this reality, the only reality, death! Was
it worth while to suffer, to desire, to strive so much, when all
ended here!'[1] The passage in *Anna Karenina* to which reference
has been made runs as follows: 'A minute later, his face brightened;
a smile played under his moustache, and the women hastened to
start laying him out. All Levin's horror at the terrible riddle of
death was awakened. . . . More than ever he realized his powerless-
ness to fathom the mystery of death, and the terror of feeling it so
near him and so inevitable.'

The theme of death is, to be sure, sufficiently commonplace; but
a preoccupation with death-bed scenes is less common in the history of the novel. Tolstoy had this preoccupation, and no other
novelist before him, save perhaps Dickens, shared it to the same
extent. But Dickens tends to veil his death-bed scenes in a mist of
tears: Tolstoy observes dry-eyed. So, too, does Rolland, painting
quite dispassionately the mysterious transformation which comes
over the face of the sufferer when he is released and the feeling of
despair in the watcher at the thought of the meaninglessness of life
which ends in the tomb. It appears not improbable that Tolstoy's
writings had a considerable influence on Rolland in this direction.

Once or twice in his life, and always at moments when he is in
great spiritual distress, Christophe encounters a humble, unassuming soul who brings him back to a realization of ultimate
values. Such souls are fatalist and heroic, not unlike Platon

[1] Rolland, *Le Matin*, p. 205.

Karataev in *War and Peace*, of whom Rolland had written that he was 'simple, pieux, résigné, avec son bon sourire dans les souffrances et dans la mort'.[1] The description fits exactly Christophe's uncle Gottfried, a pedlar, humble, submitting without murmur to the insults of the family; he tells Christophe that the only good music is 'the traditional folk-music—that Christophe's music, and the music of the classics even, is useless, means nothing—he discourages him in his dreams of becoming a great man by the same simple logic. 'You want to make songs so as to be a great man; and you want to be a great man so as to make songs. You are like a dog chasing after its tail.'[2] Later, when under the stress of an emotional crisis he starts to drink, Gottfried meets him and gives him a sermon on natural goodness, much as Platon talks to Pierre Bezukhov, only a little more coherently. Like Platon again, Gottfried dies quietly, in an out-of-the-way farmstead where he is loved for the spiritual peace he has brought: it is only by chance that Christophe learns of his passing.

When he is in Paris, friendless and ill, a woman, lodging in the same house, nurses him back to health out of charity. Sidonie resembles Gottfried in her stoicism, all the more remarkable since she is without religious faith: to Christophe she represents the 'true France'—and one remembers that Platon Karataev 'remained for ever in Pierre's mind as the strongest and sweetest memory and the incarnation of everything that was Russian'. Sidonie was 'a true member of this race, which has little or no religious faith, few intellectual reasons for living, and yet an enormous vitality—this race of the French countryside, hard-working and apathetic, in revolt under the yoke, not much in love with life, but clinging to it and not needing any outside encouragement to keep its courage'.[3] In the end she leaves him, mysteriously, probably because she feels herself becoming too attached to him. And Christophe feels himself changed—partly through his illness, partly through Sidonie's influence.

He no longer felt his old hates; he no longer thought of things that irritated him, or if he did it was with a shrug of the shoulders; he thought of his own troubles less, and had more thought for those of others. Ever since Sidonie had reminded him of the silent suffering of lowly folk, who struggled uncomplainingly in every corner of the earth, he forgot

[1] Id., *Vie de Tolstoï*, p. 70.   [2] Id., *L'Aube*, p. 177.
[3] Id., *La Foire sur la place*, p. 295.

himself in them. He who was not normally sentimental, he now had fits of mystical tenderness, the flower of weakness and sickness.[1]

It is by just such a renewal of contact with 'the people' that Levin and Bezukhov rediscover faith in life and the energy to live it. Fedor, in *Anna Karenina*, Platon Karataev, in *War and Peace*, for all the wide differences between their characters and that of Sidonie, perform a similar function.

In the ninth book of Rolland's cycle (*Le Buisson ardent*), there occurs an episode which seems to bear very distinctly the mark of Tolstoy's influence. This is the adultery of Christophe with the wife of the Swiss doctor with whom he has taken refuge after his implication in a Paris insurrection. The two works of Tolstoy which deal primarily with the subject of adultery are *Anna Karenina* and *The Kreutzer Sonata*. Rolland's Anna Braun bears no resemblance to either of the heroines of Tolstoy's two stories;[2] this woman, in whom a rigorous Calvinism has instilled a morbid fear of giving way to her natural instincts, and who becomes terrible once the dam is broken by the passion she conceives for Christophe, is a powerful and original creation of the French novelist.

The similarity with *The Kreutzer Sonata* lies in the part played by music in awakening her senses. The original theme of Tolstoy's story was the fatal aphrodisiac properties of music. Christophe discovers that Anna has a hidden talent for singing: it is as a direct result of the excitement of practising together that the two are caught up in the toils of erotic passion—'the sacred frenzy of music bore them away in its talons. . . .' Pozdnishev murders his wife when he discovers her playing the Kreutzer sonata with a musician whom he suspects is her lover. In a passage which echoes the whole sense of Tolstoy's thought, Rolland expatiates on the dangerous power music possesses to remove the stopcocks of the sub-conscious.

Oh music, thou that revealest the gulfs of the spirit, upsetting the customary balance of the mind! In ordinary life, ordinary souls are

---

[1] Rolland, *La Foire sur la place*, p. 304.

[2] Save in the two names, Anna Karenina and Anna Braun. It is not merely that the Christian names are identical: there is a similarity in the surnames that may not have been entirely fortuitous. The Russian word at the root of Karenin might be taken to be 'kariy', which means 'brown'. Rolland was not, however, a Russian scholar.

closed chambers: within, the unused energies, the virtues and vices whose practice would embarrass us, wilt away; steady practical reason, cowardly commonsense, hold the keys of the chamber. They only open a few tidily kept cupboards. But music possesses the magic wand that bursts the locks. The doors open. The demons of the heart appear. And the soul sees herself naked for the first time.[1]

This passage may be compared with Pozdnishev's outburst in *The Kreutzer Sonata* (Chapter 23).

Oh! it is a fearful thing, that sonata. Especially that movement. And, generally speaking, what a fearful thing music is! What action does it have? and why does it have that action? We are told that music elevates the soul: nonsense, it's a lie. It works—it works in a fearful way. I am speaking for my own part, but I tell you it works certainly not by elevating the soul. It works in no elevating, nor in any degrading way, but by exasperating the spirit. How can I put it? Music makes me forget what I am, what my real state of mind is, it transposes me into some other state of mind which is not my own. Under the influence of music I seem to feel emotions which are not my own, to understand things beyond my understanding, to have the power of doing things beyond my capabilities.

Tolstoy's influence on Rolland's novel is, then, perceptible, but it is by no means extensive, and does not reach down to essentials. He took of Tolstoy no more than a mature and original artist might be expected to take of a well-loved author and constant companion of his reading hours. He did not transpose Tolstoy into French in the way that the Romantics, for instance, transposed Walter Scott. Rolland's thought was more affected than his art by his prolonged meditation of Tolstoy's writings. It is in these far less tangible matters—in Rolland's general attitude to life, his Olympian vision which embraced the whole flood-stream of humanity and preferred not to narrow itself to an inspection of individual eddies; his broad judgements and broad condemnations, his lofty moral tone and occasional 'pulpit' manner, his sense of the fraternity of all mankind and his seat 'au-dessus de la mêlée'—in all these things he was a true disciple of his master Tolstoy.

[1] Rolland, *Le Buisson ardent*, p. 240.

XIII

DOSTOEVSKY AND THE YOUNGER GENERATION

I N the dozen or so years before the outbreak of the First World War Dostoevsky came into his own, and among the intellectually more enterprising members of the younger generation, came to be thought of as a figure of greater significance than Tolstoy.

This movement of re-adjustment gained even more momentum in the years immediately following the War. In the opening pages of his *Dostoïevsky* (1923) Gide compared Tolstoy to an 'enormous pile' which 'still darkens the horizon': but, just as when a traveller, journeying away from a mountain, sees other and loftier peaks emerging, so 'a few adventurous spirits are perhaps already aware of Dostoevsky reappearing behind the giant Tolstoy and gaining more and more in stature'.

The apotheosis of Dostoevsky is, however, confined, as Gide says, to 'a few adventurous spirits'—a small group of younger men. It is not the less important for that, since the group included many of the 'rising stars' in contemporary literature: one may number, among Dostoevsky's devotees, besides Gide himself, Claudel, Proust, Duhamel, Lenormand, and the poets Alexandre Arnoux and André Salmon. Among the mass of the reading public, Tolstoy doubtless had as great a retinue as ever. In 1911, a reviewer writing in one of the more progressive organs of thought at that time[1] declared him to be so great a figure as to be beyond ordinary praise or criticism. Nevertheless, Tolstoy's influence on formative thought, one may say, was at an end. It had had its hey-day in the nineties and in the first decade of the twentieth century: the reasons why Tolstoyism could not survive into the post-war era have already been suggested.

In 1913, Serge Bernstamm conceived the idea of conducting an inquiry to find out which writer was considered in France to be

---

[1] J. Saint-Hubert, 'Le *Cadavre vivant* de Léon Tolstoï', *Nouvelle Revue Française*, Nov. 1911, p. 632.

the greatest, Tolstoy, Dostoevsky, or Turgenev. As a trustworthy means of assessing current opinion on a given subject there is perhaps little to be said for the 'enquête littéraire'. But the device has the effect of focusing attention on certain subjects, and the replies produce most of the possible debating-points. Bernstamm's results[1] may not reflect with unimpeachable fidelity the division of affection in France among the Russian novelists, but they do at any rate give us most of the reasons why certain people preferred Tolstoy and others Dostoevsky.

The reason most often given, in one form or another, by those who put Tolstoy first, was that his genius was wider. Vogüé's verdict on Dostoevsky, that he was a man who described admirably what he had seen, but who travelled only by night, still swayed many readers. Tolstoy's novels give, in the opinion of Daniel Lesueur,[2] 'a larger and more complete mirror of humanity than those of his two illustrious rivals. . . . Dostoevsky saw only the darker side of the soul and of destiny'; and J.-H. Rosny[3] gives much the same reason for preferring Tolstoy. Paul-Hyacinthe Loyson[4] gives the palm to Tolstoy 'who has excluded nothing of what is reality, not even the soul', while Paul Adam[5] bases his preference for Tolstoy on *War and Peace*, a great work of synthesis. Maurice Pottecher[6] says that Turgenev's dominant characteristic is his mind, Dostoevsky's his heart, while Tolstoy unites heart and mind; and similarly Auguste Dorchain[7] feels that Tolstoy 'joins the art of Turgenev to the pathos of Dostoevsky, with a greater epic strength and a vaster thought'.

Tolstoy was preferred by some for his psychological analysis

---

[1] Published in *La Plume*, 1 Nov. and 15 Dec. 1913.

[2] Pseudonym of Mme Lapauze, then aged 49, who wrote plays, poetry, and novels.

[3] This was the elder of the Rosny brothers, then aged 57. The pair collaborated in the writing of a number of novels.

[4] Aged 40, a publicist who also wrote for the theatre. He was less famous than his father, Hyacinthe Loyson, a priest who renounced his vows and founded an independent sect in 1879 to put into practice the principles of primitive Christianity.

[5] The well-known novelist, author of *Le Mystère des foules* (1895), *Le Trust* (1910), and many other works. At this time he was aged 51.

[6] Aged 46. His name is associated (together with that of Rolland) in the movement for the establishment of a popular drama. He created an open-air theatre in the Vosges.

[7] Poet and literary historian, aged 56. Published *La Jeunesse pensive* (1881), *Vers de lumière* (1894), and a study of Corneille (1918).

which seemed to ring more true. Thus the two novelists Henri Bordeaux and Paul Margueritte, the latter, however, putting in a word of admiration for Dostoevsky's 'harsh genius'. Others again prefer Tolstoy for the moral tone of his writings, his charity, and the loftiness of his message for society.

The minority who declare allegiance to Dostoevsky do so for a variety of reasons too. A few are attracted by his pathos, his compassion with suffering humanity. Émile Fabre[1] has 'quite a special liking' for Dostoevsky, because of 'his power and inventiveness, his vivid pictures, his keen psychology, his pathos, and his grim eloquence, especially the pity that he everywhere extends to the lowly and downtrodden'. Here obviously we have not moved far from Vogüé's analysis of Dostoevsky in 1885. Jules Bois[2] probably means much the same thing as the preceding writer when he calls Dostoevsky 'un Daudet qui serait hyperesthésié d'un Verlaine'.

Dostoevsky's powers of psychological penetration are given as a reason for preference by one or two more. Han Ryner,[3] while he admits that 'Tolstoy moves me more' being 'the stricken hero whom I salute as the third great Christian after Jesus and St. Francis of Assisi', suggests that 'it is not impossible that Dostoevsky introduces a greater perspicacity into his study of other men. Tolstoy . . . does not perhaps reach the level of his rival as a psychologist and a creator'. Henri-René Lenormand[4] gives as his reason for preferring Dostoevsky that the latter made immense discoveries in the realm of psychology. Lenormand realizes that these discoveries are bound to disconcert the French public whose 'maniacal distrust of everything out of the ordinary prevents it from understanding many a masterpiece'. But once it is generally recognized that no profound psychological study can avoid the stigma of morbidity, then 'perhaps the extraordinary insight into the subterranean world that Dostoevsky possessed will cause him

---

[1] Aged 43 (it can be observed how Dostoevsky's supporters are on the whole somewhat younger than Tolstoy's). Fabre was the author of plays with a marked social tendency, the most notable being *Les Ventres dorés* (1905).

[2] Of the same age as Fabre. Wrote verse plays.

[3] Specialized in the short story. Aged 52.

[4] Lenormand, aged 31 at the time of this 'enquête', was an enthusiastic admirer of Dostoevsky. He dramatized one of the novels (*Les Possédés*, published in the collection, *Trois Drames*, 1918), and in many of his plays his characters and the atmosphere in which they move bear distinctly the signs of Dostoevsky's influence.

to be considered the creator with the greatest genius in the nine-teenth century'.

The poet Saint-Georges de Bouhélier[1] thinks Dostoevsky is the greatest of the three since it is by him that 'the loftiest human poetry manifests itself in the novel'. The novelist Pierre Mille,[2] allowing for the immense effectiveness of Tolstoy as a social reformer, yet finds that at the end of it all he is more attracted to Dostoevsky: 'it seems to me—am I wrong?—that he was the greatest as an artist. But that's simply my impression. . . .' Equally diffident is Henri Duvernois[3] who starts by saying he is secretly inclined to favour Dostoevsky, but is frightened at the idea of giving any Russian writer precedence over Tolstoy. Duvernois concludes (very prudently): 'classifications are most often unfair and always dangerous. . . . I declare myself unable to measure these giants.'

If any conclusion can be drawn from this random set of opinions, none of which is satisfactorily amplified, it is that in 1913 Dos-toevsky was at any rate a serious challenger to the fame of Tolstoy.[4] But he needed a sympathetic and convincing commentator, such as Tolstoy had not lacked; he needed more faithful translators; and he needed above all the demand (which the catastrophe of the First World War was to provide) for a sceptical attitude to the accepted scale of moral values, for a kind of mental anxiety, a sense of urgency and a willingness to go down untried avenues of thought which might lead to a new understanding of the spirit of man—a spirit much more complex, dangerous, and unpredictable than its pre-war observers had imagined.

By 1913 a start had already been made with the task of exploring Dostoevsky afresh, in the light of more up-to-date knowledge of

[1] One of the leaders of the 'naturist' school of poetry which dated from a literary manifesto in 1897, and was inspired by Zola chiefly. In 1913 Bouhélier (aged 37) had just published his crowning work *La Romance de l'homme*. 'Il y chante le tragique quotidien qui l'obsède, les rêveurs et les vagabonds, le senti-ment du mystère dans les cœurs privilégiés, l'incertitude des destins, et tout l'univers qui a l'air d'une vaste attente.' (Henri Clouard.)

[2] Remembered for his creation of Barnavaux, the type of gay, unscrupulous colonist. Mille's age: 48.

[3] Author of a series of novels, stories, and plays of a light, sentimental nature; 38 years old.

[4] Turgenev finds very few adherents. Only Henri Walschinger, Jacques Nor-mand, and Jules Claretie prefer him to either of the other two novelists—the last two because of their personal recollections of him.

his thought and a more kindly disposed attitude towards his work. André Gide began the series with an article on 'Dostoïevsky d'après sa correspondance', published in the *Revue des Études franco-russes*, June 1908. This article was reprinted, in 1923, in Gide's *Dostoïevsky, articles et causeries*. In the same volume is included another brief article, entitled 'Les Frères Karamazov', written as an introduction to Copeau and Croué's dramatization of Dostoevsky's famous novel: this appeared originally in *Le Figaro*, 4 April 1911.

Gide's 1908 article was occasioned by the publication in French of Dostoevsky's letters. The critic is more concerned with burying the past than with heralding a future, more enlightened period of Dostoevsky criticism: we have already touched on Gide's acrimonious comments on Vogüé's presentation of the author of *Crime and Punishment*: they were all contained in this first article. In 1908 Vogüé still remained, for the French, the chief native authority on the Russian novelists. Hennequin's essay had been largely forgotten: it deserved perhaps a better fate, but the slight prestige this critic had won himself during his short span of life, and the uncouthness of his style of writing, had condemned him to almost complete oblivion.

The main intention of this first article of Gide's was to establish that a vast deal remained to be said about Dostoevsky; and that much of what had already been said was untrue or true to so limited a degree that it falsified the ordinary man's conception of the writer and his works. Dostoevsky's progress to fame in France had been slow, too slow for Gide's liking: he conducts an inquest on the reasons for this 'refusal of certain minds to admit the genius of Dostoevsky'.

Gide's main grievance against Vogüé is that the viscount depicted Dostoevsky as a man of gloom and sorrow: Gide, on the other hand, regards Dostoevsky as an essentially joyful figure, with the 'joy that lies beyond sorrow' which 'Nietzsche had scented perfectly well' in the Russian's works (p. 56). It is questionable whether in fact, at this stage, Gide would have been inclined to welcome Dostoevsky if he had not been able to extract from his writings an underlying expression of faith in life and acceptance of it as an experience to be enjoyed. The phase through which Gide was passing was basically a hedonistic one. *Les Nourritures terrestres* (1897), full of passionate formulations of the ecstasy of life, inaugurates the period. *L'Immoraliste* (1902) can be regarded as the testament of hedonism, while in *La Porte étroite*, published after he wrote the first article on Dostoevsky, Gide incriminates that conception of life which places sanctity above happiness, and hopes, by a restriction of the vital forces, to squeeze through the 'strait gate'. Gide, in his article, insists on Dostoevsky's vigorous vitality, quoting from his letters: 'I always seem to be making ready to live. Ridiculous, isn't it? The vitality of a cat . . .' and: 'I have so great a store of life in me that it is hard to exhaust it' (pp. 25–6).

It was not on the strength of this essay, nor of the much shorter and insignificant article of 1911, that Gide established himself eventually as the keenest and most illuminating intermediary Dostoevsky ever had in France. He owes these titles to the 1923 lectures at the Vieux-Colombier. Gide, in fact, as a critic of Dostoevsky, belongs properly to the post-war period.

The very considerable influence of Dostoevsky on Gide's art and thought can certainly be detected at a much earlier date than 1914. But it was also prolonged far after that date, and any study of the repercussions that Gide's reading of Dostoevsky had on his own original work cannot be satisfactory if it is arbitrarily lopped off at the outbreak of the First World War. The time has perhaps not yet come for this subject to be treated, Gide being still with us, and matters of this nature requiring, more than others, the advantages of a proper perspective.[1]

In 1911 Suarès published his first study of Dostoevsky, in the *Cahiers de la Quinzaine*, reproducing it in *Trois Hommes* (1913).

Among Dostoevsky's latter-day commentators Suarès was certainly sympathetically disposed, but he did not exert himself greatly to disseminate this sympathy. The main vice of his study of Dostoevsky is the same as that which marred his essay on Tolstoy: he gives far too little consideration to the works of the author, and is almost exclusively concerned with what he conceives to be his ideas and with his personality. In the case of Tolstoy this mattered less: but Dostoevsky is interesting, at all events to the general public, solely by what he wrote. It is lawful occasionally to explain

[1] Certain aspects of the questions have, however, received the attentions of at least one highly competent literary historian. M. H. Fayer's *Gide, Freedom and Dostoevsky* (1946) nominally treats only of the way in which the theme of freedom was taken over by Gide from Dostoevsky and incorporated with modifications in his own work; but Fayer is naturally led to consider other directions in which the Russian novelist influenced the French artist.

Dostoevsky's works in the light of his experiences—but Suarès neglects the works themselves almost entirely. Instead, he attempts to conjure up an image of the great Russian by setting forth what he knows about his life, about his matrimonial experiences, what he has read of his correspondence, even the impressions he has received by gazing at Dostoevsky's portrait. The result is an essay sometimes highly suggestive, full of quickening oratory, but a piece of writing which cannot really be classed as literary criticism.

There is, in fact, some question whether Suarès had studied the novels of Dostoevsky at all deeply. Gide gives us to understand that it was only as the result of certain hints that he gave Suarès that the latter 'discovered' Dostoevsky for his own count. Suarès admitted to Gide during this conversation that he knew only *The House of the Dead* and *Crime and Punishment*; it appears he subsequently read up hastily the other four or five major works and then dashed off his essay.[1] And the little foreword in which Suarès says 'up till now, I have not named Dostoevsky . . . I was keeping back his name and countenance for some long night when I could brood on him'[2] is there only as a cover, according to Gide, to conceal the fact that his admiration was a plant of recent growth.[3]

However, even if Suarès does proceed by intuition rather than by exact knowledge, his study of Dostoevsky leads him to present a highly illuminating synthesis, in which it is difficult to believe that all is froth and affectation.[4] The enthusiasm is not held in check by any reservations of the kind that dashed his fervour for Tolstoy. He felt he could completely identify himself with the creator of Prince Myshkin and Alyosha Karamazov: he associated himself, with some show of modesty, with Dostoevsky, saying that together they composed 'the antidote to rationalistic tyranny, to the philosophers, to all inhuman poison' (p. 363).

For Vogüé, Dostoevsky had been supremely the apostle of the 'religion of human suffering'; and in his turn, Suarès salutes Dostoevsky as 'the man of sorrow'—a sorrow which is not passive, but

---

[1] Gide, *Journal*, 14 Dec. 1921 (Éd. de la Pléiade, p. 707).

[2] *Trois Hommes*, p. 257. All references to Suarès' writings in this chapter are, unless otherwise stated, taken from the 5th edition (1919) of *Trois Hommes*.

[3] Gide, op. cit., 2 July 1913 (p. 389).

[4] Gide himself conceded that 'il dit à propos de Dostoïevsky des choses extraordinairement perspicaces et telles que lui seul aujourd'hui sait en dire' (op. cit., same entry).

which is 'the active and purifying force' (p. 340). The long misery
of Dostoevsky's life was compensated by the realization he reached
of the fruitfulness of pain. No one owed more to his sufferings than
Dostoevsky. Illness, the heart-rending anguish of the spirit, and
death always at his elbow, were needful to him that he might
'acquire what I call the appetite for a universal life and its whole-
someness' (p. 344). The hardships of life endear life to Dostoevsky.
The constant risk of losing it makes its possession the more
precious.

As the ransom of Suffering there is Love. Suarès had noticed
how unhappy Dostoevsky's lovers are: and he learnt how unhappy
Dostoevsky was in his own marriages. There was an ascetic mysticism behind this inability (or refusal) to accept the unrepining
sensuality of pagan love. 'I only believe in love when it entails
suffering' writes Suarès. 'Without pain, love is but the shadow of
itself' (p. 318). And it is not merely love that demands suffering as
an indispensable ingredient: greatness and beauty are of value only
when attained through suffering. It is because they love that
Raskolnikov and Sonya are the hero and heroine of *Crime and
Punishment*—he, the murderer, is purer, and she, the prostitute,
chaster than their respectable neighbours: it is not the infamy of
Sonya that Dostoevsky celebrates, but the suffering which this
infamy costs her (p. 348).

Thus Dostoevsky is led to an entirely new conception of right
and wrong, in Suarès' view, based on the redeeming quality of love
and the ennobling force of expiation. Suarès, who turned against
Tolstoy in part because of the narrowness of his ethical system,
applauds Dostoevsky for the breadth of his.

Dostoevsky condemns only loveless wickedness. Desire he thinks
sacred, provided only it burns with a flame—even if it is impure. For
him, nothing is mean in itself; for in him everything, even carnal trans-
gressions, are heart and soul, or at least contain these elements. In his
eyes, nothing is vile on earth save nations and men that lack soul. Let us
commit all the sins, if need be, so as to be able to make atonement for
them . . . [p. 324].

It is a system of values splendidly affirmative. 'Dostoevsky, master
of all the passions, keeper of all the keys of hell, locks up the gates
of annihilation. Tempted to make every denial, he destroys nothing
but affirms everything' (p. 352). In this, Suarès thinks, lies Dostoevsky's superiority over Nietzsche: for all Nietzsche is implicit

in Dostoevsky, but all Nietzsche's negations resolve themselves in Dostoevsky into an invincible affirmation of the beauty of life (p. 357).

From a consciousness of all-pervading sin and degradation, with which his experience of life had invested him, Dostoevsky was led to cherish a great pity for the victims of sin—a pity which sprang from, or was equivalent to, Love. It was a pity 'not vague nor mawkish; it involves no weakness, no tearfulness; it is the eminently human virtue, the virtue of virtues, the charity without which everything is drab and empty' (pp. 348-9). The experiences he had had of living with criminals in Siberia had taught Dostoevsky that crime was not unmixed with goodness, that there is no guilt that cannot receive absolution once atonement has been made, that punishment, 'horrible in those who venture to administer it, is necessary to every guilty man, in order to restore his pride and his human dignity' (p. 345).

Dostoevsky's solution of the problem of evil on earth is summed up by Suarès in this sentence: 'La vie, perdue dans la faute, se retrouve dans l'expiation. Le crime égare le cœur, et n'a peut-être pas d'autre horreur que cet égarement.' Love, more than any sense of justice, compelled Dostoevsky to believe that, in some mystic sense, the sufferings inflicted by human agency (including self-inflicted sufferings, or suicide) wipe out the stain of a crime. 'All chastisement is . . . just and wholesome, in the sinner who accepts it: for his heart cries out for it. One needs the strength to punish oneself, or else one must be punished (*ou avoir la force de se punir soi-même, ou être puni*)' (p. 324). This seems to be Suarès' last word on the ethics and metaphysics of Dostoevsky: and there is small wonder that Gide found it unsatisfying. It can hold true only for the two works of Dostoevsky's that we know Suarès was most familiar with: *The House of the Dead* and *Crime and Punishment*; in fact, the phrase quoted, 'ou avoir la force de se punir soi-même, ou être puni', seems to have direct reference to the two criminals in the latter novel: Svidrigailov, who blows out his brains, Raskolnikov, who gives himself up to the police. But there is no mention of, and certainly no attempt to work out, the idea which Dostoevsky strove to elaborate in his later works, that the most upright and noble of men may have to expiate crimes which they themselves never committed, but which their sinister *alter ego*s perpetrate; further, that the responsibility for the sins of all humanity is fixed on every single individual, however innocent, expiation thus becoming a cosmic exercise.

If Suarès added little to our understanding of Dostoevsky's metaphysical outlook, his appreciation of the influence Dostoevsky might have on the development of French literature is, by contrast, very keen, and goes far beyond anything which had been suggested previously.

The 'classical' (using the word in its broadest connotation) process of psychological analysis involved the intellectual approach. The artist remained clear-headed and keen-eyed, and used his reason, his faculty for logical deduction, his specialized knowledge of the machinery of action and reaction, in order to demonstrate the rise and flourishing of passions and emotions. Dostoevsky's method of psychological analysis involves the intuitive approach. The author allows himself to be caught up in the tornado of passions which grips his characters. He stands aghast with them, he cannot understand, he does not wish to bring his understanding into play. His perceptive faculty is not his mind, but his heart, the seat of his emotions or, as Suarès calls it, his intuition.

This was something new in French prose fiction: its value lies not merely in its novelty. The intellect is an inadequate instrument for the perfect perception of emotions. The image it renders of the emotions is similar to a monochrome photograph of some particularly vivid tropical landscape. The picture produced by Dostoevsky, on the other hand, is like the painting of the same scene by a gifted artist with an immense feeling for colour.

The type of intellectual psychologist in literature, and the most accomplished exponent of the method, according to Suarès, is Stendhal; and what Stendhal is to the mechanics of passions, Dostoevsky is to their organic life.

Stendhal and Dostoevsky deal in passions, and nothing interests them or retains their attention outside these. Stendhal holds them up for inspection, he is like a sculptor chiselling shapes. Dostoevsky animates them, and lives in them like another Pygmalion. Stendhal holds all the strings of the puppet-show, and sometimes laughs at the performance. Dostoevsky, far from acting the drama of passions, is on the cross with them [p. 279].

Dostoevsky's art is 'a direct painting from intuition' (p. 280) and by no means an easy art to accept; but it must be accepted, if progress in the knowledge of man is to be made: for intuition can reach down into hidden depths which the intellect, content with superficial reasons for behaviour, will never plumb.

The intellect having been abdicated, one must not expect to recognize the hallowed traditions of order and method in demonstration. Dostoevsky explores the human soul as an insect explores the calyx of a flower: hesitating between one pistil and another, gradually it penetrates to the centre, and sucks the nectar (p. 300). His form is that of the living curve, composed of an infinite number of angles: hence its appearance of slowness and uncertainty: hence, too, his preference for colloquy instead of narrative, which renders more delicately the sinuosity of his line (p. 301). Dostoevsky is for ever engaging on voyages of discovery in quest of unknown emotions: he quivers with apprehensions, presentments, forebodings. In this 'monde de la conscience profonde' everything takes on the illusion of exaggeration, because life, once the conventional layer has been stripped off, is far more complex than the rational eye can measure, 'simplicity being but the slumber of reality'. But when Dostoevsky pulls off the comfortable blanket, a world is revealed to us in which passions appear frenzied because they resist the hand that strips off their veils: 'a world in which the emotions are carried to the uttermost point of sharpness and ardour . . . where everything is intense, there everything is excessive' (pp. 290–1). It is a dream-world, a Bedlamite's world, or may so appear to the reasoning intellect. 'But this world of madness is the sphere of a supreme reality' (p. 292).

Suarès feels that this art, which springs from the emotions and not from the thought, for which 'the universe is created by intuition', is the art of the future.

Here is the new art. Here, at least is the art I should like, the art I am questing and which we are founding, if the gods are so minded. . . . To dip all ideas in a sea of love, and to render their atmosphere, not to describe their nature as such (*en donner l'émotion, non plus la notion telle quelle*), that is the music I am meaning. In such an art, we want everything to be emotion, and we want the proofs whittled down to nothing [pp. 293–4].

Whether the image Suarès offers us of his author is accurate or not, it is evident that in these pages Dostoevsky is emerging as a figure of an altogether different calibre from the mentally deranged sentimentalist, oscillating between sadistic frenzies and maudlin lamentations, the picture which had obsessed too many of his nineteenth-century readers in France. Suarès reconsecrates Dostoevsky as the patron of all those who felt that the last word in the study of man could not be spoken by the intelligence alone.

In this cross-section of 'progressive' opinion about Dostoevsky on the eve of the War, a final word must be said about Élie Faure. It was in his collection of monographs called *Les Constructeurs* (1914) that he formulated his views of the Russian novelist.

Faure, unlike Suarès, genuinely attempts an appreciation of Dostoevsky the man of letters, apart from Dostoevsky the ex-convict, the ill-married husband, the epileptic, the gambler, the religious mystic. *The Idiot* and *The Possessed* are more to the forefront than Siberia or Baden-Baden. Like Suarès, however, he will have nothing spoken against Dostoevsky, and in the teeth of all cavilling traditionalists asserts that his style, form, construction, if they are different from what the French are used to, have their own special value and their own type of excellence.

Faure sees in Dostoevsky primarily the brilliant psychologist, who showed that 'the merest sketch of a gesture is a tragedy able to light a train of others'. There are no descriptions in these novels, Faure reminds us—'the drama creates the world around itself, evokes the darkness of the streets, the hushed footfalls on the snow, the sordid dampness of landing and corridor' (*Les Constructeurs*, p. 136).

The strangeness and unreality of Dostoevsky's characters is one of the first things that strike his reader. This had been explained by earlier apologists who postulated something akin to a flaw in Dostoevsky's own mind, projected on to his creation. Faure maintains, however, that the characters are as 'real' as those of any imaginative artist, only they are divested of every veil which shrouds them from the eye of the beholder. Dostoevsky's heroes differ altogether from the Westerner, who lives shackled in conventions. They stand outside the social edifice, their souls are naked, they are blown whither the wind of passion listeth. Are they saints or criminals? The reader has no clue: Dostoevsky is concerned with creating life, not with delivering moral judgements. The only voice heard is that of passion, drowning the still speech of reason. Are Dostoevsky's characters madmen, or are they not rather ordinary beings from whom Dostoevsky has torn off the masks of custom? With such creations 'impulse is the regular law, man is a total being, not hindered in his search for knowledge of himself by any protective social covering' (p. 129).

Hence the importance, in Dostoevsky, of the slightest pretext to behaviour. In the novels incidents occur, events take place which apparently have no possible artistic reason for inclusion. But 'the insignificant act becomes, with the circumstances that prompt it unawares, which accompany and follow it, a kind of vibration whose reverberations spread far and wide and are lost in the vibrations awakened by the act that follows' (p. 137). And this, of course, makes for vastly inflated books in which it is impossible to say that any one line is superfluous, works of art of an indescribable structural complexity. Faure instances in particular *The Possessed*, the novel in which Dostoevsky undermines all the foundations of certainty, order, and rationalism, and shows the soul continually bursting the bonds of the law. In this sombre book, swollen by the spectacle of an entire society in dissolution, 'the spirit of the West is thrown on to the furnace of the spirit of Russia with a triumphant guffaw, and there melts like an ingot of gold in a river of fire' (p. 127).

This disregard of the traditional social safeguards puts Dostoevsky under an obligation to reforge his moral values. Since effects are so incalculable, what do our acts or even our intentions matter? The essential is to have a basis of 'nobility':

In truth [declares Faure] there are among us men in whose depths is nobility, and they shall be forgiven. They are, more than all others, at the mercy of the uncertain flow and contradictory ebb of life, but being noble, they are a centre of strength, and attract around them the love of all those who have experienced their magnetism [p. 142].

A prostitute (Nastasya Filippovna) throws a packet of bank-notes on to the fire and offers them to a sordid wretch (Gavrila Ardalionovitch), who, for a moment, masters his nature and allows them to burn. Nobility consists—not in idle gestures—but in possessing the clarity of vision which discerns the superhuman moral order: even if one never or scarcely ever conforms to it. These gestures reveal simply, in flashes, that the shady characters who perform them possess this clear-sightedness.

Thus, in this reshuffle of values, it is sincerity which emerges the supreme, the only real virtue; the others, chastity, strength of will, wisdom, self-respect, goodness even, have only a relative reality.

The abstract virtues cannot, in fact, exist in practice, because every virtue is an alloy of good and evil. 'There is no Justice, only men who are just, no Truth, only beings who are sincere, no Beauty, only artists' (p. 142). In the House of the Dead Dostoevsky learnt, once and for all time, 'that intentions are what count, not actions, that innocence may exist in the midst of crime, ignominy in virtue, that there is no reason why the murderer should be of a different sort from other men, and other men of a different sort from the murderer' (p. 111). *Letters from Underground* is there to show that 'the heinousness of crime depends on the sensibility of him who commits the crime, but he alone can judge' (p. 118). The wretched idyll of Raskolnikov and Sonya demonstrates that crime is purified of evil when it creates of the perpetrator 'an absolutely new creature who unearths now, at every minute, depths of sensibility and passion in him which he had never known before'. The tragedy which overtakes these two characters 'makes them many times more sensitive than before to the lower reaches of things, makes of them delicate and resonant centres in whom the most fleeting glimpses reveal yawning gulfs and inaccessible summits. Does that justify their crimes? Dostoevsky does not assert it, and that is no doubt because he cannot know for sure. . . .' (p. 120).

For Faure, Dostoevsky is important principally as the herald of a new morality: it is in that sense that he is a 'constructor'. A Christian, yes: 'if there is any Christianity anywhere . . . it is only, since Jesus, in St. Francis of Assisi and in Dostoevsky' (p. 116).[1] But Dostoevsky's Christian charity has been so enlarged that indulgence swallows up the usual distinctions between virtue and vice, and only love remains, dominant and omnipresent.

To fix the starting-point of the history of the fortunes of Dostoevsky and Tolstoy in France was a relatively simple matter, dictated by the facts. In bringing the narrative to a close at the outbreak of the 1914–18 War I have been obliged to consult convenience instead of letting myself be guided by the natural flow of events. Strictly speaking, since the influence of these two writers continues to this day to be a living force in French literature, any terminal point is necessarily arbitrary.

The longer a foreign model is used, the more diffuse does his influence become, and the less easy to trace and measure. The

---

[1] Curious that Han Ryner had said exactly the same thing about Tolstoy! (see above, p. 224).

Russians when they first came to France meant, practically speaking, one thing only: the introduction of sentiment into realism. But as time wore on, they came to occupy more and more chambers in the mansion of art. Tolstoy was held to typify utilitarian or social art as opposed to 'aesthetic' art, and those in France who inclined to the former, elected him their champion. He also stood for a kind of Confucian morality, opposed at once to positivism which neglected moral values and to traditionalism with its moral code based on revealed divine commandments. Both Dostoevsky and Tolstoy, with their laborious and 'protean' artistic methods, authorized new experimentation in style and form. And in our final chapter we have seen how the new critics kept on uncovering fresh aspects of Dostoevsky's thought and art. Now obviously, as a literary figure is discovered to be more and more complex, so naturally the directions in which he may influence other artists become more and more numerous, and the task of plotting them all grows more and more unmanageable.

It may also be advanced in favour of 1914 as a demarcation line that there can be no comparison between the French public's attitude to the Russian novelists before the War and afterwards. It is a generalization more acceptable than most that Tolstoy and particularly Dostoevsky are writers not enjoyed by complacent minds. Dostoevsky mirrors spiritual states that are essentially insecure, unstable, interrogative; and such a condition was incomparably more widespread after the war than before. One of the principal functions of literature is to reassure the unassured by crystallizing in words and works their inarticulate doubts and hopes: hence Dostoevsky's significance went on reaching ever greater proportions after the War.

The events, cross-currents of thought, quirks and shifts of fashion of these thirty or forty years assume, now that the chronicle is done, a kind of order in their historic fixity. The broad course of development appears (perhaps illusively) harmonious, organic, and inevitable.

First of all, there was, back in Russia, in a Siberian convict-prison, in a country-seat lost in the birch-woods of Tula, the conception, gestation, creation of the great works of art: this stage ans the mid-century, chronologically. It is the grouping of forces under the cover of night.

Then follows a period—in France now—of unconfirmed and

uncoordinated reports, to which little attention was paid: all sorts of rumours, anticipatory tremors, which begin to fill the air and shake the earth.

Then come the translations, tumbling forth in a torrent. Within three or four years, thanks in some degree to a successful commercial speculation, an important portion of the two novelists' work is placed within the reach of the French reading public.

Simultaneously, the essential commentary takes shape. Essential, firstly, because, being written by so unmistakable a 'gentleman' (in every sense of the word) as the Vicomte Eugène-Melchior de Vogüé, it gives the new literature *droit de cité* in every drawing-room and reading-room in Paris—it ensures that Tolstoy and Dostoevsky do not become, at the start, the exclusive cult of a diminutive mistrustful clique. Essential, secondly, because by the very mass of what it left unsaid, the *Roman russe* allowed the busy, tidy minds of the French to tabulate the newcomers comfortably and tuck them away in convenient pigeon-holes. If Vogüé had not succeeded in reducing Dostoevsky to a few happy formulas—'the apostle of the religion of human suffering', 'a man who travelled everywhere, but travelled only by night'—then the chances are that Dostoevsky would have had a far longer struggle to win readers. There would be time enough, later, to work out a more adequate and trustworthy conception of what the Russians stood for and what they tried to say in their books.

The success of Vogüé's book surpassed expectations because it coupled the 'revelation of the Russians' with a most telling critique of the methods and aims of the naturalists—the *Roman russe* was perhaps the most effective piece of anti-naturalist propaganda that had ever appeared. Vogüé thus enrolled on the side of the Russians a strong corps of humanists, traditionalists, and idealists of many a hue.

This was a paradoxical and precarious situation. Tolstoy and Dostoevsky had no roots in humanism (of the French sort, that comes down from Rome and took its consecrated form in the seventeenth century). They were more revolutionary than traditionalist in many ways. And their ideals were not the ideals of a great many Frenchmen in any camp. There was much misconception in the early attitude, and the reaction, which ended the 'honeymoon' period and robbed the Russian novelists of much of their inflated appeal, was inevitable and on the whole healthy.

It cleared the air and left the Russians free to be loved on their own merits by those who felt naturally drawn towards them. There was never any shortage of such men in France. Not harassed by the need to 'sell' the Russians (as to some extent Vogüé was), they sought out the truth about their real significance and tried to enlighten their countrymen about this alone.

Such was the course of the incursion of the novels of Tolstoy and Dostoevsky in France. What of the imprint they left on the French novel? The general lines of the story are scarcely different. In the first few years, while the 'craze' was strong, there was more or less transparent imitation on all sides, but particularly among novelists who were just beginning their career. Anxious to work on something different from the rather stale recipes of naturalism, they seized on Vogüé's formulas. The adherence of these novelists appeared to be a fulfilment of certain prophecies of Vogüé's. In fact, it was symptomatic of something widespread in the eighties and nineties: an increasing dissatisfaction with the bareness, the greyness of materialist creeds, a feeling of having been cheated by 'science' (a better term would have been technology) because its reign had not immediately ushered in a golden age. Thus far, the inspiration that certain French writers found in Tolstoy and Dostoevsky joins up with that found by other authors at the same time in occult lore, in neo-Catholicism, in music, or, later, in Bergsonism.

But as time went by, the influence became less and less immediate, less and less obvious and demonstrable. Saturation-point was quickly reached, the public grew tired of the fashion, the prestige of the revelation was dimmed. Hereafter the influence is perceptible only among writers with strong natural affinities to one or other of the Russians. The influence on the mass of writers is still there, but it has seeped down below surface-level.

And there, to this day, it remains. As long a catalogue could no doubt be drawn up—if not a longer one—of the books, essays, and articles written about Tolstoy and Dostoevsky in the thirty years that followed the War, as in the thirty years that preceded it; and this fact is surely sufficient indication that during this later period the Russian novelists continued to find in France as large and enthusiastic a circle of readers as ever.

As for the future, only surmises are admissible. It seems likely that Tolstoy will continue to be appreciated for what he essentially is: a magnificent creator of living human types, one of the world's greatest tellers of tales. It is not impossible that at some future date there will be a renewal of interest in his simple philosophy of love, brotherhood, and gentle forgiveness: but it seems no creed for the present age of iron. As for Dostoevsky, it is safe to say that so long as the workings of the subconscious forces in man remain something of a mystery, then readers in France and the world over will continue to come to him, as the men of the ancient world to the oracle of Delphi, to receive answers, some satisfying, some dissatisfying, but nearly all of them—enigmatic.

BIBLIOGRAPHY

A. TRANSLATIONS

FULL details of translations into French which have been made of the works of Tolstoy and Dostoevsky are given in Vladimir Boutchik, *Bibliographie des œuvres littéraires russes traduites en français* (1935).

As a picture of a developing process, the main drawback of M. Boutchik's compilation is that his lists are not arranged according to the dates of publication of the translations. This may serve as excuse for the following list, the details of which are largely taken from M. Boutchik's findings.

In drawing up my list, I have made a rigorous selection among the spate of translations which appeared in France up to 1914. Only the *first* translation of any one work finds mention; and no reference is made to works which, for the influence they may have exerted on French thought or literature, were of slighter importance.

TOLSTOY

1878 *Katia* (i.e. *Family Happiness*). Trans. Comte d'Hauterive.

1884 *Ma Religion*. Trans. anon.

1885 *La Guerre et la Paix, roman historique.* Trans. 'Une Russe' (i.e. Princess Paskevitch). This edition had been published at St. Petersburg in 1879.

   Anna Karénine. Trans. anon.

1886 *Les Cosaques: Souvenirs de Sébastopol.* Trans. anon.

   À la recherche du bonheur (contains seven didactic stories). Trans. É. Halpérine.

   La Mort (contains *The Death of Ivan Ilyitch* and other 'death-scenes' extracted from Tolstoy's writings). Trans. É. Halpérine.

   Enfance et adolescence. Trans. M. Delines.

   Deux générations (i.e. *Two Hussars* and *A Prisoner in the Caucasus*). Trans. É. Halpérine.

   Polikouchka (contains also *The Snowstorm*). Trans. É. Halpérine.

1887 *Souvenirs: enfance, adolescence, jeunesse.* Trans. A. Barine.

   La Puissance des Ténèbres. Trans. Ch. Neyroud.

   Que faire? Trans. M. Polonsky and G. Debesse.

   Ma Confession. Trans. 'Zoria'.

   Ivan l'imbécile (contains eleven didactic stories). Trans. É. Halpérine-Kaminsky.

1888 *Le Joueur.* Trans. H. Olivier.

   Contes et fables (selected stories from *The Four Russian Reading Books*). Trans. É. Halpérine-Kaminsky.

1889 *De la Vie.* Trans. Countess Tolstoy.

1890 *La Sonate à Kreutzer.* Trans. J.-H. Rosny aîné and I. Pavlovsky.

1893 *Le Salut est en vous.* Trans. anon.

1895 *Maître et serviteur.* Trans. É. Halpérine-Kaminsky.

1896 *Les Évangiles.* Trans. T. de Wyzewa and G. Art.

      Zola, Dumas, Guy de Maupassant. Trans. É. Halpérine-Kaminsky.

1898 *Qu'est-ce que l'Art?* Trans. T. de Wyzewa.

1900 *Résurrection.* Trans. T. de Wyzewa.

1902 *Lettres du Comte Tolstoï.* Trans. J. W. Bienstock and P. Birukov.

      Œuvres complètes. Édition littérale et intégrale, d'après les manuscrits originaux. Trans. J. W. Bienstock and P. Birukov. This edition was never completed. Between 1902 and 1913 there appeared the following volumes: i–x, xiii–xix, xxi, xxii, xxvi–xxviii.

1904 *Théâtre complet.* Trans. T. de Wyzewa.

1907 *Correspondance inédite . . . réunie, annotée et traduite par* J. W. Bienstock.

      Shakespeare. Trans. J. W. Bienstock.

1912 *Le Père Serge et autres contes.* Trans. J. W. Bienstock.

      Hadji Mourad et autres contes. Trans. J. W. Bienstock.

DOSTOEVSKY

1884 *Humiliés et offensés.* Trans. É. Humbert.

      Le Crime et le Châtiment. Trans. V. Derély.

1886 *Souvenirs de la maison des morts.* Trans. Ch. Neyroud.

      Krotkaïa (contains *A Gentle Soul* and two other short stories). Trans. É. Halpérine.

      Les Possédés. Trans. V. Derély.

      L'Esprit souterrain (i.e. *Letters from Underground*). Trans. É. Halpérine and Ch. Morice.

1887 *L'Idiot.* Trans. V. Derély.

      Le Joueur et Les Nuits blanches. Trans. É. Halpérine.

1888 *Les Pauvres Gens.* Trans. V. Derély.

      Les Frères Karamazov. Trans. É. Halpérine-Kaminsky and Ch. Morice.

1895 *Le Rêve de l'oncle.* Trans. É. Halpérine-Kaminsky.

1896 *L'Éternel Mari.* Trans. N. Halpérine-Kaminsky.

1902 *Un Adolescent.* Trans. J. W. Bienstock and F. Fénéon.

1904 *Journal d'un écrivain.* Trans. J. W. Bienstock and J. A. Nau.

1906 *Carnet d'un inconnu* (*Stépantchikovo*). Trans. J. W. Bienstock and Ch. Torquet.

      Le Double. Trans. J. W. Bienstock and L. Werth.

1908 *Correspondance et Voyage à l'étranger.* Trans. J. W. Bienstock.

B. PUBLICATIONS CONCERNING TOLSTOY AND DOSTOEVSKY

Once again, this list is representative, it is anything but exhaustive. In particular, there will be found no reference to articles which appeared in the daily press or in any of the fortnightly or monthly periodicals save those which had the widest circulation. And, unless the prior date appears significant, no separate mention is made of articles which were subsequently embodied in a volume-publication.

An asterisk beside a title signifies that the book deals only in part with one or both of the Russian novelists.

The following abbreviations have been used:

Corr	= Le Correspondant
MF	= Mercure de France
NR	= La Nouvelle Revue
NRF	= La Nouvelle Revue Française
RB	= La Revue Bleue
RBche	= La Revue Blanche
RDM	= La Revue des Deux Mondes
RH	= La Revue Hebdomadaire
RR	= La Revue des Revues

1875 *COURRIÈRE (C.). *Histoire de la littérature contemporaine en Russie.*

1879 VOGÜÉ (EUGÈNE-MELCHIOR DE)— '*La Guerre et la Paix* de Tolstoï', *RDM* 15 June.

1881 FLEURY (JEAN). 'Deux romanciers russes contemporains: Dostoïevskii et Pisemskii', *RB* 26 February.

1883 *BADIN (ADOLPHE). *Un Parisien chez les Russes.*

CYON (E. DE). 'Un Pessimiste russe: Lew Tolstoï', *NR* 1 June.

1884 VOGÜÉ (E. M. DE). 'Le Comte Léon Tolstoï', *RDM* 15 July.

BARINE (ARVÈDE). 'Un grand romancier: Dostoïevsky', *RB* 27 December.

1885 VOGÜÉ (E. M. DE). 'Dostoïevsky', *RDM* 15 January.

DOUHAIRE (PHILIPPE). 'Revue critique', *Corr* 25 February.

SARCEY (FRANCISQUE). 'Les Livres', *NR* 1, 15 August, 1 September.

*DUPUY (ERNEST). *Les Grands Maîtres de la littérature russe.*

BARINE (A.). 'Le Comte Léon Tolstoï: à propos d'*Anna Karénine*', *RB* 5 December.

1886 SARCEY (F.). 'Les Livres', *NR* 15 January, 15 April, 15 May, 1 September.

*VOGÜÉ (E. M. DE). *Le Roman russe.*

*PONTMARTIN (ARMAND DE). *Souvenirs d'un vieux critique, 7e série.*

VOGÜÉ (E. M. DE). 'Les Livres russes en France', *RDM* 15 December.

1887 *SICHLER (LÉON). *Histoire de la littérature russe depuis les origines jusqu'à nos jours.*

FRARY (RAOUL). 'Le Mouvement littéraire', *NR* 1 July.

*DELINES (MICHEL). *La France jugée par la Russie.*

*LEMAÎTRE (JULES). *Impressions de théâtre, 1ère série.*

1888 HALPÉRINE-KAMINSKY (ÉLIE). 'La Puissance des Ténèbres sur la scène française', *NR* 1 February.

*PONTMARTIN (A. DE). *Souvenirs d'un vieux critique, 9e série.*

VOGÜÉ (E. M. DE). 'La Puissance des Ténèbres de L. Tolstoï: réflexions des spectateurs', *RDM* 15 March.

SOREL (ALBERT). 'Tolstoï historien', *RB* 14 April.

1889 *HENNEQUIN (ÉMILE). *Écrivains francisés: Études de critique scientifique.*

*LEROY-BEAULIEU (ANATOLE). *L'Empire des Tsars et des Russes, tome III.*

1890 LAPAUZE (HENRI). 'Le Comte Tolstoï, son œuvre pédagogique', *RB* 3 May.

HONCEY (JEAN). 'La Notion du péché dans la littérature russe' and 'L'Ascétisme philanthropique dans la littérature russe', *RB* 24 May and 4 October.

*LEMAÎTRE (J.). *Impressions de théâtre, 4e série.*

1891 GIDE (CHARLES). 'Les Idées sociales de Tolstoï', *Revue du Christianisme pratique*, 15 November.

1892 VOGÜÉ (E. M. DE). 'Les Cigognes', *RDM* 15 February.

*ROD (ÉDOUARD). *Les Idées morales du temps présent.*

1893 DUMAS (GEORGES). *Tolstoy et la philosophie de l'amour.*

BEHRS (ÉTIENNE). 'La Vie de famille du comte Tolstoï', *NR* 1, 15 September.

DAUDET (LÉON). 'À propos du roman russe', *NR* 15 October.

WYZEWA (TEODOR DE) 'Les Revues étrangères', *RDM* 15 October.

SCHROEDER (FÉLIX). *Le Tolstoïsme.*

1894 DAUDET (L.). 'Les Grands Évolutifs', *NR* 1 January.

MICHAILOVSKY (N. K.). 'Le Mouvement littéraire en Russie', *RR* 15 January, 1 February.

MANACÉINE (MARIE DE). *L'Anarchie passive et le comte Tolstoï.*

LEMAÎTRE (J.). 'De l'influence récente des littératures du Nord', *RDM* 15 December.

1895 HALLAYS (ANDRÉ). 'De l'influence des littératures étrangères', *Revue de Paris* 15 February.

CHARBONNEL (VICTOR). 'Les Mystiques dans la littérature présente: les Prédécesseurs', *MF* December.

1896 FAGUET (ÉMILE). 'Tolstoï et Zola' and 'Tolstoï et Maupassant', *RB* 23 May and 13 June.

*COMBES (ERNEST). *Profils et types de la littérature russe.*

KORSAKOV (IVAN). 'Le Mouvement des idées en Russie', *RBche* 15 August.

MAFFRE (P.). *Le Tolstoïsme et le Christianisme.*

*WYZEWA (T. DE). *Écrivains étrangers.*

1897 *WYZEWA (T. DE). *Écrivains étrangers, 2e série.*

1898 DOUMIC (RENÉ). 'Les Idées de Tolstoï sur l'art', *RDM* 15 May.

BERTHA (A. DE). 'Lettre ouverte au comte Tolstoï', *NR* 1 August.

OSSIP-LOURIER. *Pensées de Tolstoï.*

GAULTIER (JULES DE). 'Tolstoï', *RBche* 15 September.

WENGUEROW (ZINAÏDA). 'La Parenté de Dostoïevsky avec Théodore Sollogoub', *MF* November.

1899 WENGUEROW (Z.). 'Le 70e anniversaire de Tolstoï', *MF* January.

KOVALEWSKY (MAXIME). 'La Morale de Tolstoï', *Revue Internationale de Sociologie*, May.

OSSIP-LOURIER. *La Philosophie de Léon Tolstoï.*

MAJAL (ÉLIE). *La Pensée religieuse de Léon Tolstoï.*

SUARÈS (ANDRÉ). *Tolstoï.*

LEBLOND (MARIUS-ARY). 'La Justice russe, d'après les œuvres de Gogol, Dostoïevsky, Tourguéniev et Tolstoï', *RB* 4, 11 November.

BESNARD (LUCIEN). *L'Œuvre dramatique de Léon Tolstoï.*

*BRUNETIÈRE (FERDINAND). *Études critiques sur l'histoire de la littérature française, 6e série.*

BRUNETIÈRE (F.). 'La Littérature européenne au XIXe siècle', *RDM* 1 December.

1900 BORDEAUX (HENRI). 'La *Résurrection* de Tolstoï', *RH* 6 January.

*WYZEWA (T. DE). *Écrivains étrangers, 3e série: Le Roman contemporain à l'étranger.*

DOUMIC (R.). 'Le Nouveau Roman de Tolstoï', *RDM* 15 February.

GERFAULT (MARGUERITE). 'La Philosophie de Tolstoï', *Revue Internationale de Sociologie*, March.

*WALISZEWSKI (KASIMIR). *La Littérature russe.*

1901 *JEANROY-FÉLIX (VICTOR). *Études de littérature étrangère.*

VOGÜÉ (E. M. DE). 'Au seuil d'un siècle: Cosmopolitisme et nationalisme', *RDM* 1 February.

WYZEWA (T. DE). 'Le Comte Tolstoï et la critique russe', *RDM* 15 March.

*BEAUNIER (ANDRÉ). *Notes sur la Russie.*

ROUX (FERNAND). *Magistrature et justice dans Tolstoi.*

BORDEAUX (H.). 'L'Invasion étrangère dans la littérature française', *Corr* 25 December.

1902 *Ossip-Lourier. *La Philosophie russe contemporaine.*

Le Breton (André). 'La Pitié sociale dans le roman: l'Auteur des *Misérables* et l'auteur de *Résurrection*', *RDM* 15 February.

Rolland (Romain). *Tolstoï: une lettre inédite.*

Rachilde. 'A propos de *L'Adolescent*', *MF* August.

Bentzon (Thérèse). 'Autour de Tolstoï', *RDM* 15 August.

Arnauld (Michel). '*L'Adolescent* par Dostoïevsky', *RBche* 1 September.

Ernest-Charles (J.). '*L'Adolescent* par Dostoïevsky', *RB* 20 September.

*Faguet (É.). *Propos littéraires.*

1903 Ossip-Lourier. *Nouvelles pensées de Tolstoï.*

*Lionnet (Jean). *L'Évolution des idées chez quelques-uns de nos contemporains.*

Merejkowski (D. S.). *Tolstoï et Dostoïevsky* (translation).

*Strannik (Ivan). *La Pensée russe contemporaine.*

*Brunetière (F.). *Études critiques sur l'histoire de la littérature française, 7e série.*

1904 Bajenow (Dr. N.). 'Dostoïevsky et de Maupassant', *Archives d'Anthropologie criminelle*, January.

*Bourdeau (Jean). *Les Maîtres de la pensée contemporaine.*

Loygue (Dr. Gaston). *Étude médico-psychologique sur Dostoïevsky.*

Trégouboff (Ivan). *Lettre ouverte d'un tolstoïen à un anti-tolstoïen.*

*Reggio (Albert). *Au seuil de leur âme: Études de psychologie critique.*

Bourdon (Georges). *En écoutant Tolstoï.*

1905 Miomandre (François de). 'Trois révélateurs d'âme: Balzac, Tolstoï et Dostoïevsky', *Les Gerbes*, January.

*Ossip-Lourier. *La Psychologie des romanciers russes du XIXe siècle.*

1906 Garcia-Mansilla (Édouard). *Tolstoï et le communisme.*

Grasset (Dr. Jules). 'Demi-fous et demi-responsables', *RDM* 15 February.

Birukov (Paul). *Vie et œuvre de Léon Tolstoï* (translation).

1907 Séménoff (Eugène). 'Lettres russes', *MF* 15 January.

Ossip-Lourier. *Tolstoï . . . le Tolstoïsme.*

*Leger (Louis). *Histoire de la littérature russe.*

1908 Gide (André). 'Dostoïevsky d'après sa correspondance', *Revue des Études franco-russes*, June.

Halpérine-Kaminsky (É.). 'Léon Tolstoï jubilaire malgré lui', *RH* 19 September.

1909 *Gourmont (Rémy de). *Promenades littéraires, 3e série.*

Persky (Serge). *Tolstoï intime.*

Séché (Alphonse) and Bertaut (Jules). *Tolstoï.*

1910 Vogüé (E. M. de). 'Lettre inédite sur les études russes', *RH* 9 April.

Copeau (Jacques). 'M. Baring et Dostoïevsky', *NRF* June.

*Haumant (Émile). *La Culture française en Russie (1700–1900)*.

Tavernier (Eugène). 'Tolstoï', *Corr* 25 November.

Chervet (Henri). 'Tolstoï', *NR* 1 December.

Ségur (Nicolas). 'Tolstoï', *RR* 1 December.

Leroy-Beaulieu (A.). 'Léon Tolstoï', *RDM* 15 December.

*Vogüé (E. M. de). *Les Routes*.

1911 Jaurès (Jean). 'Léon Tolstoï', *Revue Socialiste*, March.

Monod (Wilfred). *Tolstoï*.

Suarès (A.). *Tolstoï vivant*.

Serre (Joseph). *Le Penseur dans Tolstoï*.

*Maury (Lucien). *Figures littéraires*.

Rolland (Romain). *Vie de Tolstoï*.

Monod (Léopold). *Léon Tolstoï*.

Suarès (A.). *Dostoïevski*.

Gide (A.). *Dostoïevsky d'après sa correspondance*.

1912 Wyzewa (T. de). 'Les Écrits posthumes de Tolstoï', *RDM* 15 February.

*Persky (S.). *Les Maîtres du roman russe contemporain*.

Dwelshauvers (Georges). 'Rousseau et Tolstoï', *Revue de Métaphysique et de Morale*, May.

*Bourget (Paul). *Pages de critique et de doctrine*.

Vettard (Camille). 'Les Écrits posthumes de Tolstoï', *NRF* July.

Thibaudet (Albert). 'L'Esthétique du roman', *NRF* August.

Halpérine-Kaminsky (É.). *Tolstoï par Tolstoï, avant sa crise morale*.

Strakhoff (V.). *Le Vrai Tolstoï*.

1913 *Suarès (A.). *Trois Hommes*.

Bernstamm (Serge). 'Une enquête: Tolstoï, Tourguéneff ou Dostoïevsky?' *La Plume* 1 November and 15 December.

1914 *Muret (Maurice). *Les Contemporains étrangers, tome II*.

Wyzewa (T. de). 'À propos de la correspondance de Dostoïevsky', *RDM* 15 June.

*Faure (Élie). *Les Constructeurs*.

Tolstoy (Ilya). *Tolstoï, souvenirs d'un de ses fils*.

INDEX